The Politics of Belonging

CHICAGO STUDIES IN AMERICAN POLITICS
A series edited by Benjamin I. Page, Susan Herbst, Lawrence R. Jacobs, and Adam J. Berinsky

Additional series titles follow index

Also in the series:

CHANGING MINDS OR CHANGING CHANNELS?
PARTISAN NEWS IN AN AGE OF CHOICE *by Kevin
Arceneaux and Martin Johnson*

POLITICAL TONE: HOW LEADERS TALK AND WHY
*by Roderick P. Hart, Jay P. Childers, and
Colene J. Lind*

THE TIMELINE OF PRESIDENTIAL ELECTIONS:
HOW CAMPAIGNS DO (AND DO NOT) MATTER *by
Robert S. Erikson and Christopher Wlezien*

LEARNING WHILE GOVERNING: EXPERTISE AND
ACCOUNTABILITY IN THE EXECUTIVE BRANCH *by
Sean Gailmard and John W. Patty*

ELECTING JUDGES: THE SURPRISING EFFECTS
OF CAMPAIGNING ON JUDICIAL LEGITIMACY *by
James L. Gibson*

FOLLOW THE LEADER? HOW VOTERS RESPOND TO
POLITICIANS' POLICIES AND PERFORMANCE *by
Gabriel S. Lenz*

THE SOCIAL CITIZEN: PEER NETWORKS AND
POLITICAL BEHAVIOR *by Betsy Sinclair*

THE SUBMERGED STATE: HOW INVISIBLE
GOVERNMENT POLICIES UNDERMINE AMERICAN
DEMOCRACY *by Suzanne Mettler*

DISCIPLINING THE POOR: NEOLIBERAL
PATERNALISM AND THE PERSISTENT POWER OF
RACE *by Joe Soss, Richard C. Fording, and
Sanford F. Schram*

WHY PARTIES? A SECOND LOOK *by John H.
Aldrich*

NEWS THAT MATTERS: TELEVISION AND
AMERICAN OPINION, UPDATED EDITION *by
Shanto Iyengar and Donald R. Kinder*

SELLING FEAR: COUNTERTERRORISM, THE
MEDIA, AND PUBLIC OPINION *by Brigitte L.
Nacos, Yaeli Bloch-Elkon, and Robert Y.
Shapiro*

The Politics of Belonging

Race, Public Opinion, and Immigration

NATALIE MASUOKA AND JANE JUNN

THE UNIVERSITY OF CHICAGO PRESS   CHICAGO AND LONDON

NATALIE MASUOKA is assistant professor of political science at Tufts University.
JANE JUNN is professor of political science at the University of Southern California.
She is coauthor of *Education and Democratic Citizenship in America*.

The University of Chicago Press, Chicago 60637
The University of Chicago Press, Ltd., London
© 2013 by The University of Chicago
All rights reserved. Published 2013.
Printed in the United States of America
22 21 20 19 18 17 16 15 14 13   1 2 3 4 5

ISBN-13: 978-0-226-05702-6 (cloth)
ISBN-13: 978-0-226-05716-3 (paper)
ISBN-13: 978-0-226-05733-0 (e-book)

Library of Congress Cataloging-in-Publication Data

Masuoka, Natalie.
    The politics of belonging : race, public opinion, and immigration/Natalie Masuoka and Jane Junn.
        pages. cm.—(Chicago studies in American politics)
ISBN 978-0-226-05702-6 (cloth : alk. paper)—ISBN-978-0-226-05716-3 (pbk. : alk. paper)—
ISBN 978-0-226-05733-0 (e-book)   1. United States—Emigration and immigration—
Government policy. 2. Race—Public opinion. I. Junn, Jane. II. Title. III. Series:
Chicago studies in American politics.
    JV6483.M334 2013
    325.73—dc23

                                                                        2013005907

♾ This paper meets the requirements of ANSI/NISO Z39.48-1992 (Permanence of Paper).

Contents

Acknowledgments   ix

Introduction: Conditional Welcome   1

CHAPTER 1. Public Opinion through a Racial Prism   13

CHAPTER 2. Development of the American Racial Hierarchy:
Race, Immigration, and Citizenship   36

CHAPTER 3. The Pictures in Our Heads: The Content and
Application of Racial Stereotypes   63

CHAPTER 4. Perceptions of Belonging: Race and Group
Membership   88

CHAPTER 5. The Racial Prism of Group Identity: Antecedents to
Attitudes on Immigration   122

CHAPTER 6. Framing Immigration: "Illegality" and the Role of
Political Communication   156

Conclusion: The Politics of Belonging and the Future of
US Immigration Policy   185

Notes   199

References   219

Index   241

Acknowledgments

We like to think of our partnership as one that was meant to be; Masuoka's parents, Jane and Jun, together share the second author's name. Beyond the names coincidence, our collaboration in researching and writing this book has spanned eight years and three US presidential elections, beginning with data collection in 2004 and ending in the completion of the book in 2012.

During the time we have spent together researching and writing this book, much has changed for us: babies were born, PhD dissertations were completed, first jobs started, coast-to-coast moves made, loved ones passed, and unions formed. Throughout, we have relied on the steadfast support of colleagues, friends, and family who invited us to present our work, listened to our ideas, suggested improvements to the analysis and writing, and generally helped us write this book both through conversations and their own work. For close readings and extended comments on earlier drafts of the book manuscript, we are very grateful to Jeb Barnes, Dennis Chong, Lisa García Bedolla, Bernie Grofman, Jennifer Hochschild, Catherine Paden, Kay Lehman Schlozman, and Ron Schmidt, Sr. Thanks to both Efren Perez and Nimah Mazeheri for expert advice on research methodology. We thank Mike Dennis and Bill McCready at Knowledge Networks for helping us administer our 2006 Faces of Immigration Study. For excellent research assistance, we thank Peter Kim, Sehreen Ladak, Vladimir Medenica, and students in the University of Southern California (USC) political science honors seminar.

We also express our appreciation for comments and conversations with Marisa Abrajano, Mike Alvarez, Saladin Ambar, Kristi Andersen, Sara Angevine, Jeb Barnes, Matt Barreto, Justin Berry, Cristina Beltran, Ben Bishin, Denise Blood, Larry Bobo, Jake Bowers, Rachelle Brooks,

Nadia Brown, Niambi Carter, Dennis Chong, Juvenal Cortes, Jeronimo Cortina, Kareem Crayton, Vicky DeFrancesco Soto, Louis DeSipio, Marika Dunn, Alexandra Filindra, Luis Fraga, Megan Francis, Lorrie Frasure, Andra Gillespie, Christina Greer, Christian Grose, Zoli Hajnal, Ange-Marie Hancock, Kerry Haynie, Rodney Hero, Marc Hetherington, Krista Jenkins, Martin Johnson, Michael Jones-Correa, Alisa Kessel, Claire Kim, Peter Kim, Byongha Lee, Christine Lee, Taeku Lee, Jan Leighley, Pei-te Lien, Tehema Lopez, Lydia Lundgren, Michel Martinez, Paula McClain, Vlad Medenica, David Meyer, Sangay Mishra, John Mollenkopf, Norman Nie, Stephen Nuno, Manuel Pastor, Sasha Patterson, Francisco Pedraza, Dianne Pinderhughes, Karthick Ramakrishnan, Ricardo Ramirez, Emily Renaud, Kathy Rim, Reuel Rogers, Jen Schenk Sacco, Mark Sawyer, Kay Schlozman, Gary Segura, John Skrentny, Candis Watts Smith, Rogers Smith, Chris Stout, Liz Suhay, Katherine Tate, Dan Tichenor, Al Tillery, Sid Verba, Roger Waldinger, Marty Wattenberg, Nick Weller, Cara Wong, and Janelle Wong.

Thanks to the many places that have allowed us to present ideas discussed in this book: the political science and government departments at Duke University, Harvard University, University of California Irvine (UCI), University of California Los Angeles, University of California Riverside, University of California San Diego, University of California Santa Barbara, Texas A&M, the Department of Psychology at Brandeis University, and the Health Quality Life Lab at Tufts University. We also appreciate the feedback we received at conference presentations at the meetings of the American Political Science Association, Midwest Political Science Association, and Western Political Science Association, the New York Area Political Psychology meeting, and the Politics of Race, Immigration, and Ethnicity Consortium.

At the University of Chicago Press, we thank John Tryneski, the "green flash" of political science editors, who saw potential in our argument from the beginning and continued to encourage us to write a great book. We are very grateful to Jamie Druckman for wise, substantive, and strategic counsel at all stages of the process and for sacrificing sleep and his own work to help us meet a tight deadline. We thank Rodney Powell for his care and thoughtfulness in the preparation of the manuscript for production. George Roupe, copyeditor extraordinaire, helped us to improve the flow of the argument and the quality of writing, and we are grateful for the care he took editing the manuscript. Last, but certainly not least, we are grateful to the anonymous reviewers for the University of Chicago Press, who demonstrated that the peer-review process is alive and well, and whose trenchant and constructive critique motivated us to undertake substantial revisions and reach the full potential they recognized in our ideas.

Masuoka appreciates the advice, support, and encouragement received from all of the friends, mentors, and new colleagues acquired in her cross-country migration from California to Boston. The ideas generated for this book would not have come about without the experiences and conversations that happened over this journey. This project began while I was still in graduate school and learning the ropes of social science research. I thank those in the UCI Department of Political Science who provided an excellent foundation: my dissertation chair, Bernie Grofman, as well as Russ Dalton, Louis Desipio, Mark Petracca, Willie Schonfeld, Katherine Tate, and Carole Uhlaner. I also thank the department and UCI School of Social Sciences for research funding and assistance over those years. The Department of Political Science at Duke University welcomed me as a visiting assistant professor. Special thanks go to Paula McClain and Kerry Haynie for offering me a position at the Center for the Study of Race, Ethnicity and Gender in the Social Sciences. Finally, the Tufts University Department of Political Science has offered an inviting and engaging environment during my first years as an assistant professor. I thank my department for the financial and moral support that has allowed me to complete this manuscript. In particular, my American politics colleagues, Jeff Berry, Jim Glaser, Kent Portney, and Debbie Schildkraut are always available to offer needed advice. Outside the profession, family and friends have patiently listened, provided words of wisdom, and often a bed to sleep on as I juggled the many tasks of a graduate student and then an assistant professor. My Los Angeles–based family, Chez and Jim Shoji, Eiko and Brett Brodersen, Margie Garza and Meg Masuoka generously opened their homes throughout my time in Southern California, and my sister, Erin Masuoka, was a constant presence. I had the good luck to have a writing buddy, Grace Talusan, and many paragraphs for this book were written during our coffee-fueled workdays. Gordon Au deserves special recognition for patiently dealing with the stresses that arose from what probably seemed like an endless number of deadlines. The love and support of my parents, Jane and Jun Masuoka, has long inspired the confidence to consider big ideas and tough challenges, such as completing this project.

Junn thanks her former USC colleagues Ricardo Ramirez and Janelle

Wong for showing her how colleagueship and friendship can coexist so beautifully. Janelle Wong, Karthick Ramakrishnan and Taeku Lee, co-authors of a book on Asian American political engagement, provided welcome distraction and willing participants in stimulating and often late-night discussions on the politics of race in the United States. I both thank and apologize to my dear friends Kerry Johnson and Dedi Fel-man for engaging in conversations with me about the material in this book even when they'd already heard enough. I am grateful to former Rutgers University colleagues Nikol Alexander-Floyd, Leela Fernandes, Rick Lau, Kira Sanbonmatsu, Dan Tichenor, and Al Tillery for years of support and friendship through thick and thin. Special thanks go to my lifelong friend and mentor Norman Nie and to Pei-te Lien for being first and never giving up. I thank Bob Fagella, Esq., for his legal acumen in pursuing redress for violations of the law in employment discrimination and for understanding better than anyone but Leela Fernandes why I did what I did. The Legal Advocacy Fund of the American Association of University Women and its 2009 honoree Lilly Ledbetter provided inspi-ration to continue to fight on. I am grateful to my new intellectual home, the University of Southern California, for the opportunity to be a part of and contribute to this community. My family, David Champagne, Eve Champagne Junn, and Juliet Junn Champagne, made the journey west to Los Angeles with no complaint. They are the source of meaning and joy in life for me, and I thank them from the bottom of my heart. I am also grateful to Annie Grischuk, Amy Luger, Leily Mendez, and Maria Vergara, who helped care for our children when David and I were work-ing. My parents, Robert and Sue Junn, themselves immigrant newcom-ers to America, made my sisters and I aware that despite our conditional welcome, we were still Americans who could dream big. Thanks, Mom and Dad. This book is for my parents-in-law, Theresa and Roger Cham-pagne, who from the start gave me an unconditional welcome to their family. Roger, a historian of the American Revolutionary War, also gave me his carefully cared for copy of Edmund Morgan's *American Slavery, American Freedom*. I cherish it and his memory.

Introduction: Conditional Welcome

Imagery of the immigrant coming-to-America story often revolves around a door, the signifier of entrance to the United States. But the fable of an open door to a "nation of immigrants" belies the reality that membership in the polity has long been a conditional welcome. The door has been guarded against the intrusion of the "dregs" of Asia and peasants of eastern and southern European origin (Daniels 2004a; Gyory 1998).[1] American territorial expansion to include what are now the southwestern states of Nevada, Utah, New Mexico, and Arizona changed the focus to keeping the door shut against immigrants from Mexico (Rodriguez 2008; Glenn 2002; Ngai 2004). In contemporary politics, this exclusion is symbolized by the vision of a fence stretching across the southern border of the United States.

The way a nation welcomes newcomers signifies its response to normative questions about membership and belonging. For most of the history of the United States, race has been among the most important conditions for legal entry and abode (Schrag 2010; Ngai 2004; Tichenor 2002). A long list of excluded racialized others is codified in US law, and immigration and naturalization policies are connected to race by long-standing conceptions of citizenship privileging whiteness (Bosniak 2006). Designations of some as deserving and eligible for membership and of others as unworthy and unwanted are closely intertwined with how race perception has developed in the United States (King and Smith 2011; Smith 1997; Hochschild, Weaver, and Burch 2011; Bonilla-Silva 2010). Although the category of "white" has changed over time, those who are classified as such have traditionally faced the fewest barriers to entry and were most likely to enjoy the benefits of full membership in the American polity (Gross 2008; Haney López 2006; Hattam

2007; M. Jacobson 1999). Members of groups classified as nonwhite have been granted incomplete membership, their political experience mediated by de facto and de jure discrimination as a function of their racial categorization.

The racial hierarchy—an ordering of political power among groups classified by race—is the key structural characteristic differentiating who is a full member of the American polity. Racial categorization and position in the hierarchy structure the life chances of individuals as a function of their group classification, which in turn influences the contours of political, economic, and social inequality (Massey 2007; Schmidt et al. 2009, Sidanius and Pratto 1999). The racial hierarchy in the United States is powerful and persistent, its presence so pervasive that it often seems invisible to Americans living in the midst of its structural influence. But the legacy of the institutionalization of exclusion by race is visible in widely recognized racial-group stereotypes. Groups with the highest position in the racial order have fewer and more positive stereotypes compared with other groups ranked lower in the hierarchy. Individuals in highly ranked groups are less constrained by their racial classification when forming opinions and expressing attitudes on policies governing immigration. Groups lower in the racial order experience more constraint as a function of their position of relative powerlessness and the negative stereotypes associated with their race. A person's position in the American racial hierarchy thus creates systematic variation in group identity and sense of belonging, which in turn influence attitudes on immigration. Public opinion on immigration at the individual level is therefore a reflection of one's position in the racial hierarchy as moderated by racial-group identity.

The role of racial-group identity in explaining Americans' attitudes on immigration is a relatively recent phenomenon because until the last several decades, the population was overwhelmingly white. The dramatic growth of the nonwhite population in the United States since passage of the 1965 Immigration and Nationality Act has resulted in a population that is now one-third African American, Asian American, Latino, or other race. Blacks are no longer the largest minority group, having been overtaken in number by Latinos at the turn of the twenty-first century. The size of the Asian American population has grown dramatically since 1965 and is approaching 5% of the nation's population. In a diverse and multiracial polity, looking at a single group is limiting.

Even Americans residing in highly racially segregated areas do not exist in a political vacuum away from other groups. Instead, categorization in a racial-group structures both how people see themselves and how they evaluate other groups. The sociologist Herbert Blumer's (1958) insights on the group basis of racial prejudice remain the best statement of this position:

> Race prejudice exists basically in a sense of group position rather than in a set of feelings which members of one racial group have toward the members of another racial group. This different way of viewing race prejudice shifts study and analysis from a preoccupation with feelings as lodged in individuals to a concern with the relationship of racial groups. It also shifts scholarly treatment away from individual lines of experience and focuses interest on the collective process by which a racial group comes to define and redefine another racial group. (3)

Studies of public opinion in the United States can no longer persist in testing inferential models about the antecedents of political attitudes with the white population alone. Instead, public opinion is about all Americans, and models of political attitudes must account for systematic variation in perspectives by race.

Approach to Public Opinion on Immigration

Studying political attitudes on immigration policy in a diverse American polity requires a framework that both considers the contextual environment of racial-group categorization in which opinions are formed and allows for variation at the individual level within a group. Contemporary political attitudes are embedded in historical contingencies of identity development and group acceptance. When measured at the individual level, public opinion is the product of group interactions and historical memory structured by the person's position in the American racial order. A comprehensive approach to public opinion on racial issues in a diverse polity must acknowledge the American racial hierarchy and model the influence of this structural constraint on individual-level attitudes through the moderating influence of group identity. A new approach to political attitudes on immigration thus needs to specify and implement

a methodological strategy for comparative relational analysis in order to
anticipate and make sense of distinctive patterns of results for different
racial groups in the United States.

Theory of racial hierarchy

For questions of immigration policy, the American racial order is the
structural context in which individual opinions are formed. Instead of a
simple binary of being American or not, belonging exists on a continuum
that reflects the racial hierarchy. Higher position denotes more powerful
status as the assumed in-group, or those who comprise the default category as American. The construction and maintenance of racial groups
rely on the imperatives of preserving the privileges of higher-status
groups. To keep the order intact, negative characteristics of lower-status
racial groups are imputed to individuals classified by race and ethnicity
to justify their unsuitability for full belonging in the American polity.
In contrast, positive stereotypes provide reason to continue to include
and embrace higher-status groups (Sidanius and Pratto 1999; Tilly 1999;
Steele 2010). Group characteristics by race are widely understood by all
Americans, and stereotypes provide both the content and lingua franca
of the American racial hierarchy.

The powerful impact of group categorization and racial prerequisites
to belonging is most visible when one considers the circumstances of African Americans. Historically defined as second-class citizens at best,
blacks continue to suffer systematic discrimination, segregation, and
poverty. The disproportionate number of blacks in disadvantaged positions is not a function of innate inability to attain social mobility but is
instead indicative of structural barriers based in racial position. In this
respect, African Americans' political experience illustrates how full citizenship has not been achieved, even with federal constitutional protections and statutory mandate. Racial categories have been used to create
distinctions among groups of individuals and to justify unequal treatment and citizenship rights for those deemed racially inferior. The racial hierarchy serves as a framework that ranks the desirability of groups
and delineates who is a full member and who must continually fight to be
perceived as one.

Our theory of racial position in public opinion is embedded in two
premises: that individual attitudes are constrained by the racial hierarchy and that higher position on the hierarchy denotes more powerful sta-

tus as the in-group "default category." For the first premise, race is not simply a demographic characteristic or a product of personal preference but a structural attribute imposed on an individual with important consequences for individual life chances and political experiences. As a result, political attitudes are fundamentally shaped by racial classification. Racial-group position is the key structural feature that places individuals within groups at particular positions from which to view political phenomena. One can present a given situation to everyone—that is, present the same set of images, the same news story, the same speech, or the same policy proposal—and opinions on that situation will vary systematically by group. While racial patterns in opinion are not present for all issues, for those with clear racial undertones such as immigration policy, position in the racial hierarchy is the key feature to explain differences in public opinion. The racial hierarchy is a dispersive prism in public opinion on racial issues, and like a beam of white light that refracts into a spectrum of colors when passed through a prism, political attitudes form distinctive patterns once passed through the lens of race.

On the second premise, we assume the hierarchical ordering of racial groups is widely recognized by Americans. As we discuss in detail in the next chapter, the contemporary American racial hierarchy has a diamond shape with whites on the top, blacks on the bottom and Latinos and Asian Americans in between. While the exact position of groups has changed over time, the relative ordering has remained constant. The diamond shape of the American racial hierarchy is the result of institutional practices defining race in discrete categories (i.e., "white," "black," "Chinese," etc.) as well as the distinctions created by the introduction of the concept of ethnicity. While the term "racial hierarchy" is not commonplace in the everyday vernacular of Americans, people nevertheless understand the content and ordering of racial groups in the hierarchy.

Our identification of the implications of the racial hierarchy for public opinion on immigration represents an important departure from traditional scholarship both for its explicit consideration of the structural conditions of racial position and for its comparative analysis across racial and ethnic groups. Leading models of public opinion and attitude formation—on issues of race as well as many others—either are silent about the context of power that structures individual agency or they control away racial differences in the estimation of inferential models. Our theory situates racial hierarchy as a core foundation of public opinion on immigration.

Modeling immigration attitudes: specifying group identity

Who is considered part of the in-group is not simply a matter of being born in the United States or being a naturalized citizen; legal status is a necessary though insufficient condition for full membership in
the American polity. Modeling political attitudes on immigration must
therefore account for the influence of group identity. Belonging is structured by the default racial category of white, and those classified as nonwhite have more complex and conditional perceptions of American
in-group identity. In this respect, racial diversity exists in tension with
conceptions of being American because of the close association between
whiteness and belonging. The racialization of Latinos, African Americans, and Asian Americans as nonwhites produces an incomplete correspondence between their racial-group identity and being American.
Those who are from groups characterized by high foreign-born concentration experience a tension between their minority-group status and
perceptions of Americanness. Levels of group identity vary systematically across American racial groups, and the sense of commonality with
others in one's racial group acts as a moderating force on public opinion
on immigration.

Given the racial foundations of American identity, position in the racial hierarchy structures the context in which people make judgments
about immigration policy. The critical moderating factors at the individual level are perceptions of boundaries of what constitutes an American
and the level of racial and ethnic group identification. One's recognition
of his or her racial categorization and that group's position in the racial
hierarchy are salient factors for determining how individuals perceive
and make judgments about US immigration and naturalization policy.
Distinct stereotypes create incentives and costs for adopting these politically salient identities. Groups stereotyped as outsiders feel less American and have more incentive to identify with others in a group who are
also excluded from belonging.

For whites, racial categorization and being American are closely intertwined. Their position as the most advantaged racial group and status as the assumed default category of who constitutes an American
makes issues related to immigration more of an issue about acceptance
of outsiders. A strong racial identity in correspondence with a strong
sense of boundaries of what constitutes an American would predict at-

titudes about immigration consistent with an embrace of racial prerequisites to citizenship. In contrast, whites with weaker group identities
may rely more heavily on egalitarian norms in forming attitudes about
immigration.

In contrast, members of racialized minority groups experience a tension between being perceived as fully American and their own experiences as a racial minority. Attitudes about immigration and naturalization policy cannot be described simply as a function of nationalism or
ethnocentrism for African Americans, Latinos, and Asian Americans
because their racial status places them apart from the default understanding of American. Stronger attachments to a racialized status suggest
a greater openness to outsiders because of a shared experience of exclusion. Alternatively, those who feel less attached to their racial group and
who practice a higher degree of assimilation with whites may have stronger feelings of American identification and reflect more similar attitudes
to whites with strong national identities. Despite the shared status of being situated in a lower position in the racial hierarchy than whites, members of minority groups will not have uniform attitudes on immigration
and naturalization policy. Instead, the relative placement of the groups,
the unique history and experiences of racialization by group, and the valence and application of racial stereotypes create distinctive contexts in
which public opinion on immigration is formed in each group.

Method of study: comparative relational analysis

Analyzing attitudes on immigration at the individual level based on the
theoretical premises of a racial hierarchy and its structural influence on
the context of racial-group identification implies a method of analysis
distinctive from earlier and existing treatments of public opinion in the
United States. Our task in adopting a comparative relational perspective
for the study of public opinion in a diverse polity is not to forge simplic-
ity out of complexity but to make the complex comprehensible. To this
end, the analytical strategy in *The Politics of Belonging* incorporates a
number of distinctive methodological imperatives. In order to make sustained and accurate claims about US public opinion, analysts must consider all Americans, regardless of whether they are difficult to locate and
interview. Simply controlling for race does not tell us whether and where
to expect different relationships and instead only specifies that groups

will differ. It might be the case, for example, that identification with the Republican or Democratic Party has the same influence on immigration policy attitudes for everyone, but using an approach to control for race by definition obscures the possibility of observing a different set of relationships between party identification and political attitudes for blacks than for Latinos, for example.

The use of control or "dummy" variables for racial categorization is an appropriate and useful strategy in circumstances where the significance of race is either empirically unknown or not theorized. However, when testing a theory specifying the impact of the racial hierarchy, inferential models including control variables for racial categorization are inferior to those born of an analytical strategy that allows for the estimation of structurally different relationships between explanatory variables and political attitudes among individuals classified by race. A comparative relational analytical approach requires estimating models of public opinion separately by racial group and then analyzing the results across groups. This methodological strategy is therefore most appropriate for generating empirical analysis based in strong theoretical assumptions. In this case, we expect to see structurally different relationships for Americans categorized by race for the moderating effects of group identity as well as other antecedents to political attitudes on immigration.

This approach places race at the center of analysis and reflects the axiomatic position that the American racial hierarchy continues to structure social relationships and individual behavior. Our work is thus situated at the heart of the contemporary debate over the extent to which the United States is beyond race. The perspective we take is consistent with scholars including Bowler and Segura (2012), Dawson (2011), King and Smith (2011), Fraga et al. (2010), HoSang (2010), Schmidt et al. (2010), Tesler and Sears (2010), Kinder and Kam (2009), Bobo and Tuan (2006), Smith (2003), Williams (2003), and Claire Kim (1999), who argue that the racial order remains a potent factor in politics. A key assumption driving our analysis is that the structure of the racial hierarchy works to maintain the power of those individuals associated with the group on top while systematically reinforcing unequal access and less influence to groups lower down in the racial order. Thus the comparative relational perspective adopted here acknowledges group-based inequality and treats individuals in dynamic relationship both with groups and in the context of power.

Outline of the Book

To develop and illustrate the argument that location in the American racial hierarchy structures conceptions of belonging as well as the exercise
of individual agency, the book begins by laying some theoretical and empirical foundations. We delineate a theory of the context of racial-group
position and its influence on public opinion on immigration by specifying the moderating influence of racial-group identity in a model we
call the "Racial Prism of Group Identity" (RPGI). Chapter 1 begins by
highlighting distinctive patterns of contemporary immigration attitudes
among Americans classified by race. Although traditional public opinion theories often explain political attitudes on immigration as a function of party identification, the most apparent differences in opinion are
across racial groups. The remainder of the chapter articulates why race
serves as the most important division on immigration attitudes. We discuss the implications of the distinction between race and ethnicity for
the placement of racial groups within the diamond-shaped racial hierarchy. The hierarchy and a group's position within the racial order form
the foundation for our explication of the RPGI model of public opinion on immigration and our methodological strategy of comparative relational analysis.

Chapter 2 examines the development of the American racial hierarchy, policies and practices delineating political belonging, and the meanings attached to each racial category. Taking a historical perspective,
the analysis documents the interaction of race, immigration, and citizenship and their influence in the development of the American racial
order. Both the shape and the meanings of the categories that anchor
the diamond-shaped hierarchy have changed over time, and the historical analysis in this chapter tracks major developments that have contributed to the contemporary shape of the racial hierarchy. We describe
the links between economic growth and territorial expansion, the racial
basis for citizenship, and the path-dependent consequences of privileging whiteness for political attitudes at the individual level. Belonging to
the American polity—whether through racial categorization as white or
otherwise—is dynamic and continually being redefined, and the analysis in this chapter underscores the significance of immigration policy in
the content of racial stereotypes and the construction of group identities.

The chapter ends with a discussion of how racial shades of belonging are perceived in contemporary American politics.

In chapter 3 we delineate how the racial hierarchy created out of historical processes of American political development continues to structure contemporary social practices through the widespread and consistent association of negative and positive racial stereotypes. Our analysis of survey data from the Multi-City Study of Urban Inequality as well as the 2006 Faces of Immigration Survey collected by the authors demonstrates striking agreement about the content of stereotypes attached to each racial category. Racial tropes explain the meanings attached to each racial category, and the data support a structural explanation for the development and application of racial stereotypes among all Americans. However, while there is general agreement on the content of stereotypes, the analysis also demonstrates that the rates of stereotyping do vary across racial groups, with whites more likely to stereotype by race than Asian Americans, Latinos, and blacks. These findings reflect how racial position structures individual reliance on group-based stereotypes. The findings on the content, prevalence, and application of racial stereotypes by group serve as an important foundation for understanding the contours of group identity discussed in the next chapter.

Chapter 4 begins the specification of the RPGI model by identifying the important but often omitted antecedent to attitude formation: group identity. In the context of immigration policy, we consider in detail both national identity and racial-group identity. Given the racial prerequisites for American citizenship, members of different racial groups have experienced varying degrees of inclusion that inform group attachments. To document the variation in national and racial-group identities expressed by respondents, we analyze data from the Twenty-First Century Americanism survey and compare the different levels of national identity among whites, blacks, Asian Americans, and Latinos. The chapter then considers how exclusion from the national polity has encouraged greater emphasis on racial-group identity and solidarity among minorities. Using data from the 2004 National Politics Study we compare the rates of racial-group identity across the four groups. The analysis lays the foundation for the hypotheses we test in the next chapter that both national and racial-group identities will work concurrently but in distinctive ways for different racial groups in political attitudes on immigration.

Chapter 5 analyzes the antecedents of racial attitudes by identifying and testing our individual-level model of RPGI on questions about im-

migration policy. We begin by providing an overview of existing literature on immigration opinion and racial attitudes more generally in order
to identify the range and influence of explanatory measures. In so doing,
we analyze the limitations of existing frameworks, arguing that conventional scholarship does not sufficiently take into account the position of
individuals in the American racial order in inferential models of racial
attitudes. We use data from the 2006 Faces of Immigration Survey and
employ the comparative relational approach described above. We estimate a set of inferential models separately for each racial group and discuss how and why national identity and racial-group identity influence
political attitudes on immigration in different ways for Americans classified by race.

Chapter 6 documents how racial groups respond differently to political messages on immigration. Like any other set of political and social issues, public opinion on immigration policy is highly susceptible
to framing and priming in political communications by elites and the
mass media. We focus on two strategies employed by political elites today: framing immigrants as "illegal" and priming citizens to think about
the race of the immigrant. We analyze data from the Pew 2006 Immigration Survey and compare responses to "illegal" immigration across
whites, blacks, and Latinos. The analysis demonstrates that whites are
much more concerned about "illegal" immigration than either blacks or
Latinos. In the second half of the chapter we analyze data from an embedded survey experiment designed to prime respondents to think about
a particular racial group when considering immigration policy. Strikingly, we find that racial priming does not have uniform effects across
the four racial groups. Instead, racial priming succeeds in making respondents of some racial groups more positive toward immigrants and,
in other cases, eliciting more restrictive attitudes on immigration among
whites.

The concluding chapter summarizes the main empirical findings presented from the data analysis and returns to the three critical theoretical
and methodological interventions made in the book: the presence and
structural significance of the American racial hierarchy, the moderating
influence of racial-group and national identity on attitudes on immigration, and the methodological strategy of comparative relational analysis.
We end by considering the implications of diversity on American policy
formation and discussing the role of public opinion on contemporary immigration reform.

In the chapters that follow, *The Politics of Belonging* provides a systematic account of why people hold distinctive opinions about immigration and weaves a narrative from analysis of historical developments and empirical opinion data to uncover the dynamics of contemporary political attitudes on who should be allowed to be American.

CHAPTER ONE

Public Opinion through a Racial Prism

Political attitudes on immigration and naturalization defy simple explanation, and making sense of public opinion among a racially diverse polity has become more challenging. While opinion polls routinely show variation in preferences for immigration policy by political party identification, the most obvious and consistent differences in public opinion are visible among Americans classified by race. Consider the variation in responses by race in a recent survey that asked people how concerned they were about the "rising number of immigrants in the United States." Among whites, 77% reported being somewhat or very concerned. In contrast, smaller proportions of African Americans (57%), Asian Americans (57%), and Latinos (52%) replied similarly.[1] A 2010 Pew survey found that 73% of whites favored the Arizona immigrant-profiling law (SB 1070), while 51% of blacks approved.[2] When asked whether the number of immigrants should be reduced, remain the same, or be increased, Asian Americans and Latinos were less likely to say that the number of immigrants should be reduced a little or a lot than were African Americans and whites.

Regarding other aspects of immigration policy such as eligibility for social services, a somewhat different pattern of opinion among racial groups is apparent. When asked if all immigrants in the United States should be eligible for social services provided by state and local governments—an issue approved by a majority of California voters when they passed Proposition 187, the "Save Our State" initiative, in 1994— well over 80% of whites nationally voice opposition.[3] In contrast, the opposite pattern of support for immigrant eligibility for social services is apparent among minority Americans. Three times the proportion of Asian Americans and Latinos and two and a half times the percentage of African Americans compared to whites agreed that all immigrants should be eligible for social services.

Explanations for the systematic divergence in political attitudes on immigration often rely on partisanship as a reason for the differences in attitudes between racial groups. Whites might be more favorable toward restrictionist immigration policies because they are more often Republicans than are African Americans, Latinos, and Asian Americans. But as have other polarizing issues, such as campaign financing, the politics of immigration has often brought together strange bedfellows, alliances of conservative Republicans and liberal Democrats. Immigration policy reform since the 1965 Immigration and Nationality Act has always been a bipartisan affair, resulting in federal legislation such as the Simpson-Mazzoli Act (also known as the Immigration Reform and Control Act of 1986), which both criminalized hiring unauthorized workers and provided a path to citizenship for some immigrants. At the same time, policies of restriction, opposition to amnesty for unauthorized aliens, and withholding public education and social services are most closely associated with the Republican Party. While Democratic politicians are more likely to favor progressive policies such as the Development, Relief, and Education for Alien Minors (DREAM) Act, they do not do so in lockstep, and Democrats joined Republicans in support of stronger border control and deportation enforcement aimed primarily at Latino immigrants under the Illegal Immigration Reform and Immigrant Responsibility Act (1996). In these important ways, elite cues about Democratic and Republican Party positions on immigration are not always clear cut (Tichenor 2002).

Despite these complexities, Democrats are nevertheless perceived to be more progressive on immigration reform than Republicans. If white Americans are more likely to be Republican than are African Americans or Latinos or Asian Americans—and they are—the differential in partisanship could explain the divergence in policy attitudes. As we discuss in detail in the empirical chapters that follow, partisan affiliation does influence public opinion on immigration, but it does so in distinctive ways among whites, Latinos, Asian Americans, and African Americans, the patterns reflecting the intersection between partisanship and race. For example, the 2006 Faces of Immigration Survey shows nearly perfect correspondence between strong Republican Party affiliation and concern about immigration among whites; 99% of white Republicans say they are somewhat or very concerned about the rising number of immigrants in the United States. Consistent with partisan differences, fewer whites who identify with the Democratic Party have the same response, and 75% reply similarly.

Partisanship does not explain positions on immigration to the same degree among racial minorities, however. Among Latinos, Asian Americans, and African Americans who identify with the Republican Party, the proportions who are somewhat or very concerned about increasing numbers of immigrants are more comparable to attitudes among Democratic whites; 65% of Republican Latinos are concerned, 74% of Asian American Republicans are concerned, and 57% of Republican African Americans (a small proportion of the party) are somewhat or very concerned about the rising number of immigrants in the United States. So while party identification influences individual attitudes about immigration in predictable ways, it does not do so to the same degree for all racial groups.

Understanding contemporary public opinion on immigration is a complex task that requires broadening the range of theoretical perspectives as well as the methodological strategies utilized to understand the dynamics of political attitudes. In a nation far beyond the black-white divide, models of public opinion built so heavily on that binary are not well suited to explaining variation in political attitudes amidst the racial diversity in the United States today. Traditional analytical strategies are characterized by estimating a multivariate model to explain variation in attitudes and specifying "control" or "dummy" variables for being black, Latino, or Asian American in addition to measures of partisanship and other relevant controls. The results often yield significant results for the race control variables given that the excluded category of white is the reference category to which all of the other groups are compared.

Absent stronger theoretical justification for analysis conducted with this setup, however, showing a significant result for a control variable representing an individual's racial-group classification indicates only that race matters. Important as these findings are, this strategy does not generate either expectations or explanations about why the patterns of difference are visible. A control-variable strategy in the absence of interaction effects specifies only differences in intercept rather than systematic variation in slope, where race is treated as an individual-level trait to control for rather than a structural feature that produces differential outcomes because of group position. For example, labor economists know that higher formal educational attainment is positively related to income earnings in much the same way that political scientists can demonstrate that strong Republican Party identification is related to support of restrictive immigration policies at the individual level. But economists also know that education has weaker effects on income for women than on earnings among men. Women continue to earn seventy-seven cents for every dollar earned by men in the United States, and not only do female workers earn less to start in many occupational sectors, but the rate at which income earnings increase with levels of education is not as steep for women as it is for men. Economic models of income earnings therefore either estimate models separately by sex or specify interaction effects to account for intercept and slope differences between relevant categories of analysis. In contrast, political scientists studying public opinion rarely take steps to specify a theoretical position of expected differences based in hierarchically structured groups such as race.

Our approach in *Conditional Welcome* takes as axiomatic the unequal structural context of the racial hierarchy in the United States and models the significance of group position for public opinion on immigration. We argue that political attitudes are structured by the racial hierarchy, are formed at the individual level through the lens of group identity, and are the product of group interactions and historical memory. Public opinion on immigration at the individual level is filtered through a racial prism, moderated by social-group identity in terms of perceptions of what it means to be an American and racial-group consciousness. In the following section we discuss the framework of race as it is perceived in the United States and analyze the significance and shape of the American racial hierarchy. We next articulate an individual-level theory of the context of racial-group position, the Racial Prism of Group Identity (RPGI) model, and specify how relative status among groups has consequences for political attitudes. In the final section of this chapter we explicate a methodological strategy of comparative relational analysis for studying public opinion in a diverse American polity and specify empirical expectations generated by the RPGI model.

The American Racial Hierarchy and 'Its Consequences for Public Opinion

The American state has since its inception classified and ranked people by race for political purposes. The founders' decision to preserve the practice of slavery set the stage for subsequent federal policy that would grant citizenship based on racial-group status. African slaves, Native Americans, Mexicans, and Chinese, among other groups, were excluded from political membership because they were considered undesirable for membership in the polity. The first federal law governing citizenship in 1790 established whiteness as a condition of membership, and the institutionalization of a racial hierarchy in the United States was codified by a steady stream of constitutional protections of slavery, federal and state legislation, Supreme Court and lower court rulings, international treaties and agreements, and executive actions supporting the ranking of nonwhites as inferior to whites (Schrag 2010; Bosniak 2006; Ngai 2004; Tichenor 2002; Smith 1997). Counted as three-fifths of the white population for legislative apportionment in article I, section 2, of the US Constitution, African slaves were described as "other persons." Political personhood and citizenship rights were unthinkable for a human population of slaves owned by whites. Deemed inferior, blacks have been at the bottom of the racial hierarchy in the United States for centuries, initially not free and not citizens, and not meaningfully enfranchised for one hundred years after the ratification of the Thirteenth, Fourteenth, and Fifteenth Amendments to the Constitution. These racialized formations solidified the role of group categorization and the racial hierarchy as a powerful stratifier and constant of social structure in the United States.

People classified as white, on the other hand, are positioned at the top of the hierarchy. The groups of people included in the white category have expanded over time from the narrow conception of whiteness in Anglo-Saxon Protestant terms to include formerly "less than white" Irish, Italian, Catholic, and Jewish Americans (Gross 2008; Haney López 2006; Ignatiev 1995; M. Jacobson 1999). While the composition of the white racial category has changed, the placement of the group at the top of the hierarchy has remained constant. The category of Hispanic or Latino is a relatively new addition to the American racial taxonomy and currently exists as a designation of ethnicity rather than race. While

Mexicans were enumerated as a separate race for one decennial census, the category disappeared after 1930. The designation of ethnicity as Hispanic or Latino first appeared in the census in 1980 and in official government reporting after 1977 on the basis of an administrative directive from the Office of Management and Budget (Hattam 2007).[4] The category of Latino or Hispanic includes new immigrants from Mexico, El Salvador, and Cuba, for example, along with Americans with multigenerational histories on American soil whose ancestors came to the United States from countries in Latin America or who resided on the land before it became part of the United States. Racially, Latinos can choose from any of the categories of enumeration provided by the census: "White," "Black, African Am., or Negro," "American Indian or Alaska Native," and a long list of Asian national-origin groups including "Asian Indian," "Chinese," "Japanese," "Korean," and two categories of "Other Asian" and "Other Pacific Islander." For Latinos, then, ethnicity and race are mutually exclusive.

In contrast, for Asian Americans national origin is counted by the US government as race rather than ethnicity. The only category of ethnicity in the American racial taxonomy is Latino or Hispanic, and the census counts Asian Indians, Japanese, and Koreans, for instance, as separate races. The practice of distinct racial categorization by country of origin in Asia has been in effect since the late 1800s and was put in place to support the construction and maintenance of federal Asian exclusion laws. Over time, and since 1870, the four categories of race that have remained consistent in the census are white, black, Indian, and Chinese (Nobles 2000). The racial category of Japanese was added two censuses later and has remained through 2010. The persistent and official categorization of Asian Americans as distinctly nonwhite racial outsiders has therefore been part of the official racial taxonomy since before the term "ethnicity" became part of the American racial lexicon. The staying power of these separate Asian race categories comports with explicit anti-Asian discriminatory immigration policies based in white racial privilege present until the mid-twentieth century.

The place of ethnicity and its relationship to race in the American racial taxonomy is equally illuminating. In her brilliant comparative study of the development of Jewish ethnicity and the Latino/Hispanic category in the United States, Victoria Hattam argues that race and ethnicity are mutually constitutive, each constraining and making the other possible. Ethnicity anchors difference rooted in culture and language and is—in contrast to race—malleable, open, and the basis for claims to pluralism in the United States. It is because of this construction that 2012 Republican presidential candidate Mitt Romney could have, in the 2010 census, counted himself as "Latino or Hispanic or Spanish origin" because his father was born in Mexico. In contrast to ethnicity, race is the language of difference that is fixed, phenotypically distinctive, and based in blood quantum. In its distinction from ethnicity and its ties to inequality, race is defined as bounded and unchanging.

It is this relationship that fuels what Hattam calls "associative chains" of language connecting ethnicity with pluralism and race with persistent inequality and hierarchy. It is no coincidence that blacks and Chinese and Indians were fixed as races in the American taxonomy prior to the development of the concept of ethnicity in the early twentieth-century environment of eugenics. To the extent that racial classification has been used in service to and in tandem with policies of exclusion, the logic of the taxonomy need only be relevant to justifying difference. At the same time, there is a similar absence of logic and consistency in the distinction behind Hispanic/Latino as an ethnicity, though as Hattam argues, there are both discriminatory and egalitarian impulses behind the race and ethnicity distinction of the American racial taxonomy. The content and persistence of the racial taxonomy and the explicit connection to normative conceptions of desirable characteristics for political belonging set the stage for shape of the American racial hierarchy.

The shape of the American racial hierarchy

Hattam's argument about the mutually constitutive process of the formation of Jewish identity and the ethnic category of Hispanic/Latino provides an important window of insight for developing a theory of the shape of the American racial hierarchy that includes Asian Americans and Latinos along with blacks and whites. In particular, and while it is clear that whites are at the top of the racial hierarchy and blacks at the bottom, the place of Asian Americans and Latinos in the order remains in question (Omi and Winant 1994; Bonilla-Silva 2010). We conceptualize the position of the four groups in the shape of a diamond where whites are at the top, blacks are at the bottom, and Latinos and Asian Americans are between African Americans and whites (figure 1.1). Placement is indicative of desirability for entrance and full membership in the American polity that has been articulated and reinforced by the American state in immi-

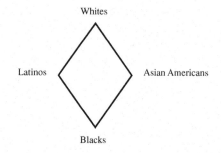

FIGURE 1.1. Diamond shape of the American racial hierarchy

gration and naturalization policy. Desirability is a multidimensional and relative phenomenon, and as Claire Kim (2000) argues in her influential work on race relations in New York City, belonging is structured on the dual axes of superior/inferior and insider/foreigner.

Whites have the benefit of default-category status as the racial insider and as superior, automatically eligible for citizenship in terms of racial categorization. Blacks, on the other hand, have a long history of being systematically shut out of the US political system and disproportionately represented in the lower economic class in the United States. Racially, Asian Americans are closer to African Americans because of their clear status as racialized others. Like blacks, their inability ever to become white under the American racial taxonomy reinforces the racial stereotype of their status as "forever foreigner." At the same time, US immigration policy, inadvertently rather than by design, has created incentives for highly skilled workers with accompanying educational credentials and professional skills to legally enter and remain in the United States. Recipients of H1-B visas under the occupational preference category of the 1965 Immigration and Nationality Act and its amendments are disproportionately from Asian countries, and the policy has created a selection bias of highly skilled and higher-status Asian Americans. Many Asian American immigrants, who during Asian exclusion were derisively stereotyped as "coolies," are now on the other side of economic class, closer in proximity to whites in terms of income and social status and more likely than other minorities to marry, live, work with, and go to school with whites (Junn 2007). High social class is not enjoyed equally by all Asian Americans, however, and those who are both poor and racially marked as other slide further down in desirability toward the placement of African Americans (Bonilla-Silva 2010).

The placement of Latinos in the American racial hierarchy is also driven by US immigration and naturalization policy and is apparent in many indicators of economic and social status. Blacks and Latinos are worst off in terms of wealth, income, education attainment, life expectancy, and infant mortality. The trajectory of Latinos, a group of Americans only recently characterized as such, has been influenced by the colonial experience of discrimination and disadvantage, exclusionary federal and state laws, and exploitation in labor practices of American employers (Jiménez 2010; Perlmann 2005). Latinos are the most diverse of the racial categories in terms of national origin and generation of immigration. In her provocative book *The Trouble with Unity* (2010), Cristina Beltrán urges care in treating Latinos as an undifferentiated political category. Latino, she argues, is not a pre-existing thing—a phenomenon waiting to emerge—but instead, Beltrán argues that "Latino is a verb" (157). Racially, and as a function of the distinction between race and ethnicity for this group in the American racial taxonomy, Latinos have the option of identifying racially as white. Doing so can move those so declared higher up the racial order closer to whites. But only Latinos who are light skinned and of higher social and economic status have effectively done so and, in the process, have distanced themselves from the stigma of the negative stereotype of "illegal" immigrant closely associated with Latinos (Bonilla-Silva 2010). Working in tandem with the relative valorization of newcomers from Asian countries, US immigration policy has helped to create the context of demand for low-wage workers and the perception of Latinos as poor, unauthorized aliens. In this respect, lower class status exerts a powerful pull down the racial order for Latinos in the United States.

Thus the contemporary shape of the racial hierarchy in the United States is not a perfectly aligned diamond shape. As depicted in figure 1.2, Asian Americans are positioned higher than Latinos and closer to whites. Latinos are pushed further down, closer to African Americans and further away from whites and Asian Americans. Different alignments of the diamond of American racial position are not only possible but to be expected as the dynamics of the politics of belonging are shaped by race and immigration. Historical precedent, subsequent development, and contextual circumstances exert continuous pressure on the shape of the hierarchy as well as on the meaning of the racial categories that anchor the order. Just as the stereotypes of Asian immigrants as "coolies" have been replaced over time by perceptions of Asians as the

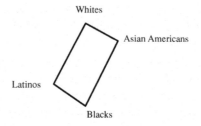

FIGURE 1.2. Contemporary shape of the American racial hierarchy

"model minority" and "forever foreigner," perceptions of Latinos and the meaning of this category have also undergone transformation.

While the racial hierarchy represents racial categories of white, black, Latino, and Asian American, other axes of categorical difference and desirability including gender, religion, and sexuality could be analyzed in similar fashion. US immigration policy is populated with other ignominious characterizations of new entrants deemed unfit for entry and political membership. In particular, Native Americans, who exist today as a separate category in the American racial taxonomy, have unique circumstances of exclusion as a function of the state-sanctioned genocide of their ancestors as well as a legacy of profound discrimination.[5] Women were long excluded from full political membership and voting enfranchisement as a function of their sex. The Page Act of 1875 explicitly prohibited the entry of immigrants defined as undesirable, among the categories of which were Chinese women who would engage in prostitution (Gardner 2005). Contemporary furor over birthright citizenship and the construction of Latinas crossing the US-Mexico border to give birth to "anchor babies" is evidence of the extent to which gender and race remain intimately intertwined in rhetoric on immigration policy. Being gay was grounds for exclusion until the 1990 Immigration Act, though the original provision excluding people "afflicted with sexual deviation" was not widely applied (Minter 1993). Likewise, the anti-Semitic immigration policies of the United States before and during World War II and the conflation of American Jews and communists are eerily similar to the present of the construction of Arab Americans and Muslims and their purported links to Middle East terrorists.

Despite the movement toward more egalitarian policies in the United States, the racial order remains sticky, continuing to produce returns for whiteness through perceptions of legitimate political membership in the default category of racial status. In contrast, minorities are still ranked lower in the racial hierarchy, systematically disadvantaged as a result of being declared nonwhite with conditional acceptance in the polity. The content of racialization and the relative placement of groups within the American racial order create different forms and degrees of constraint for Americans classified by race. We turn next to the individual-level consequences of this relative positioning.

Structuring agency through group position and perception

The persistent power of the American racial hierarchy in creating distinctions between Americans is evident in the everyday constructions and perceptions of group difference. Despite the widespread acceptance of the notion that race is a social construction, racial stereotypes remain commonplace and justified on the basis of natural traits. Blacks have a genetic ability to jump higher than whites; Asians' quantitative acumen is rooted in the survival of the fittest among ancestor rice farmers (Gladwell 2008). Despite distinctions in national origin and strong individual-level identifications with these groups, minority Americans are classified into racial groups (Greer 2013; Rogers 2006; Waters 2000; Wong et al. 2011; DeSipio 1996). There are more negative racial stereotypes of Native Americans, Latinos, African Americans, and Asian Americans than there are positive ones, but the point is that the codification of racial difference within the American racial taxonomy serves to both categorize and reinscribe as fixed distinctions rooted in race.

The strength of racial stereotypes is perhaps best illustrated in the responses to survey questions asking Americans about the traits of people in racial groups. The 2000 Multi-City Study of Urban Inequality (MCSUI) posed questions about stereotypical traits to a large sample of respondents in major metropolitan areas in the United States (Bobo and Massagli 2001). While we analyze the racial stereotypes data in detail in chapter 3, a brief preview of the findings is instructive. When respondents were asked to assess how well members of each racial group speak English, all Americans identify whites as the group that speaks English best. Indeed, the two most heavily immigrant groups of respondents, Asian Americans and Latinos, give whites the highest rating. On this insider/foreigner dimension of desirability, Latinos and Asian Americans are seen by Americans as lacking in English-language ability. On another dimension of desirability, that of superior/inferior in terms of wealth, data on racial stereotypes reveal a different pattern. Whether white, black, Asian American, or Latino, respondents view African Americans and Latinos as poor. In contrast, all Americans rate whites as being rich, followed to a lesser degree by Asian Americans.

The overall patterns in the MCSUI stereotypes data are striking, and the influence of the racial hierarchy on the everyday fortunes and opportunities of Americans classified by race is reflected in the perceptions individuals hold about racial groups. Structured by practices of exclusion at the political and institutional level, unequal individual-level perceptions of desirability are, according to more than a half century of systematic social psychological investigation, endemic to the human condition. People across the world and in societies and political systems of many varieties are susceptible to social organization by category. These patterns of categorical thinking among Americans are visible in the reflection of the racial hierarchy mirrored in perceptions of racial stereotypes.

Stereotypes are important because they are used in public narratives to justify and uphold group-based inequalities (Sidanius and Pratto 1999; Steele 2010; Fiske 2011). The powerful associations between racial-group membership and status in terms of class and being an insider are embedded in existing social norms and assumptions and communicated through legitimizing myths. These stories further exacerbate inequality through hierarchy enhancing practices that result in "durable inequalities" observed in all societies (Tilly 1999). The consistency of in-group and out-group designations, combined with a system of structural inequality embedded in the racial hierarchy, creates the context in which public opinion on immigration is formed at the individual level in the United States.

Relative group position and normative perceptions of racial groups are the aggregate-level manifestations of the American racial hierarchy. It is the context of this constraint that structures individual-level agency for Americans classified by race (Bobo and Tuan 2006; Williams 2003). For individuals in each of the four racial groups in the United States, position in the racial order has consequences for the type and degree of constraint they experience when forming attitudes about immigration policy. The decision to support or oppose a policy such as the requirement to show documentation of citizenship status in Arizona's SB 1070 law is not the same for whites as it is for Latinos. Widely perceived as the target for the law because they are stereotyped as unauthorized immigrants, Latinos are more constrained in how they view and respond to this political issue. Whites are less likely to be personally and adversely affected by such a law and as a result have broader agency in the range and degree of individual-level attributes that influence their opinion. While Asian Americans are heavily immigrant, their racial group has not been stereotyped as "illegal" and is not the target of the Arizona law. For African Americans, frames of "racial profiling" surrounding the Arizona law are relevant because blacks systematically experience higher scrutiny and surveillance as potential criminals as a function of their racial-group membership (Baldus et al. 2001; Bowers, Steiner, and Sandys 2001; Somers and Ellsworth 2001). Thus Americans classified by race develop attitudes about politics and immigration policy in the structural context of group position and perceptions of racial stereotypes.

The insight that the context of the racial hierarchy and relative group position structures individual agency in attitudes on immigration reflects an important departure from the assumption of equality of agency implicit in most analyses rooted in the "behavioral" tradition in the study of American politics. While scholars of public opinion are aware of the legacy of racial discrimination and the social and political inequalities that follow, the notion that there is uniformity in political agency—in one's ability to participate, to be mobilized by political parties and elites, to consider political alternatives, to seek and consume political information, to form positions on political phenomena—is nevertheless widely held. While analysts routinely acknowledge substantial differences in resources and motivation, the underlying premise that Americans have equal agency in the US political system is rooted in the normatively appealing liberal democratic emphasis on equal opportunity. But just because we want it to be equal does not make it so.

Who one is racially, where one's group is positioned relative to others, and what stereotypes are associated with one's group systematically structure political attitudes. For example, as appealing as it would be for women to have the same degree of freedom as men to take public transportation or walk city streets alone late at night, their decisions to do so are constrained by the reality of disproportionately high rates of violence against women. In this case, the observation of individual-level behavior such as a woman leaving a party earlier than a male guest in order to catch a train while it is still safe to ride public transportation should be analyzed with the recognition of the constraint embedded in the context of gender hierarchy. Simply put, agency at the individual level is constrained by relative group position. To account for this systematic variation in explaining public opinion on immigration, we developed the RPGI model.

The Racial Prism of Group Identity

Building on the argument that position in the racial hierarchy structures the context in which people make judgments about immigration and naturalization policy, we now articulate the logic and measurement of the moderating influence of group identity on public opinion. At the individual level, variation in one's recognition of his or her racial categorization and that group's position in the racial hierarchy are salient factors in explaining differences in public opinion on immigration across groups. The racial hierarchy creates incentives and costs for adopting politically salient identities, with those ranked at the bottom more constrained in their identity choices than those ranked at the top. Because of this, group identity works as a prism through which political stimuli about immigration policy are filtered in distinctive ways for Americans classified by race.

Racial-group identity measured through a sense of linked fate—the sense that an individual's fortunes are linked to others in his or her racial group—is the first of two important aspects of identity that we define as the racial prism through which Americans view the politics of immigration. How people understand traits that characterize an American is a second important way in which public opinion is reflected through the racial prism. These two forms of group identity together create a lens through which individuals interpret issues of political belonging in the United States. Group identity acts in much the same way as a refractive prism, into which white light enters and a rainbow of colors exits.[6] Public opinion on immigration is often treated as a unitary entity similar to the beam of white light, but in a diverse polity, relative location in the racial hierarchy and the RPGI causes attitudes to refract into distinctive form among whites, Latinos, blacks, and Asian Americans.

Members of racial groups hold systematically different perceptions of national inclusion and vary in their perceptions of characteristics and boundaries of what it means to be an American. Because the norm of Americanness is structured by the default racial category of white, those classified as nonwhite have more complex and conflicting feelings of national attachment (Schildkraut 2011; Theiss-Morse 2009). Their racialization as nonwhite makes the correspondence imperfect between their racial-group identity and being American. The common experience for Asian Americans and Latinos of being asked the question "Where are you from?" typifies the context of the tension between minority-group status and perceptions of Americanness. Rarely are whites asked the same question about their origins, nor is their answer that they are "American" scrutinized to the same degree as it is for minorities, because their race corresponds with the default racial category of American. Those who enjoy full membership as Americans will seek to protect their national group. Among minority Americans, their degree of attachment as peripheral in-group members who have not always enjoyed the full benefits of national membership will vary systematically from whites.

African Americans, Latinos, and Asian Americans experience conditional membership in the nation as a function of their racial categorization and therefore develop stronger awareness of the racial hierarchy and its effects. Peripheral-group membership structures everyday experiences and life chances, and minority Americans with a strong sense of racial linked fate recognize their status (Dawson 1994). The extent to which individuals perceive their life chances are connected to the status of their racial group is an important but overlooked factor in explanations of public opinion on immigration. Strong perceived linked fate will influence attitudes in opposition to exclusionary and restrictive laws that seek to maintain the status quo.

An example of the RPGI model at work occurred during the spring of 2006 when the US Congress debated legislation that would make immigration without government authorization a felony and increase funding to monitor the US-Mexico border. In opposition to the bill, advocacy groups organized nationwide protests. Thousands of people marched in streets, and a few held Mexican flags and signs written in Spanish. In the age of twenty-four-hour news programming, the national media repeatedly broadcast images of the protests, often accompanied by commentary and debate. The content of discussion is illuminating because it demonstrates how immigration-related images trigger different norms, values, and ideas among Americans of different racial groups. This is the text of one exchange between journalist Lou Dobbs and Janet Murguia, president of the National Council of La Raza:

DOBBS: Why are all those demonstrators out there carrying Mexican flags?

MURGUIA: Well there's a sense of pride with anybody. We just had St. Patrick's Day. Are you saying that Irish, because they're holding up their Irish flags, that all of a sudden they're not loyal or they're un-American? It's a double standard to say that people from one country can wave their flag, but people who want to be Americans can wave another flag but they're not being loyal. That's a double standard. . . .

DOBBS: I don't think that we should have any flag flying in this country except the flag of the United States. And let me tell you something else, since we're talking about double standards and I think you're right about people who would believe that.

But let's be clear. I don't think there should be a St. Patrick's Day. I don't care who you are. I think we ought to be celebrating what is common about this country, what we enjoy as similarities as people. And as Peter Viles was reporting, talking about the culture and heritage of their people and that's why they want to hold up the Mexican flag or Ecuadorian flag.

MURGUIA: No, this is about the American dream, this is about the aspirations of being Americans.[7]

These two commentators have starkly different evaluations of what they are witnessing. The conflict in their interpretation of the images is based in their distinctive understandings of what it means to be an American and the incorporation pathways immigrants should take. Dobbs defines American as similarity—his version of neutrality—over difference and foreignness, in this case, the Mexican flag. In contrast, Murguia sees being American as the practice of free expression. The two differ starkly in their conceptions of American boundaries and, despite looking at the same images, focus on different issues to make their arguments.

In the interaction between Dobbs and Murguia, both are looking at the same pictures of the protesters, but how they interpreted the events depends on their racial categorization, position in the racial order, and group identity. They have divergent perspectives because they rely on different assumptions and perceptions of membership. As a white American, Dobbs takes the position of those in the majority group. He promotes a vision of assimilation in which expressing ethnic or national-origin identities threaten that goal. By promoting assimilation, Dobbs privileges the identity and culture held by the existing white majority population. Murguia, who is Latina, sees the same pictures of the protesters but from the position of a racial minority. She rejects the goal of commonality with existing norms and instead argues that individuals can simultaneously identify with both their ethnic and national identities. The connection between race and citizenship is also raised in this interaction, and Murguia defends the Latino protesters as American, while Dobbs attacks their "un-Americanness."

The RPGI model takes the context of relative structural position seriously and specifies the indicators of constraint on attitudes as measures of perceived linked fate with one's racial group and perception of American boundaries. These two factors are key antecedents that explain attitudes on immigration as well as the systematic variation between racial groups in opinion on immigration policy. Priming individuals to think about the racial hierarchy is a potent strategy used by political elites to mobilize voters. Political appeals framing immigrants as racially distinctive and emphasizing negative tropes continue to be used to mobilize anti-immigrant sentiment (Abrajano 2010). Political communications strategies bank on the idea that voters will support more punitive policies when targeting groups stereotyped as outsiders and ranked low in the hierarchy. The RPGI model thus draws from both the American racial hierarchy and the dynamics of group identity in developing systematic expectations about the contours of public opinion on immigration.

Revealing Why Racial Differences Exist: Comparative Relational Analysis

A persistent public opinion divide between whites and blacks, particularly on issues pertaining to racial inequality, is well documented (Schuman et al. 1997; Sears, Henry and Kosterman 2000; Tate 2010). But the "public" in American public opinion has undergone dramatic change since the early days of survey research in the United States. In the mid-1960s, the population was defined by a clear black-white binary of roughly 10% African American and 90% white. The proportion of the population defined racially as white is today roughly two-thirds, and the size of the minority population has more than tripled since the mid-twentieth century. With this growth has come an explosion in research on minority public opinion, a welcome development to match the demographic changes, but one that has also been described as "downright alarming" in terms of keeping current on research (Burns and Kinder 2012, 139). Difficult as it may be to document the presence of racial differences in public opinion and then explain why the variation exists, scholarship on American public opinion can no longer legitimately be described as such without including all Americans—whites, blacks, Latinos, and Asian Americans—in the analysis. Despite the visible racial diversity of the US population, analysis of political behavior and attitudes is still characterized by analyses that demonstrate that racial groups are different while providing relatively little reasoning to explain the variation. The conventional method of using control variables to identify group differences presents race as a figurative black box. In this section, we review existing strategies employed to study racial-group differences in public opinion and then describe a method of comparative relational analysis we argue is well suited to revealing why groups vary in political attitudes on immigration.

Analytical strategy of race as a "control" variable

A common analytical strategy in public opinion research is to include race as a "control" variable in a multivariate model. Survey respondents are coded into dichotomous "dummy" variables signifying their racial status as African American, Latino, or white.[8] Whites are most often designated the reference group and excluded from the estimation. In this setup, whites are by definition the comparison group, and the observation of statistically significant estimated coefficients on the race control variables (while accounting for other individual-level effects) demonstrates the importance of being a minority for public opinion. The analytical strategy of using race as a control variable is inherently comparative because the coefficients on minority control variables are assessed against the reference category of white, making it possible to observe whether there are racial-group differences across different dependent variables. Using this method, scholars have produced a running tally of the measures for which racial-group categorization matters and have identified other attitudes for which race is not significant. Indeed, much of the public opinion literature in political science is not expressly concerned about explaining racial differences and instead focuses on identifying a particular factor, such as personality or partisanship, that explains a significant amount of variance in the dependent variable of interest.[9]

Despite its popularity in political behavior analysis, the strategy of controlling for race has important limitations. Model estimates yielding a significant coefficient on a dichotomous race control variable indicate only that racial classification is relevant, but not why it matters. Equally important, when the model controls for race without specifying inter-action terms for other explanatory variables with racial categorization, the control-variable strategy defines all other individual-level character-istics as functioning in the same way for everyone regardless of racial-group status. So when predicting attitudes on immigration with party identification, demographic characteristics, and control variables for race, the results indicate only whether the intercept varies significantly for whites, African Americans, and Latinos. This specification cannot account for potential differential effects of partisanship by racial group, and the setup of the model defines Republican Party affiliation as having the same effect on white respondents as it does for Latinos, for example. As discussed earlier, the relationship between political partisanship and attitudes on immigration for whites and Latinos is not uniform.

Viewed from this vantage point, the analytical strategy of controlling for race has the potential to yield inaccurate results for the magnitude of antecedents predicting political attitudes. The blind spot that has allowed this strategy to become so popular is the result of the widespread but si-lent assumption about equality of individual agency and, by extension, what constitutes "normal" in political behavior research.[10] Often, and al-most reflexively, researchers include control variables for racial minori-ties in regression models. The statistical justification for doing so, at least in the case of racial minorities in analysis of data from a national sample of Americans, is that whites are numerically the largest racial group. As a result, whites are defined as the "reference group" to which the other groups are compared. Although this is not necessarily intentional, inter-pretation of the coefficients on the race control variables for minority groups are often framed as deviations from the normative baseline de-fined by whites.[11] Control variables for Latinos typically show a negative coefficient in equations predicting voting, indicating that, all else being equal, Latinos do not turn out to vote at the same level as whites. Thus not only does the model specification define "normal" within the con-text of white behavior, but the substantive interpretation of the negative coefficient on the Latino control variable is stymied by a model specifi-cation that treats the antecedents as all having the same effect on voting regardless of racial group. And because whites represent the overwhelm-ing majority in most national samples, the estimated coefficients of the independent variables in the multivariate model ultimately reflect patterns that characterize white respondents.[12]

Using control variables is not always problematic, however, and taking this perspective does not imply the practice itself is flawed. There are important questions the control-variable strategy is well suited to answer. It is most useful for determining whether individual attributes vary systematically by race. Analysis yielding significant coefficients on the race control variables demonstrates that group differences persist, even when accounting for other factors and assuming the same slopes for the other independent variables specified in the model. These are important finding to establish race as a critical moderating variable on political attitudes and behavior.

A comparative relational analytical approach to race and public opinion

Our analytical approach to the study of race and public opinion begins with the axiomatic position that systems of social stratification such as the racial hierarchy create a context of unequal constraint that influences attitudes and behavior at the individual level. We reject the assumption of equality of individual agency in the estimation and interpretation of inferential models, and the assumption is only defensible if the political system itself is neutral, not favoring one or another for any particular characteristic or category.[13] Instead, agency operates in a social context of power relations as well as within the constraints of democratic political institutions and practices developed through the lens of racial hierarchy and discrimination (Katznelson 2005; Lieberman 1998). Because of the power of the racial hierarchy, different racial groups do not develop political attitudes in the same structural context, and this creates the need for a methodological strategy that recognizes the role of race as a structural characteristic.

Our strategy of comparative relational analysis is to disaggregate respondents by racial category and estimate separate models.[14] Doing so allows us to observe distinct configurations of explanatory factors both for individual-level attitudes and for the magnitude and direction of antecedents to be different across groups. Estimating separate models yields results that can be compared across groups for differences in intercepts as well as in slope for explanatory variables of political attitudes on immigration. For example, racial diversity of the respondent's neighborhood is a significant predictor of restrictionist attitudes among members of all racial groups, but the direction of the effect may be different. Among whites, neighborhood diversity enhances support for decreasing immigration, while for Asian Americans racial diversity in one's neighborhood attenuates restrictionist opinion.

A comparative relational analytical approach considers how the construction of each racial category results in the creation of unique experiences that influence attitudes on political belonging and immigration policy. For African American respondents, models must appropriately account for racial marginalization that influences perceptions of group position and group identity relevant to the black political experience (Dawson 1994; Tate 1998). Research on Asian Americans and Latinos suggests that factors related to group identity and immigrant acculturation include other relevant considerations (see for example de la Garza et al. 1992; Fraga et al. 2010; Hero 1992; Lien, Conway, and Wong 2004; Wong et al. 2011; Sanchez and Masuoka 2010). Thus the context of racial groups in relation to one another is important in the approach to specifying inferential models of political attitudes.

Including all Americans in the analysis and using a strategy that allows for meaningful comparisons across groups are of primary importance in the comparative relational analysis approach advocated here. Public opinion on immigration is best studied with multiple groups in action rather than by considering one group in isolation. While limitations in data on minority populations once prevented comparative analysis across racial groups, those concerns are less relevant today. In the empirical chapters to come, we analyze survey data from multiple independent sources that included large samples of African Americans, whites, Latinos, and Asian Americans. With these data, and using a method of comparative relational analysis, we show that perceptions of social advantage, group threat, and identity are formed in reference to where a group is positioned relative to others.

Expectations from the racial prism of group identity model

Utilizing a strategy of comparative relational analysis allows us to reveal a variety of relationships between racial categorization, group identity, and individual-level factors among Americans classified by race in their political attitudes on immigration. Group identity is the key moderating mechanism that explains variation in individual attitudes on immigration as well as why racial groups vary in their positions. A number of empirical expectations are generated by the RPGI model.

Because membership and belonging in the United States is structured by the racial order, relative position on the racial hierarchy dictates the strength of attachment groups hold toward both the nation and their racial group. The intimate correspondence between race and nation has meant that those classified as white are automatically assumed to be American. We will show that whites see a nearly perfect overlap in their perception of themselves as core members of the nation and as members of their racial group. Racial minorities on the other hand experience a tension between feeling American and being perceived as American. Their nonwhite status creates a context in which blacks, Latinos, and Asian Americans perceive peripheral as opposed to core in-group member status. Because racial categorization has long been used to justify the incomplete inclusion of minorities in the American polity, racial-group identities are continuously reinforced. Racial minorities will thus report stronger recognition of their racial-group-linked fate than whites. Relative position on the hierarchy is also significant, and groups positioned at the bottom of the order will report stronger identities as a result of their persistent experiences with race-based exclusion.

The racial hierarchy structures the intensity of group identities and in turn influences how individuals respond to the political issue of immigration. For whites, status as the top-ranked group in the racial hierarchy and the correspondence between white racial categorization and idealized characterizations of Americanness reinforce bias against groups characterized racially as out-groups. With respect to the inferential analysis predicting antecedents to public opinion on immigration among whites, a stronger racial-linked fate in correspondence with perceptions of strict American boundaries will predict attitudes about immigration consistent with their embrace of the racial prerequisites to citizenship. Their status at the top of the racial hierarchy encourages whites to uphold the existing order. As a result, whites are more likely to accept and respond to narratives justifying exclusion, including negative racial stereotypes. Political communication strategies designed to mobilize restrictive attitudes on immigration will have the strongest effects on whites by framing immigration as a threat to the status quo and priming negative stereotypes about racial minorities.

For racial minorities, stronger perceptions of racial-linked fate reflect an understanding of the non-egalitarian structure of the racial hierarchy and the implications of racial position for the life chances of individuals. This recognition of structural position supports greater openness to outsiders because of a shared experience of exclusion. Stronger perceived linked fate among African Americans, Latinos, and Asian Americans will attenuate support for decreasing the number of immigrants to the United States and enhance support for progressive immigration abode policies. Each racial minority group's relative position on the racial hierarchy will dictate the degree to which individuals have an incentive to either reject or uphold the status quo of the racial order. Racial groups ranked toward the bottom are more critical of the structure that justifies their marginalization and so will be less willing to accept political communication narratives that prime negative racial stereotypes. As a result, strategies attempting to mobilize support of restrictive immigration policy by tapping into negative stereotypes, and framing threats to the status quo will be less effective among minority Americans.

Before we proceed to analyze the quantitative survey data on political attitudes on immigration in chapters 3 through 6, the next chapter takes a step back and examines the broad contours of the development of the American racial hierarchy. We consider how race, immigration, and policies and practices of citizenship have worked together—sometimes in concert and at other times in opposition—to create distinctive contexts of political belonging for Americans classified by race.

CHAPTER TWO

Development of the American Racial Hierarchy

Race, Immigration, and Citizenship

In the shadow of the Statue of Liberty and flanked by Democratic and Republican politicians, President Lyndon Johnson signed the 1965 Immigration and Nationality Act into law. Enacted on the heels of momentous civil rights legislation, the law was passed with strong bipartisan support and minimal congressional floor debate. A sharp departure from Asian exclusion policy put in place in the 1880s and the national-origin quotas instituted in the 1924 National Origins Act, the 1965 Immigration and Nationality Act created an immigration preference system based on family reunification and occupational skills. Changes to immigration policy seemed to be neither radical nor relevant to the politics of race in America, which at the time was defined by a black-white binary. Few among the interest groups and lobbyists who influenced the bill in Congress expected the policy to have the effect that it did on the racial and ethnic composition of the United States (Gillion 2000).

Amid the social turmoil and political resistance surrounding the struggle for civil rights for African Americans, the 1965 act was not explicitly racialized. Instead, removing discriminatory barriers to entry in immigration policy was consistent with the rejection of World War II–era genocide and a symbolic move toward a tenuous embrace of equality. Championed for decades by New York City congressman Emanuel Celler and shepherded through the legislative process by Speaker of the House John McCormack from Boston, the 1965 Immigration and Nationality Act easily passed both houses of Congress. Celler, of German

Jewish descent, and McCormack, the grandson of Irish Catholic immigrants, supported the legislation for the provisions that would allow families in eastern and southern Europe to reunite in America after decades
of exclusion and also because of its rejection of the explicit prejudice of
earlier immigration policy.

American policy makers' vantage point at the time of the 1965 act was
turned toward Europe, where most white Americans' ancestry could be
traced. The law was neither aimed at other continents nor envisioned
to benefit non-European immigrants. The assumption that immigrants
of the future would mirror immigrants of the past stanched opposition
based in racial antipathy (Ngai 2004). President Johnson's remarks at the
signing of the act reflected this viewpoint and belied the significance of
the policy to future dynamics of race and ethnicity in America: "This
bill that we will sign today is not a revolutionary bill. It does not affect
the lives of millions. It will not reshape the structure of our daily lives,
or really add importantly to either our wealth or our power" (Johnson
1965). But the 1965 act was in fact a radical break from nearly all federal
immigration policy that preceded it because it did not specify in racial or
ethnic terms which groups were more or less desirable for entry into the
American polity.

The law it replaced had been specifically designed to limit immigration by Jews, Italians, and Irish, among others, all of whom were groups
of people Congress had once identified as inferior to Nordic stock and
those from northern and western Europe. In the early twentieth century,
the "science" of eugenics flourished and influenced experts advising
Congress on the impact of immigration on the United States. The now
infamous United States Immigration Commission, commonly known as
the Dillingham Commission, was influenced both by the "science" of
the international eugenics movement and by nativist public sentiment
(Zolberg 2008; Tichenor 2002). In 1911 the Dillingham Commission produced a forty-one-volume report that, among other things, enumerated
a hierarchy of the races. Exclusion of Chinese and Japanese immigrants
had been mandated decades earlier, beginning with the Chinese Exclusion Act of 1882, and an "Asiatic Barred Zone" was in effect by 1917.
It was not only political elites who relied on a hierarchy of desirability
for immigrants from most to least white. Anti-immigrant sentiment ran
high among American voters, their perceptions fanned by nativist, anti-
Catholic "Know-Nothings," the American Protective League, and anti-
Chinese mobs on the West Coast. By the mid-twentieth century, federal

actions such as "Operation Wetback" undertook the forcible removal of Mexican nationals and Mexican Americans during the mid-1950s. Restrictions on immigration and unequal treatment of newcomers have consistently been based in arguments about racial distinctiveness and the unsuitability of immigrants to belong to the American polity (Filindra and Junn 2012; Young and Meiser 2008).

Throughout the development of policies governing citizenship and naturalization in the United States, Americans grouped by categories of race have experienced varying degrees of membership. In this chapter we describe the development of political membership in the United States through an examination of the history of the dynamic relationship between race, immigration, and citizenship. The analysis demonstrates that informal norms, official rules, and social practices of belonging have been shaped by an explicit preference for whites. These institutional developments provide the foundation upon which the American racial hierarchy was built and continues to be reinscribed. The racial order remains politically significant because it systematically produces increasing returns for Americans classified racially as white and at the same time creates disadvantage for others who are declared not white. A series of contingent historical events have established a story about the nation and who is a member of the political community (Ngai 2004; Smith 1997, 2003; Takaki 2000; King and Smith 2011). Based in powerful and long-standing imperatives of American territorial expansion and economic development, the content of the assumptions of belonging is embedded in both the structure of power and normative constructions of desirability in the United States.

The racialized foundations of US citizenship have evolved over time, and while early choices made by the framers of the Constitution created a series of path-dependent processes influencing the conceptualizations of belonging and citizenship, new circumstances and political events have encouraged Americans to modify their sense of national identity. One of the most important practices influencing revisions of political membership is the creation of new racial and ethnic categories in the American racial taxonomy and the critical role these classifications have played in organizing individuals into distinct categories. The continued use of racial and ethnic group categorization has strongly influenced Americans' sense of membership and identity in contemporary politics.

While the formation of racial categories is often identified as justifications for slavery or group-based discrimination, this analysis focuses

on how racial categories have been used to structure political belonging
to the American polity. Because racial and ethnic categories were constructed in step with national territorial expansion and economic development, the maintenance of racial classification and group position was
a direct response to the political and social demands of the time. The
dynamics of race, immigration, and citizenship are traced through the
history of the United States beginning with the founding, progressing
into the time of westward and extracontinental US expansion during the
nineteenth and twentieth centuries, and finally into the civil rights movement era. We conclude the chapter by identifying the contemporary implications of these historical developments for shades belonging among
whites, African Americans, Latinos and Asian Americans.

Foundations of American Political Belonging

The foundations for American national identity have roots in the values
held by colonists who were themselves influenced by the political issues
and economic circumstances leading up to the drafting and ratification
of the Constitution. The new American colonies established a political
culture and national identity largely from the ground up, though the concept of a national identity across the colonies would be decades in the
making (Hartz 1991; Hofstadter [1948] 1989; Lipset 1997). Unlike European countries with centuries-long histories of national tradition and
heritage, American colonists created and molded their own definition for
the new territories, though it was not necessarily shared across colonies.
In contrast to national belonging in Europe, the concept of citizenship as
a "right of blood," or *jus sanguinis*, could not apply to a land newly populated by white settlers. Instead, citizenship would eventually develop in
the new world around the concept of *jus soli*, or "right of soil."

Equally important were the religious foundations of the colonies.
Early Puritan settlers in New England established a strong Protestant
culture, and religious values became integrated into political life. The
Protestant work ethic is a celebrated and central value in American culture even in modern times (Weber 1930). The historian Eric Foner (1999)
argues that Americans' attachment to concept of liberty was originally
less the result of an adherence to a political ideal than it was a religious
value based on the notion that freedom could be achieved through religious salvation. At the time, colonists strived to obtain a full state of

liberation, which meant escaping from sin and accepting the moral life intended by God. While the ideas of freedom, liberty, and the importance of communal spirit are connected to a distinctively different political logic today, the values Americans embrace today were imprinted into the political culture by early settlers in the New World.

Early definitions of national identity based in political ideals

When the American colonists demanded independence from the British Crown, they had to establish an identity distinct from Britain's, despite having carried over many of the same religious and cultural practices from their home country. American colonists rebelled over their lack of political rights and representation and, more important, the economic constraints set forth by the king of England. The political ideals of liberty, freedom, and right to property that already had roots in the colonial culture became fully ingrained in the American psyche when these concepts served as the motivation for the Revolutionary War (Foner 1999). Since this period, influential writers of the past, historians, and many Americans in the general public today claim that the unique characteristic of American national identity is its emphasis on shared political values rather than ancestral heritage. Alexis de Tocqueville (1863) is often credited with highlighting the unique aspects of American political culture. At the time, the American creation of a democratic system of governance was novel and pathbreaking. When the US Constitution was drafted, European nations were still controlled by royal families and aristocracies. National identity in the United States and the corresponding American creed could be defined by key political values of equality, liberty, and democracy.

Cultivating group solidarity: strategies for developing national identity

In his widely influential book *Civil Ideals* (1997), Rogers Smith argues that American political culture is characterized by multiple political traditions rather than simply the one advanced by Tocqueville. The notion of cohesion through shared political ideals is alluring for its egalitarian appeal where all individuals, regardless of their background, can share American political ideals. Those who engage in this form of solidarity are perceived as meritorious and deserving of membership in the political community. However, as many historians have argued, those political

ideals of freedom and equality did not apply to all individuals who resided in the United States. Although Tocqueville did not detect the same
type of aristocracy that was practiced in Europe, significant social stratification nevertheless existed in the colonies. From Smith's perspective, it
is difficult to accept the argument that all Americans developed loyalties
to the kinds of political ideals that did not apply to their experiences.

Smith thus questions the applicability of this civic vision of American national identity under circumstances where the political ideals promoted were not actually attained in practice. Nations cannot survive if
they do not retain an image of legitimacy and authority over their populations or, in Benedict Anderson's (1991) terms, "imagined political
communities." For Anderson, nationality is a cultural artifact that is invented through development of a collective consciousness: "Members of
even the smallest nation will never know most of their fellow-members,
meet them, or even hear of them, yet in the minds of each lives the image of their communion" (6). Yet the "imagining" that leads to this collective consciousness does not arise naturally but must instead be outlined and cultivated politically. Leaders foster collective consciousness
because it motivates solidarity and loyalty to the state not through force
but by promoting a sense of commonality and righteousness (Marx 1998;
Smith 1997; Taylor 1998). Smith argues that American political leaders
emphasized nonegalitarian social hierarchies based on attributes such as
race, class, and gender that more effectively promoted loyalty to the state
rather than the civic vision of America. By differentiating some individuals as virtuous and others inferior, political leaders created a logic of
exclusivity and desirability of membership in the nation based on one's
inborn characteristics.

By the time the founders met to draft the Constitution, there were
many political and social divisions, including a sharp regional divide between the North and the South, one between agrarian farmers and urban dwellers, as well as a strong cleavage between developing political
perspectives of the Federalists and Anti-Federalists. The framers faced
important compromises that could unify the colonies, among them the
Three-Fifths Compromise for the apportionment of political representation. The status of African American slaves became an important question of not only economic development but also states' rights and representation. In an effort to appease representatives of southern states,
the founders codified slavery as well as the understanding that African
slaves were not full persons and thus inferior in status to whites. Through

these laws the state systematically imposed advantages to those classified as white and disadvantages to those classified as nonwhite, fostering
a tenuous unity based in race among propertied whites and poor white
settlers, groups who would not otherwise feel solidarity with one another
(Marx 1998).

Categories with consequences: construction of
citizenship and race in the founding era

In creating the United States of America, the framers not only defined
the identity and values of the nation but also established who was a member of the polity. Through defining the rules of citizenship, state leaders
created a system that determined who belonged and who did not belong.
Citizenship defines the boundaries of the nation-state and its sense of
identity. By creating limits on who could be a member, citizenship laws
also promoted the idea of virtuousness and exclusivity. This exclusivity
served as a unifying issue for those who are included and as a mobilizing
force for shared group identity among those who were excluded. States
further promoted this sense of exclusivity by allocating rights and privileges to citizens and reserving the right to deny those same rights to
noncitizens. As Linda Bosniak (2006) notes, "Citizenship is commonly
portrayed as the most desired of conditions, as the highest fulfillment of
democratic and egalitarian aspiration" (1).

The framers of the US Constitution were hesitant to codify rules of
citizenship in the founding document itself. In practice, American colonists followed British common law of *jus soli*; citizenship was awarded to
those born within the boundaries of the nation-state (Schuck and Smith
1985). Those born on American soil were assumed to be rightful and
loyal citizens. The framers were committed to promoting a sense of civic
vision of the nation, and many, including James Madison, Alexander
Hamilton, and Benjamin Franklin, believed that foreigners were capable
of developing the necessary political ideals to be a citizen. They rejected
the existing illiberal practices of European nations that awarded rights
and advantages through bloodline (*jus sanguinis*) and heritage and did
not want to replicate these rules for membership (Brubaker 1998). Debates over who could serve as leaders in government revealed a strong
nativist spirit, however, and general distrust of foreigners led the framers to codify restrictions against allowing foreign-born residents to serve
in the national government. Residency requirements were placed on

election to Congress, and only native-born citizens of the United States could serve as president. In this way, the framers promoted a general sense of exclusion of foreigners.

Holding citizenship did not necessarily imply equality among members. Racial categories of white and black were further differentiated by classification as free, not free, or slave and resulted in the categorization of free whites, white indentured servants, free blacks, and black slaves. The racial advantage for white indentured servants over black slaves was clear, given that whites had the possibility to earn their freedom, while blacks were permanently conceived of as property. The distinction between slave and free had important implications for blacks in that free blacks were officially counted as full persons rather than property (Berlin 1992; Foner 1999). In some states, free blacks were afforded political rights including the franchise. But even blacks' status as "free" did not equate to being equal with whites. Blacks' inferior racial status led to the general social belief that blacks were in a caste class below whites. This dynamic highlights the cyclical relationship between the laws and institutions supporting slavery and the racial hierarchy and the perceptions among Americans that blacks were inferior to whites. Southern judges reversed laws that awarded freedom to blacks born to free black women, and most free blacks were required to leave the state once released from bondage. Other laws imposed special restraints on blacks with the purpose of controlling potential insurrection (Filindra and Junn 2012).

The question of how citizenship was applied to free blacks remained both a moral and legal question through the remainder of the antebellum era. Legal rulings created a distinction between citizenship awarded to blacks and the same status that was endowed to whites. Northern courts denied that citizenship implied equal rights and instead characterized multiple classes of citizenship (Smith 1997). Lawyers in the 1834 Connecticut state case *Crandall v. State of Connecticut* argued that citizenship only afforded protection of law, not the assignment of rights to free blacks. This position was later echoed in other state court cases deciding black citizenship rights. In practice, blacks' citizenship status prevented extreme forms of discrimination against free blacks in the North, while any rights they might have were nearly completely ignored in the South. In the North, free blacks were offered some individual rights such as the ability to own property. But at the same time, free blacks were not equal citizens and were denied the right to testify in court against whites or serve in the state militia in many states (Franklin and Moss

1988; Zilversmit 1967). The relationship between free and citizen was ultimately decided at the federal level in 1857 with the infamous US Supreme Court decision in *Dred Scott v. Sanford*, which ruled that free blacks were not citizens of the United States.

The framers did codify the notion that there were different levels of citizenship in the new nation, but in practice citizenship in the United States reflected the racial hierarchy (Lieberman 2008). Blacks were originally counted as citizens of the United States, but the practice of treating them as inferior and unequal members paved the way to their construction as noncitizens in *Dred Scott*. Thus the early choices made by the framers created reliance on defining citizenship in racial terms; whites were not only citizens but were afforded the full rights of membership, while those classified as black were defined as second-class citizens at best and systematically excluded from the polity.

A clearly racialized description of American citizenship was made explicit with passage of the Naturalization Act of 1790, which limited naturalization to "free white person[s]" of "good moral character." At the time, the law was considered to be inclusive because it provided relatively few requirements for white men to earn citizenship.[1] Yet the racial adjective used in this law expanded the idea that not only blacks but all those classified as nonwhite were excluded from full citizenship. Native Americans—present long before colonists arrived from Europe—were by definition not Americans and not eligible for US citizenship. By establishing and implementing the racial prerequisite to citizenship, America officially defined itself as a "white" nation or, more precisely, a nation that limited full political inclusion to those *classified* as white (Gross 2008; Haney López 2006). The issue of women in politics was not even considered, and the gendered basis defining citizen as male would require a Constitutional amendment to overturn exclusive male privilege in the franchise (Andersen 1996). The attention to and preservation of the white category has been key to maintaining the perceived exclusivity of American citizenship, helping to justify those deserving of citizenship, and in turn contributing to the characterization of others as inferior and incapable of contributing to the political community.

Social practices and the political decisions made during the founding era set in motion a developmental pathway for how Americans would conceive of the nation and national identity that was squarely based in the superiority of whites (Foner 1999). The founding set forth conceptions of citizenship based in a racial hierarchy distinguishing desirable

from undesirable in political membership and influencing the development of both racial categories and conceptions of belonging.

Building the Nation-State: Expanding
the Definition of America

In the century that followed the American Revolution, the United States
engaged in efforts at territorial expansion, political democratization, and
the spread of market relations (Foner 1999). These developments during the time of the Industrial Revolution and heavy foreign migration to
the United States during the Nineteenth Century were significant to not
only how America defined itself but how it defined who belonged to the
nation. The United States faced the challenge of molding national identity to a geographically expanding entity as well as within the context of
a rapidly growing and diversifying population.

Expanding westward and beyond

American westward expansion was motivated by a vision to expand but
also because territory was available. The Manifest Destiny narrative justified the takeover of occupied lands by describing American incorporation of western territories as providence and the opportunity to further
democracy. At the time, property-holding was a requirement for voting.
Although this was a clearly illiberal concept in conflict with principles of
democracy, the law remained unchallenged because of the ease at which
men could obtain property in new western territories. Those who would
have been otherwise excluded from participation were able to earn equal
membership in the political community by taking land.

American acquisition of some western territories was completed with
little international and military conflict, and President Thomas Jefferson purchased the Louisiana Territory for a bargain price from France.
However, American desire to enhance its territory all the way to the west
coast led to a war with Mexico beginning in 1846. Americans had already
settled in the territory that is now California and Texas long before the
advent of war, which helped support the idea that American conquest
of the southwest was inevitable. When the Mexican government surren-
dered defeat, Mexican leaders agreed to sell the New Mexico territories
to the United States in the 1848 Treaty of Guadalupe Hidalgo in return

for the guarantee of rights and protection of the Mexican citizens who had resided in the territories before the war. Once the United States had expanded westward across the entire North American continent, the nation began to engage in the acquisition of territories beyond the continent. When the United States government interceded in Cuba's war for independence from Spain, it escalated into a war with the Spanish. The American military victory over Spain resulted in American control over Spain's remaining colonies of Cuba, Puerto Rico, Guam and the Philippines. The doctrine of Manifest Destiny thus inspired not only western expansion across the continent but also the assertion of American colonial power internationally.

Populating a newly expanding empire:
developing a national immigration policy

The seemingly unlimited land in North America played a significant role in the formation of American national identity and political culture. Land offered the opportunity for the nation-state to both expand the empire and promote a national vision as inclusive and democratic. This also opened economic advancement to the poorer classes and economic opportunities to newcomers. American immigration policy during the period of western expansion was seen as relatively open and welcoming because immigrants were useful in populating the western frontier and providing labor to help construct the necessary infrastructure of the industrial economy. The first waves of immigrants arrived from the same sending countries as immigrants who arrived in the United States before the Revolutionary war (Higham 2002, Tichenor 2002). New immigrants thus assimilated quickly into a society that had similar cultures and practices as their home countries. Because western expansion created a need for all types of labor, immigrants were not forced into particular labor markets or to live in segregated areas. Instead, these early immigrants were able to integrate into American society with fewer visible traces of their foreign "otherness," and Americans continued to celebrate their identity as a nation of immigrants.

Early nativist responses to immigrants highlight emphasis of national civic identity rather than one based solely on ethnocentrism. Newcomers were evaluated on their potential to conform to American civic norms, and early anti-immigrant movements were aimed not at a specific ethnic group but rather at Catholic immigrants who were of Irish, French and German descent (Higham 2002; Schrag 2011). American antagonism against Catholics had important roots in Britain, and supported by an overwhelmingly Protestant colonial class. Stereotypes of Catholics fed fear that these immigrants embraced authoritarian practices incompatible with American political ideals of freedom and equality. By defining inclusion based in shared political values, Americans embraced the idea that they had relinquished the aristocratic practices found in old Europe. But as John Higham (2002) points out, early nativist movements also created a tradition of defining America by what it was not. By identifying those groups and ideas that were objectionable, the American habit was to target those who needed to be excluded rather than those who needed to be included. There may not have been a direct link to race in this early period, but American rejection of particular groups was based in their clear contrasts with Anglo-Saxon Protestant traditions.

When the United States expanded its border to the west coast and there was no more new land to provide unlimited economic and social opportunity, the approach to American national identity and new waves of immigrants shifted to more blatant restrictionism. Expansion offered a sense of opportunity and ability to shape a new nation and its people. Once continental expansion was complete and after the country survived the Civil War, the social and political landscape of the United States had changed. The Industrial Revolution shifted the mode of production and further exacerbated class stratification. The economic growth spurred by industrialization generated a second wave of demand for human labor and a new influx of immigrants migrated into the United States to take advantage of economic opportunities. However, unlike the first wave of immigrants, this second wave of immigrants introduced migrants from regions outside of Western Europe where earlier immigrants had originated. On the East coast, immigrants came from Southern and Eastern Europe while on the West coast, immigrants entered arrived from China and Japan.

The phenotypic and cultural differences of these new immigrants posed a clear perceptual contrast to American Anglo-Saxon traditions as compared to previous waves. Differences between immigrants and the native-born population were further exacerbated by the economic environment. New immigrants were unable to prosper solely from industrial labor, and because new land was no longer readily available for the claiming, immigrants settled primarily in industrializing urban ethnic enclaves. As a result, the growth and distinctiveness of new immigrant groups was more clearly apparent to the native-born. The relatively high rates of poverty and slower incorporation into society made it appear as if these new immigrants were less able to become absorbed into native born population. In the midst of these changes, anti-immigration groups that had been unable to influence public policy in the previous era were more easily able to rally nativist sentiment. States with ports of entry began to pass their own laws limiting immigration, forcing the government to create a national bureaucracy that would implement more uniform controls on entry into the United States (Zolberg 2008).

The first national policy to limit immigration was passed to pacify a limited but politically powerful anti-Chinese movement in California. California state officials had already tried to limit immigration into the state but were generally unsuccessful (Gyory 1998).[2] Although Chinese immigration was primarily a localized concern on the west coast, anti-Chinese sentiment became a national political issue given California's role as a "swing state" in presidential elections (Tichenor 2002). Both national political parties supported a national policy to exclude immigration from China in an effort to win California's votes, and in 1882, a bipartisan majority in Congress passed the first of a series of Chinese exclusion laws. This act banned Chinese immigration to the United States for a period of ten years and strengthened the deportation provisions of the law. Another provision introduced a new requirement for Chinese to carry government certificates of residency (Tichenor 2002; Davis 1893). While ethnocentrism motivated California's demands for exclusion, racism alone could not explain the adoption of Chinese exclusion. Other political motives, particularly the electoral gain anticipated by party leaders, helped to secure the exclusionary immigration policy.

Chinese exclusion set a new precedent of using immigration policy to control the types of immigrants entering the country as well as the assertion of American national identity. Legal scholar T. Alexander Aleinikoff (2002) argues that the United States used federal immigration policy to assert its national sovereignty. By declaring the right to police migration, leaders used their power to control national territory. Immigration policy was used strategically to define what people constituted the United States (King 2002).[3] A focus on race in the context of immigration was further encouraged by the influence of the "science" of eugenics (Haney López 2006; King 2002). The rise of the importance of science turned greater public attention to the need to classify individuals into distinctive racial groups. Theories that linked racial categories to inferior and superior individual qualities became popular in the biological and social sciences. The construction of immigrants from eastern and southern Europe and Ireland as "less than white" complicated the racial category of white and set the stage for efforts by these populations to "become white" (Ignatiev 1995; M. Jacobson 1999, 2006).

Public fear that immigrants would pollute the population with their inferior traits increased sentiment to limit immigration. The Chinese Exclusion Act only limited entry of a particular racial group, and immigrants considered undesirable from southern and eastern Europe, as well as a new wave of immigrants from Japan, continued to enter the United States. To help inform justifications for immigration policy reform, the now infamous US Immigration Commission, commonly known as the Dillingham Commission, was created in 1911 to review studies on immigrants and immigrant incorporation (Hattam 2007; Tichenor 2002). The commission recommended the establishment of numeric quotas, which helped perpetuate the racial composition of the United States as an Anglo-Saxon white nation. In response, Congress passed the Johnson-Reed Act of 1924, which established numeric quotas based on national origin.[4] This law advantaged immigrants arriving from countries of the "native stock," or those persons with the same origination of the American population at the founding. Thus there were generous quotas for immigrants arriving from western Europe, while strict quotas were imposed on those people of "immigrant stock," or those people with backgrounds of immigrants who arrived after 1790 (Ngai 2004). In the same year, Congress passed the Indian Citizenship Act, granting the right of citizenship with some limitations to Native Americans. While in some ways an interesting juxtaposition of the expansion of rights to a highly maligned population with the Johnson-Reed Act that restricted new entrants, both the numbers and political power of American Indians had decreased so dramatically that the expansion of rights for this group was not perceived as threatening.

The racial lines drawn in the 1924 National Origins Act demonstrate the clear shift from perceiving immigration as a mechanism to populate the western territories and uphold a democratic political vision to concern over preserving the nation's racial and cultural makeup. If, as

Tichenor (2002) argues, nations define themselves through their immigration policy, then the country's long history of racial exclusion reflects the national vision of its identity embedded in a racial hierarchy.

Incorporation and belonging in an era of expansion

It is clear that American territorial and economic expansion directly contributed to the diversification of the American population. This acquisition of new territories meant that the inhabitants of those territories would also need to be absorbed into the nation. Incorporating new Americans corresponded with activities aimed at preserving a particular sense of national identity.

At the founding, the primary mode of classifying different forms of national membership was by race. In practice, full citizenship was also determined by other traits such as gender and class, and categories used to classify membership and belonging relied on the social groupings that existed at the time. With territorial expansion and mass immigration, new groups of people were introduced into the existing racial classification taxonomy. There were new European ethnic groups including Jews, Italians, and Irish who arrived from areas outside of European countries of origin from which immigrants had come in decades past, other immigrant groups who arrived from Asia, and various groups who were indigenous to the colonized territories. In the process of dealing with these new groups, new pathways to acquiring political membership were created, as were new categories of membership.

Membership via territorial acquisition

American acquisition of new territories from Mexico and Spain created a new process of determining membership through international treaty. The official status and rights of incorporated people after an acquisition of territory was largely determined by the extent to which the ceding country demanded rights for its citizens (Foner 1999). When the Mexican government agreed to cede the New Mexico territory to the United States, it insisted on guaranteeing the protection of those Mexican citizens who resided in the territory at the time of transfer. The Treaty of Guadalupe Hidalgo as originally negotiated allowed Mexicans to remain in the territory and keep their Mexican citizenship or be granted American citizenship. By guaranteeing citizenship, the Mexican government hoped to protect citizens' rights and property, but America's new foray into colonialism meant that the government had not yet established how to incorporate new territories. There was some precedent developed from the incorporation of Indian tribes and territories acquired earlier.[5] In *American Insurance Company v. Canter* (1828), the Supreme Court ruled that American acquisition of a territory, whether by conquest or by treaty, transferred citizenship to those inhabitants of the territory (Smith 1997). Over time, the Supreme Court upheld this ruling and verified the citizenship status of all those territories eventually incorporated as states into the Union.

In an interesting twist of racial politics of the time, Mexicans could be recognized as "white" by virtue of their citizenship rights. According to the Naturalization Act of 1790, citizenship and naturalization rights were limited to free white persons. Thus, unlike blacks or Asian Americans, Mexicans were able to bypass the racial prerequisite and could become citizens as a result of a treaty agreement. In the 1897 *In re Rodriguez* case, the state of Texas attempted to challenge the citizenship rights of Ricardo Rodriguez, a Mexican citizen who had applied for American citizenship. Texas argued that because Rodriguez was not white, he could not qualify for citizenship on the basis of the racial prerequisite for naturalization. Defense lawyers convolutedly argued that because Mexicans enjoy citizenship status, they are legally considered white. The federal judge confirmed Rodriguez's citizenship status, citing the provisions of the Treaty of Guadalupe Hidalgo but admitted that if "the strict scientific classification of the anthropologist should be adopted, he would probably not be classified as white" (Haney López 2006). As this case demonstrates, the relationship between whiteness and citizenship was directly challenged with the incorporation of Mexicans as American citizens, but ultimately the courts decided to uphold the racial prerequisite to citizenship rather than racialize Mexicans as nonwhite (Gross 2008; Gomez 2008; Hattam 2007). Indeed, with the exception of the 1930 census, Mexicans have been and continue to be classified as white by the US Census Bureau (Hattam 2007; Nobles 2000).[6]

Since Mexicans were legally considered white, discriminatory actions could not necessarily be justified on the simply basis of their nonwhite status. State and local governments sought to create distinctions between Mexicans and Anglo Americans using other characteristics such as language. Spanish speakers were denied access to schools and could not serve on juries in California and Texas through the mid-twentieth century (Gomez 2008, Menchaca 2002). But even so, Mexicans' supposed whiteness did not ensure their treatment as equals in society (Bender 2010).[7] In the California state constitution, language to explicitly define who would be awarded voting rights excluded Mexicans. In *People v. Pablo de la Guerra* (1870), the California state supreme court ruled that government holds the power to limit political privileges to certain types of Mexicans:

> The elective franchise is denied to certain persons who had been entitled to its exercise under the laws of Mexico. The possession of all political rights is not essential to citizenship. When Congress admitted California as a State, the constituent members of the State, in their aggregate capacity, became vested with the sovereign powers of government, "according to the principles of the Constitution." They then had the right to prescribe the qualifications of electors, and it is no violation of the treaty that these qualifications were such as to exclude some of the inhabitants from certain political rights. (Menchaca 2002: 222)

Thus the application of citizenship to Mexicans paralleled the unequal treatment of African American citizens during the antebellum era. Mexicans were awarded citizenship status, but they were treated as second-class citizens and did not enjoy the full rights of citizenship afforded to European or Anglo Americans (Rodriguez 2007).[8]

In contrast to the treaty agreements with Mexico, citizenship status for the inhabitants of Cuba, Puerto Rico, the Philippines, and Guam were not guaranteed in the 1898 Treaty of Paris negotiated with Spain. The Spanish government retained some rights for Spanish citizens in the territories, but the political rights and citizenship status of the native inhabitants were to be decided by Congress. At the time of the treaty, the US government anticipated different futures for each of the island nations. This perception was largely driven by views about the international status of each nation and the perceived governing capability of the native people (Ayala and Bernabé 2002). Cuba's independence was provided for in the Treaty of Paris, but the United States retained control of the Philippines, Puerto Rico, and Guam. Congressional debate during the ratification of the Treaty of Paris revealed that American leaders perceived a moral duty to civilize the populations that were otherwise considered incapable of self-rule (Ngai 2004).

By designating Puerto Rico, Guam, and the Philippines as territories, the United States government created a new category of "unincorporated territory," and their indigenous peoples were assigned a new class of membership termed "US Nationals." (Ngai 2004). In what are now known as the Insular Cases (1901–1922), the US Supreme Court established the status of the territories acquired from Spain. Puerto Rico was particularly important because of its status as an economic port to Central America, and overall the territories were to be governed by federal legislation (Smith 1997). However, the Court also asserted that because the territories were not states, the inhabitants of those territories could not be citizens of the United States. American officials followed the rule established by the 1884 *Elks v. Wilkins* case that inhabitants of acquired territories are protected by federal law but are not guaranteed the full rights as citizens. The "US National" category thus meant that residents of the territories were members of the nation but not citizens.[9] Indeed, even when Puerto Rican residents were granted citizenship status in 1917, they were not fully enfranchised because of Puerto Rico's status as a territory rather than a state. American citizens in Puerto Rico do not have formal representation in Congress, nor can they vote in presidential elections.

Categories in the age of expansion: immigration,
naturalization, and whiteness

The introduction of populations from Mexico, the Philippines, Puerto Rico, Alaska, and Hawaii after the United States acquired those territories created a need for categories of race to distinguish these newcomers from American citizens. Naturalization law limited citizenship to those classified as white, and anti-immigrant policy proposals persistently advocated exclusion of non-Anglo-Saxon immigrants. Pressure on the white racial category to expand beyond Anglo-Saxon Protestants that had traditionally typified whiteness increased as immigration from Europe continued. Discrimination against the Irish, Italians, Jews, and other southern and eastern Europeans was justified on the basis of their "racial" inferiority (M. Jacobson 1998; Roediger 2005). Nevertheless, these European groups were also recognized as racially white despite the position of nativist groups such as the "Know-Nothings" who actually advocated for the removal of the 1790 Naturalization Act because it offered citizenship to undesirable European immigrant groups (Schrag 2010).

While there was an explicit attempt to distinguish European ethnic groups from one another, "white" was an important category to maintain, as it helped justify exclusion of the other major immigrant group, Asians. Indeed, the racial prerequisite of whiteness became a key clause in naturalization law and was used to deny citizenship to new immigrants entering from Asian countries. In 1878, the California Circuit Court ruled in the *In re Ah Yup* case that a Chinese immigrant could not naturalize because he did not meet the racial requirement. However, the definition of "white" was challenged because the category was never fully outlined by law. Immigrants from various countries including China, Japan, Syria, and India petitioned for citizenship by challenging the definition of white. Ian Haney López (2006) documented a total of fifty-two legal cases that challenged the definition of white, two of which reached the Supreme Court.[10] Using a variety of explanations that helped justify their decision, including the nascent science of anthropology, eugenicist ideas about racial hierarchies, and "common sense" understandings of race, the courts rejected the whiteness appeals of nearly all non-European claimants.[11] These decisions help to establish contemporary conceptualizations of whiteness.

The racial clause in naturalization law created two distinctive trajectories of immigrant incorporation for those defined as white and those defined as nonwhite. European immigrants experienced social discrimination because of their perceived cultural differences from native Anglo-Saxon Americans, but they were afforded formal citizenship because of their white racial classification. Early European immigrant groups were also given the right to vote upon entry into the United States and were considered important voting blocs (Andersen 1979). Thus European ethnic groups never had to formally fight for their inclusion as equal members in the political community on the basis of race. Instead, their ability to become citizens as a function of their status as whites helped to speed social and political assimilation. The ability of European ethnics to eventually lose the discriminatory weight of "otherness" attached to foreign-born immigrants has inspired many sociological and political theories about assimilation in America. The theory of straight-line assimilation most commonly attached to the writings of Milton Gordon (1964) but also upheld by other major sociological scholars predicts full integration and eventual equality for European immigrant groups. Robert Dahl's (1961) theory that social groups can compete equally in the political system for their own share of resources was in part based on his observations of European immigrants in New Haven, Connecticut, during the first half of the twentieth century.

In contrast, the explicit exclusion of immigrants from Asia from gaining US citizenship was used as justification to deny them equal rights and privileges. The race, foreign status, and lack of citizenship of Asian Americans were used interchangeably as justifications of public policies aimed at enforcing their unequal status. California's Alien Land Laws (1913) prevented "aliens ineligible for citizenship" from owning or leasing land, and similar versions of the law were later passed in other western states and Kansas (Chan 1991; Takaki 1998). Many laws targeting noncitizen Asian Americans mirrored laws used against blacks in the antebellum period. In *People v. George Hall* (1850), the California Supreme Court ruled that a Chinese man could not give testimony against a white person. In the decision, Chief Justice Hugh Murray wrote, "The same rule which would admit them [the Chinese] to testify, would admit them to all the equal rights of citizenship and we might soon seem them at the polls, in the jury box, upon the bench and in our legislative halls. This . . . is an actual and present danger" (C. Kim 1999, 113).

Naturalization law enabled nearly complete political exclusion of Asian Americans throughout this period, but the American practice of *jus soli* nevertheless provided citizenship to nonwhites born in the United States (Hing 1994). The Fourteenth Amendment, enacted to uphold the citizenship rights of black slaves after the Civil War, was interpreted to mean that second-generation Asian Americans were citizens at birth. In 1895, Wong Kim Ark, a US-born Chinese American, was denied reentry into the United States after a trip to China on the assumption that he was not a US citizen. The Supreme Court upheld birthright citizenship in 1898 and affirmed Wong Kim Ark's US citizenship status. Higham (2002) argues that Americans have long connected foreignness with threat to the nation, and the racial category of Asian was synonymous with "outsider" (Chan 1991, Takaki 1998). The suspicion that Asian Americans held stronger loyalties to their ancestral homelands than to the United States encouraged government attempts to revoke the citizenship status of native-born Asian Americans, the most egregious case being the internment of more than 120,000 Japanese Americans during World War II (Daniels, 2004b; Ngai 2004). Despite the fact that the federal government found no evidence of espionage or acts of disloyalty at the time, California state officials including state Attorney General Earl Warren promoted the idea that Americans of Japanese descent continued to serve the political and military interests of Japan (Weglyn 2000).[12]

National expansion and immigration played an important role in shaping the linkage between nation, race, and citizenship by reinforcing the ascriptive vision of American identity as racially white. But the move toward more racially egalitarian policies in the mid- and late-twentieth-century influenced movement in a different direction with respect to conceptions of belonging to the United States that was more inclusive.

Civil Rights and Beyond: Greater Alignment between Equality and Membership

While explicit racial discrimination is an enduring theme in American political development, advocates of egalitarian practices have also been a critical part of the story. Abolition movements existed at the time of the founding (Foner 1999). Pro-immigrant groups have mobilized to equalize policies of entry and protect the civil rights of noncitizen immigrants (Tichenor 2002). However, it was not until the civil rights era that this position has enjoyed significant political success. After World War II, racial inequalities in American society became less tenable (Karst 1989). Decades of racial subjugation had compelled blacks to cultivate a shared racial-group consciousness and engage in effective political action for greater racial equality (Parker 2009). The civil rights movement led to important policy changes such as the 1964 Civil Rights Act, which mandated equality for racial minorities, and the 1965 Voting Rights Act, which implemented protection of voting rights.

This shift occurred alongside important changes in federal immigration policy. It became increasingly apparent that US immigration policy, which created classes of desirable and undesirable immigrant groups, was discriminatory. Immigrant activist groups, largely representing Americans of Italian, Polish, and Jewish descent, argued that the quotas of the 1924 National Origins Act were discriminatory (Gillion 2000; Tichenor 2002). The 1965 Hart-Celler Act removed the national-origin quotas and replaced it with a preference system based on professional and technical skills, family reunification, and refugee status. The new immigration policy created a shift in the racial and ethnic makeup of the nation, as people from all over the world could come to the United States and bring their families from abroad.

Immigration reform in 1965 did not simply change the demography of the country; it also created important changes in how race was conceptualized. Categories of race and ethnicity became at once less and more complicated. The racial category of white is one inclusive category that includes a variety of European ethnic or ancestral heritages (Hattam 2007; Waters 1990). At the same time, the current preference categories can motivate the logic of connecting meritorious traits with eligibility for membership. Immigration policy may no longer discriminate simply on the basis of one's national origin but instead admits persons on the basis of their technical skills and other desirable traits such as a high level of education. This logic corresponds to the long-standing American narrative of individualism (Hartz 1991; Kinder and Sanders 1996).

Prior to the civil rights movement, racism and discriminatory treatment on the basis of race was socially acceptable. Racial inequality was seen as normal, and individuals were not reprimanded for promoting racist views or practices (Kinder and Sanders 1996; Sears, Henry, and Kosterman 2000). Tali Mendelberg (2001) labels the notion that Americans value the vision of racial equality and want to be perceived as a person who practices this vision the "norm of equality." Americans began to view explicit racism as an undesirable characteristic and racial discrimination as inappropriate, though racial antipathy has clearly not vanished from the American landscape (Dawson 2011; Kinder and Dale-Riddle 2012). Consistent with civil rights statutes, the federal government implemented new policies to prohibit discrimination on the basis of race.

"Colorblind" Categories: Egalitarian Norms and Illegality

As antidiscrimination provisions became part of the policy-making landscape and after Barack Obama was elected president of the United States, some proclaimed that Americans were "postracial" and that the nation had surpassed the need to classify by race. Despite these changes and movement toward more egalitarian norms, inequalities between people of different races persist, and scholars question whether racist thinking has really disappeared from the American landscape. Poverty affects racial minorities disproportionately to white Americans (Oliver and Shapiro 2006). Indirect racial discrimination is linked with low rates of minority political empowerment and glass-ceiling barriers that prevent minority promotions in private economic markets (Lublin 1999;

Tate 1998), While it is no longer widely socially desirable to proclaim racist visions of black inferiority, scholars contend that racial antipathy is now simply communicated in different ways (Kinder and Sanders 1996; Sears, Henry, and Kosterman 2000).

There may be significant disagreement over whether race continues to stratify citizenship in the United States, but Americans have not ended the practice of distinguishing those who deserve political membership from those who do not. Despite the significant reforms in the 1965 Immigration and Nationality Act, the United States continues to have a policy that restricts immigration. As Ngai (2004) explains, "If the principle of immigration restriction has become an unquestioned assumption of contemporary politics, we need to ask how it got to be that way and to consider its place in the historical construction of the nation" (5). The practice of immigration restriction constructs those immigrant groups that are awarded visas as deserving and virtuous and portrays those who are denied entry to be undeserving (Hing 2003; King 2002). Not every applicant will be granted legal entry, and many immigrants enter the United States without government authorization. Because those who enter without authorization are violating the law, they are characterized as even more undeserving of membership.

The vision of American citizenship as exclusive, prestigious, and virtuous drives the enforcement of restrictive immigration policies, but unlike policies enacted before the civil rights movement, contemporary policies cannot simply discriminate on the basis of race. Exclusion now requires nonracial justification, and deservingness based on compliance with the virtues of the Protestant work ethic, liberal individualism, and civic republican values have replaced explicitly racialized constructs of belonging. Thus immigrants who are admitted legally are considered to be deserving, but those who enter without authorization are construed as illegal and criminal (Ngai 2004), and discriminatory treatment against such unauthorized immigrants can be justified. Because the two largest immigrant groups in the United States today arrived under different sets of circumstances and entry strategies, distinctive meanings have become attached to their racial categories. Immigrants from Asia are stereotyped as legal immigrants, and their inclusion is justified on the basis of the important medical, engineering, and scientific skills they bring. A larger number of Latino immigrants, on the other hand, enter the United States without authorization, and many do not qualify for the visas given for occupational preferences. As a result, larger numbers of unauthorized Latino immigrants violate American law and promote an image of criminality among immigrants from Latin America (Calavita 1992; Nevins 2001).

Contemporary laws governing immigration and naturalization have important influence on Americans' opinions about who is deserving and which groups of immigrants should become part of the American polity. The dynamic interaction of these practices and Americans' perceptions of race, citizenship, and belonging create a context of belonging for each of the four major racial groups in the United States.

Racial Shades of Belonging

The role of racial exclusion throughout the nation's history has created and been created by a racial hierarchy that places whites at the top, blacks at the bottom, and Asian Americans and Latinos in between. The pervasiveness of the racial hierarchy is reflected in the perceptions of the racial order among all Americans, regardless of their racial categorization, and even in the presence of movement toward more egalitarian policies. Each of the racial categories has become strongly associated with group stereotypes, and while Americans may disagree with the veracity of these racial tropes, they nevertheless recognize that the stereotypes exist.[13] Below we summarize how each racial group is ordered in the American racial hierarchy by outlining how that racial category has been used to delineate national membership and belonging.

The white category

The United States has from its founding been envisioned as racially white. Because whiteness has implied full citizenship, whites can easily assume a place as an equal member of the polity. As a result, whites are unmarked with outsider status and reside in the "default category" of Americanness. The structure of the American racial order has presented incentives for members of this default category, lacking any label as an "other," to identify more strongly as "American" without any modifier. For whites, the concepts of race, nation, and citizenship align without contradiction. At the same time, some whites can experience discrimination in the United States on the basis of their ethnicity. European ethnicities were once ranked on a social hierarchy in the United States that had implications for how they were treated and incorporated into society, and those who deviated from Anglo-Saxon culture were deemed foreign and unassimilated. As a result, whites are more likely to emphasize ethnicity and culture as the primary basis of their social difference in the United States.[14] Alternatively, whites who do not assert ethnic differences can more easily exist as simply "American" (Hattam 2007).

The black category

The black experience in the United States demonstrates that formal citizenship does not ensure social, economic, and political equality. Throughout American history, blacks have persistently been relegated to a lower-caste status and have experienced only fleeting periods of equal opportunity. A review of the African American experience in the United States reveals systematic patterns of social, economic, and political inequality. Although African Americans have won a modicum of rights during various periods in US history, many of those rights and privileges were later rolled back. Historians have recorded three major periods in which this cycle has occurred: the first abolition movements directly following ratification of the Constitution, Reconstruction after the Civil War, and the civil rights movement of the 1960s. Arguably, African Americans have witnessed the most success in gaining equal rights as citizens in the last period, but they remain a clearly disadvantaged group. As a result, blacks have long experienced their inclusion into the polity as tenuous and uncertain. For African Americans, citizenship and belonging in the United States have always been qualified by race. Blacks are included as citizens of the United States and have been recognized as such for more than a century, but their second-class status has led to incomplete inclusion and demonstrates a far from perfect connection between citizenship and equality.

The Asian American category

Unlike African Americans, whose ancestors mostly arrived in the United States as slaves, Asian Americans entered the United States through voluntary immigration starting in the mid-1800s. Their status as immigrants is the key characteristic that has defined Asian Americans' experience in the United States. Because they were classified as nonwhite, Asian immigrants were not eligible to become naturalized citizens and so were originally labeled as "aliens ineligible for citizenship" (Takaki 1998). As noncitizens, Asian Americans were denied basic rights and civil liberties because they were constructed and treated as strangers inside the polity and undeserving of equal treatment. The inability to obtain citizenship also nurtured the perception of Asians as perpetual foreigners. Because of these historical experiences, the Asian American racial category became inextricably linked with foreignness, which has been used, particularly during times of fear, to challenge the loyalty of Asian Americans to the nation. Even native-born Asian Americans could not escape the assumption of foreignness and have continually had to reassert their membership. Recent changes in immigration law have created the perception that Asian Americans are deserving immigrants who enter the United States legally. Preferences for professional skills allow well-educated Asian immigrants to qualify for citizenship with technical, engineering, and medical skills. But even as a "model minority," the perception of Asian Americans as foreigners persists. For Asian Americans, membership and belonging in America is qualified by the perception that they are outsiders. In these respects, citizenship status does not provide full and complete membership in the American polity for Asian Americans, and perceptions of their belonging are moderated by the history of exclusion and the prevalence of racial stereotypes about them.

The Latino category

American territorial expansion into former territories of Mexico has clearly informed how Latinos understand their place and belonging in the nation. Latinos first existed as colonial subjects whose membership in the nation was never clearly defined, despite the fact that some of these inhabitants had occupied the land before it was granted to the United States. Formal citizenship status was awarded to Latino groups when the United States incorporated new territories. Because citizenship was limited to only whites when these territories were acquired, Latinos were indirectly defined as racially white. In practice, however, Latinos were considered less than white, and many did not enjoy the full rights associated with citizenship. Depending on a number of characteristics, including language, skin color, and Native American lineage, Latinos in the United States experienced a second-class citizenship similar to blacks, particularly in the American Southwest (Rodriguez 2008). The contradictions that characterize Latinos' ambivalent racial status correspond with the inconsistent treatment of Latinos; they are on the one hand integrated into the American economy, but on the other hand there is a preference to exclude them from the citizenry. Mexicans, for example, were first incorporated into the United States as formal citizens. But once the status of the newly acquired territories was decided, Mexicans were switched from being an incorporated people into foreign-born aliens. Mexicans were encouraged to enter the United States because they served as the primary labor pool for the large-scale commercial agricultural industry that ironically was made possible by the acquisition of the territories of the Southwest and California. Immigration policy did not place quotas on Mexican immigration for most of the twentieth century, and by allowing Mexicans to enter en masse, Americans perpetuated the notion that Mexicans were sojourners and transient workers who did not intend to stay (Bender 2005). Mexican immigrant labor thus helped to reframe Mexican Americans as foreigners rather than the original inhabitants of the Southwest. These historical experiences and the resulting narratives, along with the placement of Latinos lower in the American racial hierarchy than Asian Americans and whites creates a different form of incomplete membership for Latinos in the United States.

The racial and ethnic distinctions in the United States today have long-standing roots and ongoing influence in politics. The stereotypes tied to racial and ethnic groups are distinctions produced and perpetuated by the demands of American territorial expansion, economic development, and political advantage. Inequality in politics, economy, and society in the United States has since the birth of the nation been based on a racial hierarchy. While dynamic and ever-changing, political belonging is rooted in the relationship between immigration, race, and citizenship. Documenting the development of racial and ethnic categorization and exclusion resulting from group-based stereotypes provides a basis for understanding the historically contingent context within which Americans identify with the polity and with other groups. For those groups with a higher placement in the hierarchy, defining oneself as American does not come into conflict with a racial or ethnic identity because those groupings have historically not been at odds with one another. But Americans classified by a racial or ethnic category that has experienced exclusion and discrimination on the basis of that categorization have a mediated and conditional relationship to their American identity as a result of structural inequalities implicit in the racial hierarchy. This observation of structural relationship forms the basis of the next chapter.

CHAPTER THREE

The Pictures in Our Heads

The Content and Application of Racial Stereotypes

I mean, you got the first mainstream African-American who is articulate and bright and clean and a nice-looking guy . . . that's a storybook, man. — US Senator Joe Biden, 2007

Maybe that was an attempt to attract the illegal vote—I mean, the Latino voters. — US Senator Rick Santorum, 2012

If a Chinese child gets a B—which would never happen—there would first be a screaming, hair-tearing explosion. The devastated Chinese mother would then get dozens, maybe hundreds of practice tests and work through them with her child as long as it takes to get the grade up to an A. — Yale Law School professor Amy Chua, 2011

Stereotypes attached to racial categories are deeply embedded in US culture and politics through the widespread recognition of the American racial hierarchy. The power of group stereotypes is evident in the behavior and everyday language used by Americans, as well as in public statements made by people who sometimes express racial stereotypes despite their best efforts to sound neutral. The foregoing statements by Vice President Joseph Biden, former US senator Rick Santorum, and law professor Amy Chua were not necessarily intentionally racially based. Instead, they reflect the long-standing influence of racial stereotypes of African Americans, Latinos, and Asian Americans on the public imagination of the differences between people of different races.

In the first quote, Biden, who at the time was a US senator running for president in 2007, provided his assessment of Barack Obama.[1] Biden had been asked by reporters to assess the candidates running against him for the Democratic Party nomination. After the fallout from his re-marks, Biden stated that he had not intended for the use of the word "clean" to be a reference to the nature of blacks. But for Biden, Obama seemed unique because he was different from stereotypical expec-tations of an African American man. In contrast to most black men, Obama seemed smart and clean, and precisely because of these counter-stereotypical traits served as an inspiring figure for voters. In the sec-ond example, Santorum, during a 2012 Republican Party presidential primary debate in Florida made an accidental slip by using the word "il-legals" when he meant to reference "Latinos."[2] Santorum was respond-ing to a question about mobilizing Latino voters. In the final example, Chua described the assumed scholarly ability of a Chinese child.[3] Chua's portrayal of Asian Americans is presented as a prototype rather than an anecdotal case, but instead of challenging the racial stereotype, main-stream commentators and pundits accepted the "model minority" trope with little hesitation and attacked Chua for what they perceived to be improper childrearing practices within the context of racial threat from Asian Americans.[4]

These statements became newsworthy because people recognized that stereotypes were at work and understood the content of the racial tropes invoked. The pictures in our heads linking racial groups and stereotypi-cal traits are remarkably consistent among Americans, though there are important differences across groups in their application of stereotypes. Moreover, the content of racial stereotypes can be both "positive" and "negative," encompassing assumptions about groups in terms of intel-ligence, wealth and status, sociability, conformity with law, and family values. Some groups might be stereotyped negatively as poor but posi-tively as having strong family values, for example. Other racial groups are stereotyped as high achievers in terms of educational achievement and intelligence, but simultaneously defined by negative tropes of persis-tent foreignness. Still other groups have a disproportionately high num-ber of positive stereotypes and few negative tropes, while other racial groups are characterized with mostly negative stereotypes and relatively few positive group traits.

Location in the racial hierarchy corresponds with the valence and in-tensity of stereotypical traits associated with groups. The analysis in the preceding chapter identifies the mutually reinforcing relationship be-tween exclusionary practices of citizenship in the United States and the use of race to define political belonging. These dynamics in turn frame and reinforce the shape of the racial hierarchy and define the substantive content of the categories. By defining citizenship with the racial category of white, Americans have come to associate those classified as white as the most privileged and desirable members of society. Because non-whites are defined by default as less desirable and worthy of inclusion, group stereotypes for African Americans, Latinos, and Asian Americans are both more numerous and more negative than for whites. In this chapter we analyze the content and application of racial stereotypes for Americans classified by race by examining individual-level survey data on racial stereotypes from two different data collections.

The evidence demonstrates that Americans are generally in agreement about the stereotypes attached to contemporary racial categories. Situated at the top of the racial hierarchy, whites as a target group are perceived in negative stereotypes the least and in positive stereotypes the most among all Americans. In contrast, blacks, who are at the bottom of the racial order, have the highest level of negative stereotypes assigned to them by respondents and the lowest level of positive stereotypes. Consistent with their position in the racial hierarchy, Latinos and Asian Americans are in between whites and blacks, though Americans overall see more positive stereotypes in Asian Americans and have a much higher perception of negative stereotypes for Latinos.

We consider the contours of both positive and negative stereotype traits because their assignment and interaction are important reflections of the racial hierarchy and its dynamics. As Claire Kim (1999, 2000) illustrated in her comparative study of race in New York City, racial groups such as Asian Americans who occupy a position between the top and bottom of the hierarchy are valorized relative to blacks. Groups cannot be defined in isolation, and the application of stereotypical traits to racial groups is most revealing when considered in comparative relational perspective. Thus we hypothesize that individuals in racial groups of lower position will be perceived to hold relatively more deficient characteristics and negative traits than those placed higher in the hierarchy. Likewise, high standing in the racial order corresponds with stereotypical traits that denote superiority and power.

Because the racial category of black is at the bottom of the hierarchy, African Americans will be perceived to be associated with numerous negative traits. Stereotypes targeting blacks are rooted in their position as an economically disadvantaged group, and the accompanying stereotypes associate this racial group with lower class status. In addition, given the tendency to emphasize individual agency over structural forces, the common American explanation for black disadvantage is deficient behavior (see Bobo, Kluegel, and Smith 1997). As a result, racial stereotypes of blacks emphasize "deviant" behaviors such as laziness, preference for being on welfare, and tendency toward crime and violence. In contrast, whites occupy the most privileged position on the hierarchy and are associated with more positive stereotype traits. Because whiteness is associated with desirability and belonging, the valued American traits including having a strong work ethic, intelligence, and friendliness are stereotypes most readily assigned to whites, and fewer negative stereotypical traits are applied to the racial group of white.

The traits attached to the two groups in the middle of the hierarchy should be a mix of positive and negative traits, corresponding to their status relative to whites and blacks. Contemporary stereotypes of Asian Americans and Latinos reflect the assumption that most are newcomers to the nation. Indeed, while not all Latinos and Asian Americans are immigrants, these two groups account for over 75% of the foreign-born population in the United States. As a function of this newcomer status, both groups are perceived as speaking a language other than English and holding different cultural values from native-born Americans that are sometimes framed as being incompatible with American life (Huntington 2004). Despite sharing the status of immigrant groups, Latinos and Asian Americans are recognized as two different racial groups. Consistent with the contemporary shape of the racial hierarchy, Asian Americans are closer to whites and have more positive stereotypes than Latinos. Federal immigration policy since the 1965 Immigration and Nationality Act privileges high-skill occupations among other preferences for legal entry. Given the relatively high geographic barriers to entry to the United States for immigrants from Asian countries as compared to those from Latin America, the immigration preference system creates a selection bias of Asian immigrants who come to the United States with high educational attainment and economic status. As a result, more Asian immigrants arrive with government authorization and can more easily assimilate into the middle class. This trajectory is consistent with the "American Dream" narrative, and Asian immigrants are framed as models of successful assimilation, in contrast to Latino immigrants, many more of whom arrive in the United States with fewer resources and opportunities for social and economic advancement. Latinos often come to work in agricultural and service sectors of the economy (Bender 2005) and are therefore more likely than Asian immigrants to come with relatively low levels of education and wealth. Because federal immigration law privileges legal status for those with high skills and formal education, Americans associate the poorest immigrants with being unauthorized (Chavez 2008). These social forces combine to place Asian Americans higher in the racial order than Latinos and, consequently, also nurture more numerous positive stereotypes and fewer negative stereotypes of Asians than of Latinos.

The data in the following sections show a remarkable consistency in the recognition of stereotype traits ascribed to racial groups among all Americans, even those groups who are negatively stereotyped. This consistency indicates that minorities are aware of their relatively lower placement on the hierarchy compared to whites, and while they may not like the stereotypes associated with racial groups, they know the tropes exist. African Americans, Latinos, and Asian Americans understand that their racial classification marks them with a degree of desirability consistent with the stereotypes associated with their group. As shown in scholarship based in the position that humans understand the world in relational terms (e.g., Blumer 1958; Bobo and Hutchings 1996; Tajfel 1981), social status is one important way individuals orient themselves. Social status and position in the hierarchy have clear effects on how individuals behave. Those who enjoy high status tend to demonstrate confidence, assert dominance, and, most important for our purposes, support existing hierarchical relationships (Fiske 2011; Anderson and Berdahl 2002; Sidanius and Pratto 1999). In contrast, those of lower status are more likely to suffer from low self-esteem and have difficulty overcoming the obstacles they experience as a function of their status (Abrams, Hogg, and Marquez 2005; Major and O'Brien 2005; Steele 2011). At the same time, because those of lower status experience exclusion and discrimination as a result of their position in the racial hierarchy, they are more critical about norms that uphold the existing order. As we show in the following analysis, while Americans are in general agreement about the ordering of racial groups in the hierarchy, groups differ in the degree to which they adhere to racial stereotypes as a result of their differing status.

Stereotypes Reflect the Racial Hierarchy

Stereotyping is most often used by researchers as a measure of individual-level predisposition to be prejudiced (Allport 1954; Devine 1989; see also Burns and Gimpel 2000; Hurwitz and Peffley 1997). Similarly, negative perceptions, stereotypes, or dislike of other racial groups are used as empirical proxies for ethnocentrism or predictors of intergroup conflict (Bobo and Hutchings 1996; Kinder and Kam 2009). When people rely heavily on negative stereotypes to make decisions, they are more likely to exhibit prejudiced behavior and attitudes (Allport 1954; Kinder and Sanders 1996). Psychologists also describe stereotyping as a cognitive tool to process complex information quickly (Hilton and von Hippel 1996; Schneider 2004). Humans categorize similar phenomena into groups and make sense of new information by considering its relation to preexisting categories (Conover 1988). Thus racial stereotypes act as a type of schemata or collection of ideas through which individuals develop frameworks for understanding how racial groups differ. For example, "poor" may become linked with a particular racial group such as blacks when an individual consistently views blacks in poverty, either firsthand or in a mediated fashion. Racial stereotypes reflect an individuals' averaging of what they perceive as representative characteristics of a racial group (Schneider 2004).

Systematic research also demonstrates that individuals are less likely to pay attention to members of an out-group and that people tend to overlook the internal diversity found within an out-group (Goldstein and Chance 1978; Judd and Park 1988). Homogenization of a group can also result in dehumanization (Harris and Fiske 2006; Haslam 2006). Furthermore, racial stereotypes reinforce associations between negative attributes and racial minorities (Dovidio, Evans, and Tyler 1986). Assumptions of deficient traits coupled with the tendency to dehumanize out-groups leads individuals to engage in discriminatory behaviors against some racial groups, and scholars have identified serious implications of racial stereotyping. Political elites can also manipulate public attitudes by evoking negative stereotypes of a targeted racial group (Gilens 1999; Hurwitz and Peffley 2005; Valentino, Hutchings and White 2002).

While stereotyping serves a cognitive purpose for individual decision making, the content of stereotypes is more than a product of the individual mind. Devine (1989) cautioned scholars to distinguish between cultural stereotypes shared by society and personal beliefs developed out of individual experiences. The argument that individual attitudes are informed fundamentally by external social forces is not new to political science, but it is a perspective that has increasingly been overlooked in favor of cognitive perspectives focusing on internal dynamics. Walter Lippmann's (1922) thoughtful discussion about the formation of public opinion placed significant emphasis on social stereotypes and the environment: "For the most part we do not first see, and then define, we define first and then see. In the great blooming, buzzing confusion of the outer world we pick out what our culture has already defined for us, and we tend to perceive that which we have picked out in the form stereotyped for us by our culture" (81).

Individuals do not create the meanings attached to politically relevant categories but instead accept or reject existing stereotypes. As a result, some categories have more influence over individual-level cognitive processing and decision making than do others. Studies in social psychology show that individuals are most likely to accentuate differences between groups when they are provided with categories that already exist in their society. For example, in a study that asked subjects to estimate the differences in value of British coins, researchers found that the British respondents were more likely to accentuate differences among those coins than the American respondents who had no prior exposure to British currency (Tajfel 1981). While people are able to create groups and develop strong in-group loyalties from very minimal standards of difference, they also perceive the highest degree of difference when the values associated with those categories have preexisting social or cultural meaning (Tajfel 1981). Because of the significance of race as a political category, the traits attached to racial categories will have strong influence on decision making at the individual level. While people are capable of ignoring racial stereotypes, the automatic activation of racial stereotypes is difficult for individuals to control (Devine 1989).

In a highly insightful article, Bobo and Massagli (2001) argue that the historical experiences and treatment of racial groups set a precedent for how stereotypes are framed:

Racial stereotypes are at once social products and social forces; they spring in part from the fact of social inequality among groups but also form constituent elements in the reproduction of inequality. Stereotypes are social prod-

ucts in the sense that they emerge from the history and context of particular relations among groups. They reflect the positioning of groups in physical
space, work or occupational roles, and the overall economic hierarchy. Yet,
stereotypes are also social forces and highly generalized, durable cognitive
constructs. They are bundles of ideas that directly influence individual expectations, perceptions and social behavior in intergroup contact settings. Social
psychological research shows that stereotypes influence what we see, what we
believe to be true, what we expect, and therefore how we tend to behave toward members of groups other than our own. (92)

Bobo and Massagli are critical of the oversights in cognitive theories on
stereotypes, arguing these approaches fail to acknowledge the structural
forces that uphold the perception of group traits. Stereotyping is not
only a product of individual cognition but a reflection of how society has
defined groups. In their analysis of empirical data, Bobo and Massagli
find that when comparing the racial stereotyping of respondents living
in different urban areas with varying levels of diversity, the content attached to racial stereotypes is strikingly similar regardless of a person's
surroundings. If stereotyping is a general indicator of in-group preferences, then respondents should hold the most stereotypes about those
they come into contact with. But this is not the case. Similarly, their data
do not show that people rate all out-groups negatively and only their own
racial group positively. Individuals not only develop stereotypes from
their personal experiences but also report those meanings as they are
defined by society.

We concur with Bobo and Massagli in their challenge of the scholarly
assumption that racial stereotyping is simply a proxy for individual cognitive processes and prejudice. We argue that adherence to racial tropes,
which include positive and negative stereotypes applied to groups,
should also be thought of as an indicator of an individual's acceptance
of the racial hierarchy and the narratives used to justify it. Americans
develop assumptions and tropes about each racial group largely consistent with visible social and economic practices, and race and class are
closely intertwined in the existing social order (Massey 2007). A hierarchy that ranks on a scale of rich to poor looks nearly the same as the
hierarchy from white to black. This is because racial categorization has
historically been utilized to exclude access to capital from some and provide the justification for access to others (Oliver and Shapiro 2006; Wilson 1987). This practice has had deleterious effects on the rates of social

mobility for those excluded. As a result, certain groups are more likely to be undereducated and poor, which helps to substantiate homogenizing perceptions and negative stereotypes about those groups. While the narratives justifying minority poverty can serve racist purposes, general economic patterns that individuals perceive in their daily lives are created by historical economic processes and are not a figment of individual imagination.

Conceiving of racial-group stereotypes as a reflection of the racial hierarchy shifts the focus toward the structural influence of long-standing social forces and away from purely individual-level antecedents. The context of constraint and opportunity forged by racial categorization and group position implicit in the racial hierarchy helps to explain the patterns of difference between groups observed in the data. As is apparent in the findings that follow, low-status groups often adhere to negative stereotypes about their own group, and Latinos, Asian Americans, and African Americans hold racial stereotypes about their own groups similar to those of whites about minorities. For example, implicit association tests reveal that blacks hold negative stereotypes about blacks (Ashburn-Nardo, Knowles, and Monteith 2003). An explanation for this finding is that blacks, just as whites, accept the existing American narrative that frames blacks at the bottom of the racial hierarchy (Arkes and Tetlock 2004). Although blacks also seek to develop a strong sense of self-esteem and group pride, societal norms still influence how they view their own group (Hughes and Demo 1989; Rosenberg and Simmons 1971).

Stereotypes Viewed through the Racial Prism

Americans are in general agreement about how the racial hierarchy is ordered, and the perception of positive and negative stereotypes across racial groups is remarkably consistent. This finding is predictable on the basis of two important theories in social psychology: social dominance theory (Sidanius and Pratto 1999) and system justification theory (Jost and Banaji 1994). Both theories begin with the assumption that individuals are distinctly aware of their status as either part of the most powerful group or relegated to one of the lower-status groups, and all individuals, regardless of their status, engage to varying degrees in activities to uphold the existing social order. Jost and Banaji (1994) explain this tendency as the result of all individuals' "social and psychological needs to imbue the status quo with legitimacy and to see it as good, fair, natural, desirable, and even inevitable" (887). Thus individual attitudes are not solely driven by self- or group interests but also demonstrate compliance with the social structure governing societal norms. Because people to one degree or another exist in their hierarchical position, there are clear attitudinal and behavioral differences between those individuals of high status and those of low status. Sidanius and Pratto (1999) find that individuals positioned at the top of the hierarchy are more likely to exhibit what they term "social dominance orientation," reflecting "the degree to which individuals desire and support group-based hierarchy and the domination of 'inferior' groups by 'superior' groups" (48). Those who benefit from the existing order are more likely to support measures or viewpoints that uphold the hierarchy. Jost and Banaji (1994) document the tendency of members of subordinate groups to hold the dominant group in higher esteem than their own, and individuals are not automatically prone to view their own group positively when their group is defined as the societal out-group. Instead, members of dominant groups display the greatest tendency for in-group favoritism, while members of subordinate groups have weaker in-group preferences and valorize dominant groups.

Fiske (1993, 2011) argues that power and the tendency to stereotype are strongly related. She finds that those who hold powerful positions are more likely to rely on stereotypes than subordinates. Using the relationship between teachers and students as an example, Fiske shows that teachers are more likely to generalize about their students, while students often provide individuating information about teachers. She hypothesizes that there are different incentives for those in powerful positions to rely on stereotypes than those in subordinate positions. Subordinates are more likely to pay attention and make detailed observations about those individuals in power because their fortunes depend on the actions of superiors. But the powerful do not have to pay as close attention to subordinates because they know that their subordinates have little control over them. Superiors' knowledge about subordinates is therefore more likely to be governed by generalized stereotypes. Since stereotyping can dehumanize, those in powerful positions can more easily engage in discriminatory behavior against subordinates. Fiske's research provides the critical insight that while there are stereotypes that the public generally accepts, social position also determines when and how individuals choose to apply those stereotypes.

Given our axiomatic position that position in the racial hierarchy structures power relationships, we expect racial categorization to influence how individuals rely on stereotypes. Because whites occupy the most powerful position as the default racial in-group, they are most likely to hold the most negative stereotypes about racial minorities. According to social dominance theory and system justification theory, whites are most supportive of narratives promoting the status quo and least likely to challenge existing negative stereotypes about racial minorities. Precisely because the racial hierarchy favors them, whites are the group most likely to exhibit strong in-group favoritism because they can attribute their relative advantages they hold to their superiority. Following Fiske's logic, as the most powerful group, whites may have less incentive to pay close attention to racial minorities because their lives are less likely to be negatively affected by them.

Racial minorities, on the other hand, will exhibit less in-group favoritism than whites. Since racial minorities know they are ranked lower than whites in the hierarchy, they also report holding those negative traits that are used to justify their racial position. Moreover, and because racial minorities are situated in subordinate position to whites, they pay more attention to their own social surroundings, and norms governing social desirability are less likely to govern how racial minorities stereotype. As Jost, Banaji, and Nosek (2004) show, when subordinate groups negatively stereotype, they apply those stereotypes to their own group, but when dominant groups negatively stereotype, they apply those stereotypes to another group. Subordinate groups who display in-group favoritism are thus combating perceptions of undesirability that are normally applied to their own group. In contrast, dominant groups who display in-group favoritism are supporting their group's status at the top of the hierarchy. Jost, Banaji, and Nosek hypothesize that because of this, racial minorities are less concerned with violating social desirability norms, whereas whites prefer to dampen their perceptions of both in-group favoritism and negative out-group stereotypes in order to present more socially desirable answers.[5]

But not all racial minority groups are the same, and because blacks, Latinos, and Asian Americans occupy different places in the American racial hierarchy, power differences exist between minority groups. Thus, we expect variation in how racial minorities apply stereotypes. When a group is ranked relatively high on the hierarchy, its members display practices closer to the dominant group of whites, and position plays an important role distinguishing stereotyping across subordinate groups. For example, since Asian Americans are framed as the "model minority" group and on average hold higher levels of education and income, their relatively higher status provides more incentive to negatively stereotype blacks and Latinos, who are currently ranked at lower levels in the hierarchy. In contrast, blacks, who historically have been placed at the bottom of the hierarchy, are more likely to reject pejorative racial stereotypes for all groups.

Multi-City Study of Urban Inequality Data

A challenge to studying public opinion across racial groups is that there are limited data sets with sizable samples of all four racial groups that allow for comparative relational analysis. In addition, with respect to racial stereotypes, most questions on racial-group traits are asked only about African Americans. With the exception of experimental case studies conducted on student samples in psychology (e.g., Cuddy, Fiske, and Glick 2007), there are few data sets with stereotype questions that target each of the four major racial groups in the United States. The most extensive collection of racial-group stereotype data asking respondents to assess the traits of whites, blacks, Asians, and Latinos is included in the MCSUI.[6] This survey was conducted between 1992 and 1994 with samples of the adult population living in four cities: Atlanta, Boston, Detroit, and Los Angeles.[7] By focusing on these urban areas, investigators were able to collect large samples of racial minorities. The MCSUI represents one of the most extensive studies in the United States to date on racial attitudes and stereotyping.

Respondents in the MCSUI were asked to rate whites, blacks, Asian Americans, and Latinos on pairs of opposing traits on a scale of 1 to 7, where a score of 1 represented the positive trait while a score of 7 represented the negative trait.[8] The range midpoint of 4 would denote that the target group represented neither the positive nor negative trait. The survey included questions about these stereotypical traits: rich or poor, intelligent or unintelligent, prefers to be self-supporting or prefers to be on welfare, speaks English well or speaks English poorly, and not involved with drugs and gangs or involved with drugs and gangs. While these stereotypical traits are not an exhaustive list of possible traits that could be applied to a racial group, the purpose here is not to identify every possible racial stereotype that exists but instead to reveal how Americans perceive social status and desirable behavior. To analyze stereotype data, we standardized each pair of traits to have a range between −1 and 1 where values above 0 denote application of positive stereotype traits and values below 0 indicate negative trait attribution.[9] A score of zero denotes that the target group was perceived to have neither the negative nor the positive trait. The data are presented in disaggregated form by race of respondent with each of the bars in the chart representing the mean rating for each target group (i.e., whites as rich or poor) for the five stereotype pairs.

Figure 3.1 compares group ratings for the stereotype of rich or poor by race and offers a clear depiction of the racial hierarchy. White targets are most likely to be rated as rich by respondents in all racial groups. Asian targets are also perceived to be somewhat rich, although the mean scores for Asian targets are closer to a neutral score of 0 than 1 (denoting "very rich"). Both black and Latino targets are rated as poor by all respondents, and racial groups, on average, rate Latinos as the poorest group though the difference between the average rating applied to black targets and that to Latino targets is small (but statistically significant). Thus ratings on the rich-poor stereotype trait indicate that black and Latino targets are both perceived to occupy disadvantaged positions.

While the data show that all racial groups report the same relative rankings of groups on the stereotype of rich-poor, with whites perceived to be the most economically privileged, Asian Americans next, and blacks and Latinos seen as the most economically disadvantaged, there are differences in how racial groups apply the rich-poor stereo-

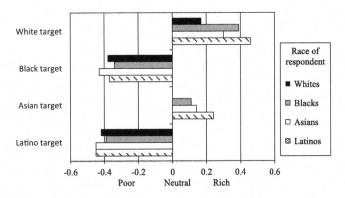

FIGURE 3.1. Stereotype of rich or poor by race. *Source*: Multi-City Study of Urban Inequality.

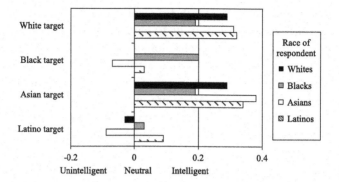

FIGURE 3.2. Stereotype of intelligence by race. *Source*: Multi-City Study of Urban Inequality.

type. Racial minority respondents give white targets significantly higher ratings as rich than do white respondents. Although white respondents also rate their own racial group as the wealthiest, they do not perceive their group to be as advantaged as do racial minority respondents. All of the differences discussed here at statistically significant at the .01 level. Latino respondents give the highest rating to white targets on the stereotype of being rich. The racial group most often stereotyped to be the poorest in this data set is also the one that sees the largest difference in wealth between their own group and whites. This is consistent with Jost and Banaji's system justification theory, which states that lower-status groups tend to award higher distinction to high-status groups, while high-status groups award the most positive traits to their own group.

Ratings differences on the other four stereotype traits of intelligence, welfare use, English language ability, and drug or gang involvement, show a similar set of clear patterns. Respondents in the MCSUI are in general agreement in ranking whites at the top of the hierarchy for all of these traits, ranking Asians in the middle, and ranking both blacks and Latinos at the bottom. Figure 3.2 shows that white respondents give members of their own racial group higher ratings on the intelligence measure, while Asian Americans also show similar in-group favoritism. Blacks assess whites and Asians about the same in intelligence, while Latinos rate Asians as having higher levels of intelligence than whites.

The pattern of the higher-ranked racial groups showing positive in-group preferences and lower-ranked groups being more likely to assign negative traits to their own group persists across the other stereotype trait questions. Focusing on the ratings provided by white respondents, we find that whites always rate their own group to have positive rather than negative traits. White respondents award higher ratings to the white target as being rich, having strong English-language ability, preferring to be self-supporting and not being involved in drugs and gangs than to any other racial group, and these differences are all statistically significant at the .01 level. The data for the stereotype of welfare use by race are shown in figure 3.3 and data for the stereotype of English-language ability by race is displayed in figure 3.4. The other group that showed positive in-group preferences was Asian Americans, who gave their own group the most positive scores as being intelligent, preferring to be self-supporting, and not being involved in drugs and gangs. The data on the stereotype of drug or gang involvement by race is displayed in figure 3.5.

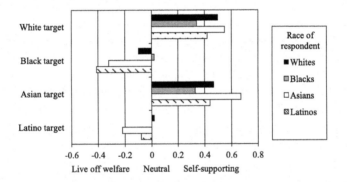

FIGURE 3.3. Stereotype of welfare use by race. *Source*: Multi-City Study of Urban Inequality.

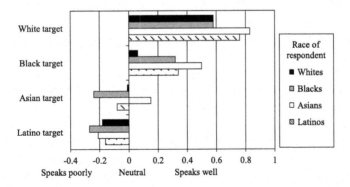

FIGURE 3.4. Stereotype of English-language ability by race. *Source*: Multi-City Study of Urban Inequality.

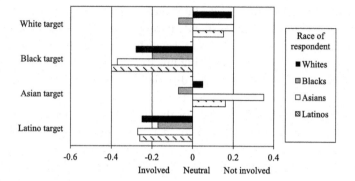

FIGURE 3.5. Stereotype of drug or gang involvement by race. *Source*: Multi-City Study of Urban Inequality.

These differences are also statistically significant at the .01 level. However, consistent with the racial order, Asian American respondents did report that on some traits, other racial groups were stereotyped more positively. They gave whites the highest score on being rich and also gave a higher rating on speaking English well to both blacks and whites.

The two higher-ranked groups in the racial hierarchy also share the viewpoint that lower-ranked racial groups on the hierarchy are associated with undesirable traits, with the only exception that both white and Asian American respondents rate English-language skills as higher among blacks than either Asians or Latinos. These differences are statistically significant at the .01 level and consistent with the content of stereotype racialization of Asians as the "perpetual foreigner" (C. Kim 2000; Tuan 1999). These results are also consistent with the placement of Asian Americans below whites in the racial hierarchy. Interestingly, Asian American respondents give black targets a higher rating on speaking English well than white respondents assess blacks on that trait, a difference that is also statistically significant at the .01 level.

In terms of the stereotype of preferring to be self-supporting than to live on welfare, Asian American respondents report that black and Latino targets prefer to be on welfare, while white respondents on average report neutral scores on black and Latino preference for welfare. This difference observed is consistent with the social desirability effect discussed above and suggests that Asian American respondents see a clear racial order in which their ratings of groups correspond with common racial tropes but are less affected by the worry of being perceived as racist. While white respondents report the same racial ordering of groups, they are less likely than Asian Americans to apply negative traits to low-ranked groups because of social desirability norms. These differences are all statistically significant at the .01 level.

Although the higher-ranked groups demonstrate strongly positive in-group biases, the two lower-ranked groups of black and Latino respondents show weaker in-group preferences. The most striking feature in the data is that blacks and Latinos rarely rate their own group to be better than whites. This is not to say that black and Latino respondents do not rate their own group positively; black respondents believe that blacks are as intelligent as both whites and Asians and also perceive blacks to speak English better than both Asians and Latinos. Latino respondents rate their own group positively compared to other groups only on the intelligence measure. But while Latino respondents perceive their own group as intelligent, they do not view their own group to be as intelligent as whites or Asians.[10]

Unlike white and Asian American respondents, both blacks and Latinos attribute negative stereotypes to their own racial group. Black respondents perceive that blacks are poor, but figure 3.5 also shows that they rate black targets as more likely than any other racial group to be involved in drugs and gangs. They also take a neutral stance on the preference of blacks to live off welfare. Latino respondents rate their own group as poor, with the lowest level of English-language ability, preferring to live off welfare, and being involved in drugs and gangs. However, black and Latino ratings show that these groups do not agree on the group ranked the lowest in the racial hierarchy. Black respondents believe that their own group is more intelligent than Latinos and vice versa. Both groups rate each other as poor, although Latino respondents perceive their own group to be poorer than black respondents do, and all of these differences are statistically significant at the .01 level. At the same time, black and Latino stereotyping of each other reflects the negative tropes applied to these two groups in society as a whole. These findings are consistent with the increasingly persistent cultural associations between blacks and Latinos with respect to welfare and crime (Gilens 1999; Hancock 2004; Mendelberg 2001).

Faces of Immigration data

To supplement the MCSUI findings on racial stereotypes, we next analyze data from a survey we conducted in 2006. The Faces of Immigration Survey was conducted with a nationally representative sample of equally sized populations of white, black, Latino, and Asian American respondents.[11] The questions on the survey asked about characteristics that applied to Latino immigrants and Asian immigrants, but do not include comparable data on black and white targets as is available in the MCSUI data. Despite the absence of the full range of racial group targets to compare, the data can nevertheless be analyzed to test how respondents from all four racial groups see stereotypical traits of Asian and Latino immigrants.

In the 2006 Faces of Immigration Survey, respondents were asked to "check the characteristics you think apply to these groups of immigrants." They were then provided a list of nine attributes including work very hard, often end up on welfare, do very well in school, significantly increase crime, have strong family values, threaten national security, keep to themselves and don't try to fit in, are mostly illegal immigrants, and have values that conflict with American culture.[12] By allowing respondents to choose traits, we did not force respondents to provide an opinion on each trait, and stereotypes are thus measured differently in the 2006 Faces study than in the MCSUI. This variation in measurement provides a validity check on the patterns of stereotypes assigned to members of racial groups. If the trait ratings provide similar results between the two studies even with different question wording techniques, then we can further confirm American views about the placement of groups within the racial hierarchy.

Table 3.1 presents the percentage of respondents in each racial group who selected each trait for Latino immigrants and Asian immigrants.[13] The table divides the stereotypes into those classified as "positive" and "negative." As in the results from the MCSUI data, we again find that clearly racialized tropes are applied to Latino and Asian immigrants.

Consistent with their racialization as perpetually foreign, sizable numbers of respondents of all racial groups indicate that both Asian and Latino immigrants keep to themselves and don't try and fit in. Large shares of respondents also believe that Latino immigrants are more likely to end up on welfare and increase crime and are mostly illegal, while no more than 10% of respondents assign such traits to Asian immigrants. The pattern of stereotypes for Latinos is consistent with their low ranking on the racial hierarchy relative to Asians. Despite the construction of Japanese Americans in particular as threats to domestic security in WWII, the theme of national security is applied to neither Asian

TABLE 3.1. **Perception of Stereotypical Traits of Latino and Asian Immigrants by Race**

Characteristics ascribed to Latino immigrants

Positive stereotypes	Race of respondent				Negative stereotypes	Race of respondent			
	White	Black	Asian	Latino		White	Black	Asian	Latino
Work very hard	66%	79%	64%	78%	Often end up on welfare	41%	21%	38%	36%
Do very well in school	7%	19%	6%	22%	Significantly increase crime	38%	20%	30%	29%
Have strong family values	68%	65%	65%	73%	Threaten national security	12%	4%	5%	7%
					Keep to themselves and don't try to fit in	38%	19%	31%	31%
					Are mostly illegal immigrants	62%	46%	38%	32%
					Have values that conflict with American culture	21%	20%	14%	22%

Characteristics ascribed to Asian immigrants

Positive stereotypes	Race of respondent				Negative stereotypes	Race of respondent			
	White	Black	Asian	Latino		White	Black	Asian	Latino
Work very hard	76%	74%	92%	72%	Often end up on welfare	4%	3%	8%	5%
Do very well in school	81%	65%	83%	70%	Significantly increase crime	5%	5%	4%	8%
Have strong family values	78%	70%	77%	68%	Threaten national security	6%	4%	2%	9%
					Keep to themselves and don't try to fit in	46%	43%	34%	49%
					Are mostly illegal immigrants	5%	9%	4%	10%
					Have values that conflict with American culture	20%	21%	18%	19%

Source: Faces of Immigration Survey

nor Latino immigrants, and only small shares of respondents perceive these two groups to threaten national security. On the positive stereotypes, consistent with the American narrative of immigrant ingenuity, an overwhelming majority of the respondents evaluate both Asian and Latino immigrants as hardworking. Respondents are also likely to say that both groups have strong family values. However, since only Asians are framed as the high-achieving model minority group, a larger share of respondents perceived Asian immigrants as doing very well in school than Latino immigrants.

The data in table 3.1 also show racial differences in how respondents apply stereotypical traits to Asian and Latino immigrants. For example, 62% of whites believe that Latinos are mostly illegal, while a smaller share of blacks (46%) and even smaller proportions of Asian Americans and Latinos (38% and 32%, respectively) consider Latinos to be in the United States without legal authorization. To assess how racial groups vary in their propensity to stereotype, we disaggregated respondents by racial group and calculated the total average number of negative and positive stereotypes assigned to Asian immigrants and to Latino immigrants for each group. These results are reported in table 3.2.[14] Different racial groups apply positive and negative stereotypes at varying rates. This pattern is most obvious in the average ratings reported by white respondents. Whites give the highest average number of negative stereotypes to Latino immigrants of all four racial groups.[15] Whites along with Asian American respondents assign a relatively low average number of positive stereotypes to Latino immigrants.[16] This is in distinct contrast to black and Latino respondents, who both give the highest average number of positive stereotypes to Latino immigrants and the highest average number of negative stereotypes to Asian immigrants.[17]

TABLE 3.2. **Average Number of Positive or Negative Stereotypes Ascribed to Latino and Asian Immigrants by Race**

Race of respondent	Positive stereotypes of Latinos (total of 3)	Negative stereotypes of Latinos (total of 6)	Positive stereotypes of Asians (total of 3)	Negative stereotypes of Asians (total of 6)
White	1.42	2.05	2.40	0.88
Black	1.80	1.69	2.39	1.19
Asian	1.41	1.76	2.55	.69
Latino	1.79	1.73	2.41	1.18

Source: Faces of Immigration Survey

TABLE 3.3. **Difference between Average Number of Negative and Positive Stereotypes Ascribed to Latino and Asian Immigrants by Race**

Race of respondent	No. of neg. Latino traits minus no. of neg. Asian traits	No. of pos. Asian traits minus no. of pos. Latino traits
White	0.87	0.92
Black	0.40	0.60
Asian	0.83	1.02
Latino	0.45	0.59

Source: Faces of Immigration Survey

Because the 2006 Faces survey asks respondents to select those stereotypes that applied to Asian and Latino immigrants, the measures allow us to construct a more direct measure of how respondents order groups.[18] We created two measures of hierarchical placement of racial groups. The first measure identifies the perception that Asians are ranked higher than Latinos on the racial order and is operationalized by taking the difference between the total number of positive stereotypes applied to Asian immigrants and the total number of positive stereotypes applied to Latino immigrants. A larger, positive difference will reflect that a respondent associates more desirable stereotypical traits to what that respondent understands as the higher-ranked group. The second measure of hierarchical thinking identifies the perception that Latinos are lower than Asians on the racial order and is operationalized by taking the difference between the total number of negative stereotypes applied to Latino immigrants and the total number of negative stereotypes applied to Asian immigrants. In this case, a larger positive difference will reflect that the respondent associates more undesirable traits with the racial group ranked lowest on the racial hierarchy.

Table 3.3 reports the averages on each of these two scores of hierarchical thinking by race of the respondent.[19] The results are consistent with our theory on racial position as well as the theories on social hierarchies articulated by Sidanius and Pratto (1999) and Jost and Banaji (1994). We find that the more highly ranked groups in the racial hierarchy, whites and Asian Americans, are more likely to engage in hierarchical thinking than the lower-ranked groups of blacks and Latinos. Whites show the highest difference on the negative stereotyping measure, and Asians hold the highest score for the positive stereotyping measure. But while the absolute averages are different across the four groups, not all of the differences are significant. Difference-of-means tests show that the most important differences are between high- and low-ranked groups.

White and Asian American respondents stereotype in a similar manner, as do black and Latino respondents. This pattern continues to be significant even when controlling for important individual-level differences such as education and gender, and only one result falls outside of this pattern.[20] Although there is no significant difference in how white and Asian American respondents assess negative stereotypes, Asian Americans are significantly more likely to associate more positive stereotypes with Asian than with Latino immigrants. This is consistent with patterns in the MCSUI data where Asian Americans are both more likely to show positive in-group bias but also willing to report a clear racial order.

Structuring Stereotype Content and Application

Regardless of their racial background, Americans' perception of group stereotypes is consistent with the order of racial groups in the racial hierarchy. What remains eerily consistent is the placement of whites at the top of the racial order and blacks at the bottom, with Latinos closely following African Americans in being assigned negative stereotypes. The composition of the white racial category has changed over time to accommodate groups once seen as "less than white," but the privilege and desirability attached to whiteness has remained constant (Haney López 1996; Lipsitz 1998; Gross 2008). Similarly, stereotypes applied to blacks in the United States have shown little content change. Historians and social psychologists document that the general message communicated through negative black stereotypes has shown striking durability over time (Devine and Elliot 1995). Negative portrayals of blacks as lazy, prone to aggression, and ignorant are persistent themes continually readapted to fit the relevant social context. During the antebellum era, when black America was relegated to chattel slavery, the racial stereotypes of blacks revolved around the behaviors of black servitude. Black women were often portrayed as "mammies"—physically unappealing, uneducated, but loving and subservient nurses who cared for their white owners' homes (Wallace-Sanders 2008). In the modern era, persistent black poverty has encouraged media images of black women as "welfare queens" (Gilens 1999; Hancock 2004; Harris-Perry 2011). While the antebellum and modern stereotypes of black women are clearly different, both stereotypes communicate similar negative portrayals of black women as prone to dependency.

We have argued that racial stereotypes are indicators of institution-alized norms embedded in the racial hierarchy, but this does not nec-essarily lead to the conclusion that racial tropes are fixed. As detailed in chapter 2, changes in the meanings attached to racial categories have occurred over the history of the United States (Omi and Winant 1994). Most often, changes occur within the context of major political and so-cial events that alter how groups interact with each other. The civil rights movement and the significant influx of new immigrants following the 1965 Immigration and Nationality Act, for example, influenced group interaction through fundamental changes in institutional arrangements and the demographic composition of the population. Immigration is a particularly important cause of shifting racial tropes because new en-trants have diversified the US population and changed the definition, meaning, and application of racial categories (Hattam 2007; Ngai 2004). Racial stereotypes are thus not obdurate constructs but specific to the time and context of political belonging.

While the position of whites at the top and blacks at the bottom of the hierarchy remains stable, the content and application of stereotypes for the racial categories of Latinos and Asian Americans demonstrate the malleability of the racial hierarchy. Not all categories can change at the same speed or in a positive direction, however, and social psycholo-gists have found that certain racial stereotypes are more likely to persist over time, while others are more likely to be context specific. One theory for why this is the case is that some stereotypes are more likely to be in-tegrated into interpersonal communications compared to others. Those stereotypes that are continually used and integrated into social conversa-tions in discussions with family, friends, and colleagues will be more cog-nitively accessible to individuals. Schaller, Conway, and Tanchuk (2002) argue that the stereotypes more often used in interpersonal communi-cations are those that represent dominant racial tropes and so are less likely to fade in memory. Another key force behind the stasis and change in racial stereotypes is the mass media. Consistent stereotypical portray-als in the media help to further embed particular tropes in Americans' minds, and evidence supports the observation that stereotypical group images and racialized narratives have strong effects on how Americans think about social policies (Dunaway, Branton, and Abrajano 2010; Ent-man and Rojecki 2000).[21]

One group whose dominant racial tropes have shifted over time is Asian Americans. These changes have occurred as a result of federal immigration policy that systematically altered the composition of Asian immigrants from laborers to high-skilled workers. From the late-nineteenth century, Asians were recruited to the United States to fulfill labor demands on the West Coast ranging from the building of the trans-continental railroad to planting and harvesting crops (Chan 1991; Takaki 1998). Asian immigrants were labeled "coolies," and by the time the rail-road was completed, unwanted workers were described as the "dregs of Asia" (Gyory 1998) by California governor and railroad baron Leland Stanford. More recently however, newcomers with engineering, medi-cal, and technical skills typify Asian immigrants. No longer perceived as day-laboring "coolies," Asian Americans today are framed as "model minorities" or highly industrious individuals with superior math and sci-ence skills (Rim 2007; Tuan 1998).

The capacity for change in stereotypes and the presence of higher lev-els of positive racial-group stereotypes for Asian Americans creates a context for group identity specific to this racial category. On the flip side, the prevalence of negative stereotypes about Latinos and the provisions in the American racial taxonomy for Latinos to be of any race including white structure group identity for Latinos in ways distinctive from con-straints on Asian Americans. The stereotype data from both the MCSUI and the Faces of Immigration Survey analyzed here underscore the rel-atively low position of Latinos compared to Asian Americans. In both data sets, and for many of the negative stereotypes, Latinos were rated by all respondents to be at the bottom of the racial hierarchy with Afri-can Americans.

Black and Latino respondents' willingness to assign their own groups negative stereotypical traits supports our claim that questions on stereo-types in public opinion surveys should not be interpreted only as indica-tors of negative out-group bias in the form of prejudice or ethnocentrism. The MCSUI and Faces of Immigration Survey data make clear that ra-cial groups do not simply assign positive trait ratings to their own group and negative trait ratings to out-groups. Instead, the responses are indic-ative of systematic and widely understood understandings about how ra-cial groups are racialized, even if that means assigning one's own group negative stereotypes. The patterns in the data on stereotypes are thus a reflection of how Americans see the racial hierarchy.

In this way, the racial hierarchy structures the context in which in-dividuals develop an identity based on their racial-group status. How groups are stereotyped is an indicator of how others in society see individuals classified by race, and this categorization creates a context of contingent expectations based in group identity. Social psychologist Claude Steele (2010) made the same point eloquently:

> I am thus proposing something simple: the sense of a given social identity arises from having to deal with important identity contingencies, usually threatening or restrictive contingencies like negative stereotypes about your group, group segregations of one sort or another, discrimination and prejudice, and so on, all because you have a given characteristic. What raises a characteristic we have to a social identity we have are the contingencies that go with the characteristic, most often threatening contingencies. (74)

The identity contingencies Steele describes are "the things you have to deal with in a situation because you have a given social identity" (3). For lower-ranked groups in the racial hierarchy, those contingencies take the form of obstacles that are a function of their relatively low status and desirability. These obstacles constrain the choices and agency for individuals in racial groups ranked toward the bottom of the hierarchy. In contrast, the context of their racial position provides opportunity and enhances the individual agency for members of higher-ranked groups. The racial hierarchy influences how each American conceives of his or her place in the nation and how one interacts with others, and it plays a role in how one responds to newcomers.

CHAPTER FOUR

Perceptions of Belonging
Race and Group Membership

When Americans express opinions about immigrants and immigration policy, they reveal their perceptions of political belonging in the United States. Despite the nation's history of racial exclusion, Americans of all races have pride in their country and express patriotic values. The uniformity in positive affect for one's country, however, exists in tandem with empirical results showing systematic variation in the sense of belonging to the nation at large as well as connection to a racial group across Americans classified by race. Those who share the default racial classification for what it means to be an American can more easily feel that they belong than can minorities whose membership in the polity was once excluded because of their race. Consistent with the racial-group stereotypes analyzed in the preceding chapter, the traits that characterize a desirable American are framed normatively by whiteness and implicitly associated with that group. As a result, there is no conflict between being an American and being white, and no racial modifier is needed for this group of Americans. Whites are simply Americans. In contrast, members of minority groups have experienced political belonging in the United States as being conditionally welcome. Their Americanness is modified by their racial-group classification as African Americans, Latinos, or Asian Americans. Minorities and whites are, to varying degrees, aware of their position in the American racial hierarchy, and the recognition of both racial-group consciousness and the parameters of what constitutes an American are relevant to political attitudes on immigration.

The variation between whites, African Americans, Latinos, and Asian

Americans in perceptions of belonging are evident in everyday interactions both private and public. During the 2008 US presidential election, controversy swirled around remarks made by Michelle Obama at
a campaign stop in Wisconsin: "For the first time in my adult life, I am
really proud of my country, because it feels like hope is making a come-
back . . . not just because Barack has done well, but because I think
people are hungry for change." Later that day, Cindy McCain, wife of
the Republican Party nominee, John McCain, said: "I'm proud of my
country. I don't know about you—if you heard those words earlier—I'm
very proud of my country." When asked whether she was responding to
Mrs. Obama's statement, Mrs. McCain replied, "I just wanted to make
the statement that I have and always will be proud of my country." The
Obama campaign quickly countered, releasing the following statement:
"Of course Michelle is proud of her country, which is why she and Barack
talk constantly about how their story wouldn't be possible in any other
nation on Earth." Obama himself weighed in and said: "Statements like
this are made and people try to take it out of context and make a great
big deal out of it, and that isn't at all what she meant."[1]

Mrs. Obama's comment was controversial because some interpreted
her statement as revealing a lack of patriotism or devotion to the United
States. While the intentions of both the First Lady and the wife of
Obama's opponent can never fully be known, Mrs. McCain's remarks
embodied a confident sense of national belonging that signified an un-
questioning allegiance to her country.[2] Born into a wealthy white family in Arizona, Cindy McCain had always felt like an American and an
insider because she had never been excluded from the benefits of political membership in the United States. In contrast, one interpretation of
Mrs. Obama's sentiment is that it reflected her position as an African
American woman. Descended from American slaves, the First Lady's
racial status as black moderated her perceptions of belonging through
the conditional political membership African Americans have experienced in the United States. African Americans' sense of full acceptance
and membership in the national community is conditioned by historical memory and the legacy of discrimination created and supported by
the American racial hierarchy. While attacked and criticized for many
things, neither of the McCains was doubted as being sufficiently American. Political challenges to the Americanness of the Obamas, on the
other hand, were both numerous and persistent.[3]

We begin this chapter on race and perceptions of belonging by acknowledging an important assumption about identity, that group membership is a crucial reference point for how individuals orient preferences. Foundational theories of social-group identity propose that humans are prone to favor and protect group boundaries (Tajfel 1981). But membership in all potential social and political groups is not relevant for political attitudes on immigration. Instead, we distinguish group membership with the nation along with a second measure of the sense of linked fate with others in one's racial group as two identities relevant to explaining variation in public opinion on immigration at the individual level. Before testing the relationship between these measures of identity and political attitudes as discussed in the next chapter, we here provide a detailed and systematic analysis of a variety of measures of national identity and racial-group identity by analyzing data from two surveys of samples of the US population collected in 2004. The Twenty-First Century Americanism survey and the 2004 National Politics Study included extensive batteries of questions on feelings of group membership with the nation as a whole and with racial groups in particular.[4] They are among the few national studies that include data on large samples of members of all four racial groups. We analyze these data to reveal the patterns in expressions of the boundaries of what it means to be an American, whether respondents see themselves as a typical American, the extent to which being an American is part of their identity, and expressions of patriotism. The contours of racial-group identity among whites, African Americans, Latinos, and Asian Americans are considered by examining responses to questions on perceptions of linked fate, feelings of closeness to others in one's racial group, and perceptions of racial discrimination.

We argue that the questions asking respondents to rate the importance of a variety of traits important to being considered American is the most suitable measurement of a sense of American national identity when predicting political attitudes on immigration. For racial-group identity, the measure of perceived linked fate is selected as the indicator of racial consciousness. Our argument for the choice of these two measures is rooted in the theoretical premise of the Racial Prism of Group Identity model that specifies the moderating influence of individuals' recognition of their position in the racial hierarchy. While we analyze both group-identity measures of perception of American boundaries and linked fate for all Americans, not everyone holds these identities to the same degree. In order to explain the differences in group identity between Americans classified by race, we begin by reviewing existing

studies on national attachment and characterize how scholars conceptualize national identity. We observe that most studies are conducted on
white Americans and therefore do not explicitly consider national identity among those who do not experience the same unconditional acceptance as members of the American polity. In so doing, we develop an explanation for why racial minorities express a sense of national identity
that is distinctive from that of majority whites by incorporating existing psychological theories on social identity theory. Next, we document
how racial-group attachment is manifested among African Americans,
Latinos, Asian Americans, and whites. The analysis demonstrates that
racial-group identity is not simply an indicator of group affect but an indicator of one's awareness of their racialized status. We conclude this
chapter with a discussion of how national and racial identities are related
to one another and why these measures of group identity should matter
for public opinion on immigration.

National Membership as a Social-Group Identity

While focus on national attachment is often defined by constructs such
as patriotism and nationalism,[5] many have argued that individuals use
national membership to describe their own social-group identity (Huddy
and Khatib 2007; Theiss-Morse 2009; Transue 2007; C. Wong 2010).
National membership can help orient how people relate to others on a
global scale and thus describes an important characteristic of the individual. Social-group identity assumes that individuals can understand
their place in society by identifying how they are socially positioned relative to others (Huddy 2003). A classic social-identity perspective describes the basic cognitive process employed by all humans as classifying
individuals into those who belong in one's own group (the in-group) and
those who do not belong in one's own group (the out-group). The most
significant consequence of the formation of social-group identity is that
it leads to strong and enduring loyalties to one's in-group and the desire
to create differentiation from out-groups. As a result, individuals hold
strongly positive and affective attachment to others in their own group
and advantage in-group members compared to those from out-groups.

National groups are generally understood as involuntary constructs
and not necessarily a product of choice for most citizens (with the exception of naturalized citizens). There are of course many other social

identities that are not chosen, and early experimental studies on social identity demonstrate that a group identity can be based on nearly any type of categorization made socially relevant, such as eye color (Tajfel 1981). However, once a social identity is relevant, individuals express strong loyalties to that group. Recent studies on American national identity have shown that white Americans not only self-identify as American but report strong positive attachments to their nation and their fellow Americans. National identities also encourage individuals to draw strong boundaries defining members and nonmembers. Those who hold strong national attachments feel the most in common with other citizens. Elizabeth Theiss-Morse (2009) found that respondents who emphasized clear definitions of who is an American were more likely to believe they agree with the American people on important issues and are more likely to help other Americans. Moreover, as Leonie Huddy and Nadia Khatib (2007) found, all Americans hold a national identity as American, while other constructs such as nationalism are more influenced by factors such as political ideology.

Because of data limitations, most public opinion studies on American identity are analyzed with data from white Americans. Studies examining national-identity attachments among racial minorities have focused on responding to political or ideological attacks framing racial minorities as "un-American" that are based on the position that identifying with one's racial or ethnic group conflicts with an identification as American (Huntington 2004; Schlesinger 1991). The intent behind scholarship on this topic has been to demonstrate that racial minorities do indeed feel positive attachments to the nation (Fraga and Segura 2006). Other research focuses on attachment to identity labels, and Lien, Conway, and Wong (2004) examine preference for the identity label "American" over other labels such as "Asian American" and find that native-born Asians are more likely to identify as American than foreign-born Asians (Wong et al. 2011). Systematic studies of racial minorities have shown that racial minorities have high levels of patriotism, and once differences in educational attainment and income are accounted for, native-born Latinos have higher levels of pride in the nation than whites (de la Garza, Falcon, and Garcia 1996; Citrin et al. 2007). Studies on black patriotism demonstrate that while blacks may feel politically marginalized, they still hold strong attachments to key American values like equality and opportunity (Carter 2007; Parker 2009). Furthermore, minorities do not simply feel patriotic, but they are willing to dedicate their lives to

their nation through military service (Armor and Gilroy 2010; De Angelis and Segal 2012).

Although research finds that all Americans, regardless of race, hold positive attachments to their nation, there are group differences in the strength of attachment. Schildkraut (2011) found that while nearly all white respondents (89%) selected an American identity over other racial or ethnic identity labels, more than half of black and Latino respondents (52% and 53%, respectively) and 47% of Asian respondents identified as American. Sidanius and colleagues (1997) found that the form of national attachment also varies across racial groups. An even greater challenge is explaining why those differences exist. In her comparison between white and black respondents, Theiss-Morse (2009) found unexpectedly that blacks were more likely than whites to agree with the idea that certain ascriptive characteristics, such as being white and Christian, were most important for being American.[6] This finding contradicted the widespread assumption in social-group identity that those with strong in-group identities should perceive the most rigid group boundaries. No generalizable theory has been generated to successfully explain racial-group differences in national-identity attachment.

This gap could be the result of a serious weakness in studies of social-group identity and national identity that generally assume individuals emphasize the same group boundaries and share the same experiences of group membership in the nation. However, as demonstrated in the example of the exchange between Michelle Obama and Cindy McCain at the outset of this chapter, some Americans experience American membership as exclusionary, while others feel an unconditional embrace with the nation. What has been overlooked is the fact that individuals vary in the type of membership status they hold within the nation.

Among the few social psychologists to take varying status within groups into account are Pickett and Brewer (2005). They hypothesize that individuals have a tendency to classify members of a social identity group into two basic subtypes. Some individuals are considered "core" members whose membership in the group is unquestioned and guaranteed. Other individuals are considered "peripheral" members. Their belonging is not obvious and has the potential to be rescinded. Groups assert their boundaries on the basis of a set of defined attributes, values, or other characteristics. The human need to experience a sense of belonging and the general desire to maintain a group's high status encourages members to police and uphold the group's defined boundaries. As a result, groups create and rely on stereotypes or prototypes that embody the group's desired image. Those members who have characteristics that mirror most closely the group prototype are perceived to be core members of the group and can maintain a sense of confidence that their status as a member will be retained. However, those who diverge from the prototype hold memberships that are perceived to be tenuous and persistently threatened.

Core versus peripheral members: effects of marginalization

If we take Pickett and Brewer's distinction between core and periphery into account, it is apparent that the most existing research on social-group identity theory is in studies on the psychology of core-group members. We know that those perceived as core members of a group believe that they represent a typical member and hold strong attachments to the group (Hogg and Abrams 1988). These strong in-group identifiers are more likely to perceive rigid boundaries distinguishing in-group members from out-group members (Castano et al. 2002; Ellemers, Spears, and Doosje 1999). These individuals are also more likely to both desire and engage in activities to uphold the norms of the group (Marques et al. 1998). In addition, there is substantial research on exclusion against those who are deemed nonmembers (Hogg, Fielding, and Darley 2005; Marques et al. 2001). Indeed, most theories on intergroup conflict (including among identities involving race, ethnicity, religion, and class) all examine group dynamics when there are assumed to be clearly demarcated boundaries distinguishing members of groups (Allport 1954; Blumer 1958; Brewer 1991; Horowitz 2000). Group memberships are for the most part conceived of as not overlapping. Studies that employ social-group identity theory have assumed that there are clear differences between in-group members and out-group members, while ignoring the distinction of core versus peripheral members within the in-group.

There is relatively little attention to the psychology and behavior of peripheral group members.[7] Peripheral group members face a different set of challenges because they are included in the in-group while at the same time being on its periphery. Sometimes individuals obtain the status of peripheral membership because they are indeed atypical compared to other group members. Other times, individuals perceive peripheral status because they do not believe they embody the same characteristics as the group prototype. Since inclusion in a group is considered among the most important of the motivating factors in social identity theory, peripheral group members feel anxiety about their status because their membership is perceived as uncertain and tenuous. As a result, peripheral group members may engage in certain behaviors in order to be perceived as unambiguous members of the group.

In their review of experimental studies conducted on college students and sorority members, Pickett and Brewer (2004) summarize that "peripheral group members seem to care more about ingroup-outgroup differences. Compared to core members, peripheral group members tend to dislike and exclude non-prototypical ingroup members more, engage in more derogation or 'sliming' of outgroup members, and tend to evaluate the outgroup less favorably, especially when they anticipate becoming more prototypical in the future" (101). According to Pickett and Brewer, physically altering oneself is often not an option for peripheral members to demonstrate their prototypicality. Therefore, to defend their status as group members, peripheral members are more likely to uphold rigid group boundaries that help them to justify their own belonging. When given power in decision-making processes, peripheral members are more likely to enforce stricter group norms and emphasize prototypical characteristics in order to decrease the threat of their exclusion. Peripheral members often prefer exclusion of newcomers to the group, since that also helps to uphold their status in the group. Thus, in contrast to core-group-member behavior outlined in social identity theories, those who are most typical of the group are not always the staunchest defenders of group boundaries.[8]

Influence of the racial hierarchy on perceptions of national membership

Once a theory of racial position is integrated with Pickett and Brewer's identification of peripheral group membership, it becomes easier to explain why perceptions of national membership are not uniform across racial groups in the United States. Because race has been used to define American citizenship, the experiences and perceptions of inclusion correspond with position in the racial hierarchy. As a result, belonging to the nation is not uniform but stratified into a continuum from core to peripheral members with whites at the center. Empirical research supports this construction, and work by Devos and Banaji (2005) demonstrates that the connection between race and core-group status exists primarily as an implicit attitude. Since whites are automatically assumed to be American, they experience national inclusion as unchallenged core members of the group. As core members, their perceptions of national membership can be more easily explained by classic theories on social-group identity. Whites with strong national attachments should thus hold strong affective sentiment toward the nation and should feel a sense of commonality with other Americans. Because their Americanness is not disputed to the same degree as it is for minorities, whites are more likely to perceive themselves to be typical Americans.

Racial minorities, on the other hand, are not as readily assumed to be American as are whites. Instead, their membership in the national polity is conditioned on their racial categorization as outsiders. As a result, African Americans, Latinos, and Asian Americans are part of the in-group of Americans (as opposed to foreigners and immigrants), but they are peripheral rather than core members. Given the dynamics of group interaction long documented by social identity theorists, this standing as peripheral members produces incentives for racial minorities to defend their membership through compensating actions designed to demonstrate their genuine Americanness. While common among nonwhite minority Americans, peripheral status is not uniform, and perceptions of national membership should not be dichotomized into a simple binary of core versus periphery. Instead, in-group status as an American is better imagined as a sphere with multiple layers in which whites are located at the center core and racial minorities are positioned in different places along the periphery. The distance from the center for each racial group is consistent with their placement in the diamond shape of the racial order described in chapter 1.

Consistent with the data on racial stereotypes analyzed in chapter 3, African Americans are perceived as Americans because of their long-standing presence in the United States and their nearly universal ability to speak fluent English. But while blacks are accepted as native-born members, they have historically been classified and treated as less than equal to whites, and their persistent struggle to achieve equality has cultivated the perception among blacks that they do not enjoy the same privileges as whites. As a result of their long-standing status as second-class citizens, African Americans are rarely seen as prototypical Americans. In terms of national group membership, African Americans are the archetypal peripheral member defined by Pickett and Brewer (2005). As peripheral in-group members whose status makes them aware of group boundaries, we expect African Americans to impose more rigid

boundaries on national identity than whites. But while blacks may perceive rigid boundaries, they nevertheless do not perceive themselves to be typical Americans as often as whites perceive themselves to be.

Asian Americans and Latinos also experience peripheral membership, but because their exclusion is framed by different forces than those used to exclude blacks, their peripheral status leads to different perceptions of national membership. Both Asian Americans and Latinos are stereotyped as non–English-proficient foreigners and by definition dissimilar to native-born Americans. At the same time, the power of the American "melting pot" narrative and the history of integration established by European immigrants of the past provide a path of assimilation for racialized immigrants. The fable of the United States as a "nation of immigrants" encourages the mythology of an inclusive nation. While Asian Americans and Latinos may not feel that they are fully accepted as Americans, their placement in the racial hierarchy encourages them to perceive more porous group boundaries than African Americans. Finally, the framing of Asian Americans as a model minority creates greater expectations for inclusion and eventual acceptance, and we anticipate that Asian Americans will perceive more porous group boundaries than Latinos.

Racial-Group Differences in American National Identity

To observe the empirical relationship between racial categorization and American national-identity attachment, we analyzed survey data from the Twenty-First Century Americanism survey. This nationally representative survey included a total sample of 2,800 adults and oversampled minority populations to result in total sample sizes of 324 African American, 396 Asian American, and 436 Latino respondents.[9] The Twenty-First Century survey is one of the most extensive studies on American identity with data on all Americans.

The typical survey item for American identity analyzed in public opinion studies measures how respondents choose to describe the key characteristics of an American. Respondents in the Twenty-First Century survey were given a list of characteristics and were asked to say which were "most important for making someone American," including: "being born in America," "having American citizenship," "being white," "being a Christian," "being able to speak English," "respecting Amer-

ica's political institutions and laws" and "feeling American." In the following analysis these measures were combined into an additive index
on a scale of 0 to 1 to form an overall measure of national identity defined by an "American boundary."[10] This measure is desirable because
it reflects how individuals choose to define the bounds of national membership.[11] The overall American-boundary measure is also the product
of multiple items rather than a single question on perceptions of identity and therefore allows for the observation of different patterns between racial groups in the selection of characteristics signifying American boundaries. Those who list more required characteristics perceive
stricter boundaries, while those who view fewer required characteristics
perceive more flexible boundaries to define American national membership (Theiss-Morse 2009). The American-boundaries question battery
corresponds with measures ordinarily used in opinion surveys.[12]

Consistent with our hypotheses on peripheral membership and the
racial hierarchy, we find peripheral members of the American in-group
have higher means on the American-boundary measure than core members. African American respondents have the highest mean of all racial
groups: 0.71 on a scale of 0 to 1 (standard deviation = 0.15).[13] As peripheral members, blacks defined the nation by a more rigid boundary than
either core members or other peripheral members ranked higher in the
racial hierarchy. Latinos, who share a similar status near the bottom of
the racial order report the next highest mean at 0.65 (standard deviation = 0.16). The two groups with the lowest means on the American-
boundary scale are whites and Asian Americans, with the latter having
the lowest mean of 0.60 (standard deviation = 0.15). Whites have a mean
of 0.63 (standard deviation = .16). These data reflect the average scores
on the American-boundary scale for US citizens. For specific characteristics important to being American, each racial group emphasizes
a unique combination of traits. Two characteristics that all respondent
groups agree signify an American are respecting America's political institutions and laws and being able to speak English. Because national
identity is a social-group identity, members will associate their own personal characteristics as valuable to being American. Table 4.1 lists all
seven characteristics and shows the proportion of each racial-group rating the characteristic as "very important" for being American.[14] Consistent with Pickett and Brewer's theory, peripheral members are more
likely to emphasize those characteristics that best describe themselves

TABLE 4.1. **Proportion Rating Trait as "Very Important" for Being American by Race**

	% Believes very important for being American			
	Whites	Blacks	Asians	Latinos
Born in America	21%	42%	11%	33%
Being a Christian	16%	39%	12%	18%
Being white	2%	10%	3%	4%
Respecting America's political institutions and laws	82%	78%	74%	80%
Having American citizenship	78%	81%	57%	73%
Being able to speak English	69%	79%	71%	73%
Feeling American	64%	59%	47%	64%

Source: Twenty-First Century Americanism survey

and correspondingly deemphasize characteristics that are likely to encourage their marginalization from the larger group.

In terms of differences by groups, African Americans emphasize ascriptive characteristics that they associate with their own group, such as being a Christian and being born in America as important to defining American boundaries. In addition, blacks perceive Americanness to include respecting America's political institutions and laws.[15] The status of African Americans as peripheral in-group members encourages more rigid ascriptive boundaries and emphasis on traits characterizing the black community. Asian American respondents in contrast are more likely to deemphasize those characteristics that could lead to their exclusion, such as being born in America, being a Christian, being white, and holding citizenship. Selection of these traits and the overall less rigid boundaries perceived by Asian Americans is consistent with their racialized status as a model minority and their relative valorization as ideal new members who take advantage of opportunities for advancement (C. Kim 2000). As a result, Asian American citizens may be more likely than other peripheral out-group members to perceive American boundaries as more porous. The pattern of responses to the American-boundaries characteristics among Latino responses is more difficult to decipher. Latinos who are US citizens are significantly more likely than whites to believe that being born in American and being a Christian are important to being American.[16] In general, however, Latinos are more closely in agreement with whites on the relevance of other traits. It is possible that, instead of reacting to their status as peripheral members,

Latinos may simply be reporting those characteristics emphasized by the majority population. Alternatively, because this analysis includes only Latinos who are citizens, they might perceive their position in the racial hierarchy as closer to whites than the population of Latinos overall.

The variation between groups is striking, and a reasonable concern is that these differences may be attributed to the vast differences in socioeconomic status such as education and other resources in the sample populations.[17] Consistent with placement on the racial hierarchy in terms of economic resources, white and Asian American respondents in the Twenty-First Century study were much more likely to be college educated and to have higher family incomes than black and Latino respondents.[18] Moreover, much larger portions of the Asian American and Latino samples than white and black samples were foreign born. While these demographic and resources differences mirror the composition in the population, it is nevertheless possible that these differences could be—more than perceptions of racial position—behind the variation observed in the American-boundaries index. Using multivariate regression, we tested to see whether those group differences on the American-boundary index are influenced more strongly by race or resource-based traits.[19] The results of the estimations show that race continues to be a significant factor in responses to the questions on American boundaries.[20] The results confirm that both blacks and Latinos perceive more rigid national boundaries than whites and that African Americans perceive the strictest boundaries to what it means to be an American. There is no significant difference in how whites and Asian Americans view national boundaries, and this finding tells us that while Asian Americans were found to have the lowest mean score on the American-boundary index among all racial groups, their perception of relatively porous boundaries is the result of disproportionately high levels of resources among Asian American respondents in the survey sample.

Peripheral members of the American in-group who are ranked at the bottom of the racial hierarchy are more likely to perceive strict national boundaries than core members. This raises the question of whether those who perceive stricter boundaries also strongly identify with the group. Social identity theory suggests that there is a direct and positive relationship between group membership and positive identification with the group. But Pickett and Brewer's distinction between peripheral and core in-group membership suggests that there may not be a direct relationship between perception of group boundaries and group identification.

Instead, following Pickett and Brewer's insight, we would expect peripheral members to perceive strong group boundaries but weaker affective attachments to the group as a result of their experiences of exclusion. Alternatively, core in-group members should feel stronger attachment.

To examine the relationship between identification as American and the perception of group boundaries, we examine two other measures of national identity measured in the Twenty-First Century survey: feeling like a typical American and affective attachment to the nation and its citizens. We rely on two measures originally developed and tested by Theiss-Morse (2009) and Huddy and Khatib (2007), which we call "typicality" and "national identity." The typicality measure is an index created by combining responses to the statements "When I think of the American people, I think of people who are a lot like me," "I would feel good if I were described as a typical American," and "In many respects, I am different from most Americans."[21] The typicality questions measure the extent to which respondents perceive themselves to be in the core or at the periphery of Americanness. Respondents who say they are typical members feel confident that they belong in the group. The measure of national identity was created by combining responses to the statements "Being an American is important to the way I think of myself" and "I feel strong ties to the American people."[22] Those who score highly on the national identity index hold strong in-group identification with the United States.

There are clear differences in the extent to which members of different racial groups perceive themselves as typical Americans. Whites have the largest proportion of respondents who score the highest possible value on the typicality index (42%), and they report the highest average score of 0.66 on a scale of 0 to 1 (standard deviation = 0.23). Asian American respondents reported the lowest mean of 0.54 (standard deviation = 0.2), while black and Latino respondents fell in the middle with average scores of 0.61 (standard deviation = 0.25) and 0.60 (standard deviation = 0.24) respectively. To determine if the demographic characteristics of the samples explain these group differences, we again ran multivariate regressions to control for the differences in age, gender, socioeconomic status, foreign-born status, and ideology across racial groups.[23] When controlling for these factors, we find that Asian Americans and Latinos are significantly less likely to feel typical when compared to whites.[24] However, we found no statistically significant differences between responses among African Americans to the typicality measure compared with whites. This suggests that the stereotype of foreign outsider applied to Asian Americans and Latinos influences perceptions of their typicality. African Americans are not stereotyped as foreigners, and they hold perceptions about their typicality similar to those of whites.

For the measure of national identity, all racial groups rate strong affective attachments to the nation and their fellow citizens. Indeed, this measure has very low variance; half of all respondents (51%) have the highest possible score on this index. This finding is expected because membership in a group should encourage positive attachments to that group, regardless of one's core or peripheral status. Nevertheless, there were differences between racial groups. Whites had the highest average score on the index of national identity (0.87 on a scale of 0 to 1, standard deviation = 0.18). Both Asian Americans and African Americans had lower means, of 0.78 (standard deviation = 0.26) and 0.77 (standard deviation = 0.20), respectively. The average group scores of Latinos fell in the middle: 0.81 (standard deviation = 0.23). Controlling for socioeconomic and demographic differences, the results show that racial minorities are less likely to have positive national affect than whites, though there were no significant differences between racial minority groups.[25] Thus, core members of the nation (whites), feel the highest degree of national identity.

Although members of racial groups, on average, respond differently to the three varieties of national American identity, perception of group boundaries and group affect may be highly correlated for all respondents regardless of their race. Table 4.2 reports the correlations between perceptions of strict boundaries with the measures of typicality and national identity.[26] The relationship is positive between the American-boundary index, typicality, and national identity, indicating that strong identification with the nation is related to the perception of stricter group boundaries regardless of the racial background. When comparing differences in correlations across racial groups, however, there is further evidence to support the presence of peripheral group membership. The correlations show that there is a strong relationship between perception of strict boundaries with feelings of typicality ($r = 0.43$) and national identity ($r = 0.47$) for whites. For core members of the nation, strong in-group identification and perception of rigid group boundaries are strongly related. In contrast, the correlation between perception of strong boundaries and typicality is weaker for racial minorities. For the relationship between American boundaries and national identity, African Americans and La-

TABLE 4.2. **Correlations among National-Identity Measures by Race**

	Typicality	National identity	Patriotism	Ideology
Whites	.43	.47	.39	.39
Blacks	.32	.42	.42	.16
Asians	.26	.19	.24	.25
Latinos	.33	.41	.43	.23

Source: Twenty-First Century Americanism survey

tinos look similar to whites, but the relationship between these two identities for Asian Americans is weak. So while Asian American respondents were more likely to report higher levels of group affect toward the
nation than other racial minority groups, group affect is only weakly related to how Asian Americans perceive group boundaries.

Finally, we analyzed whether racial groups differ in the relationship
between perception of American boundaries and other concepts traditionally considered in studies on national identity such as pride in the
nation (patriotism) and conservative political ideology.[27] Pride in one's
nation is considered an important outcome of positive identification,
and it is expected that in-group identities lead to positive perceptions
of the respondent's country. Scholars have demonstrated that patriotism
and national identity are positively correlated among whites. Furthermore, there is evidence of an ideological component to how individuals respond to national symbols and values in which conservatism is correlated with patriotism (Huddy and Khatib 2007). Among whites, there
also appears to be a relationship between partisanship and patriotism:
Republicans are more likely to assert patriotism than Democrats (Sullivan, Fried, and Dietz 1992).

While the results are consistent for whites, it is not clear whether
the same patterns will be present among minorities, and few consider
what effect marginalization within a national group may have on these
perceptions. Our analysis of the relationship between the measures of
American boundaries, patriotism, and ideological conservatism among
African Americans, Latinos, and Asian Americans demonstrates that
the correlations between all three measures are positive. Recall that
among whites, the correlation between the American-boundary index
and patriotism is nearly the same as the size of the relationship between
the measure of perceptions of American boundaries and political ideology. The same pattern of relationships does not exist for racial minor-

ity groups. While the same as whites in terms of direction, Asian Americans show a weaker magnitude of the relationship between perceptions of American boundaries and both the measures of patriotism and political ideology. For blacks, there is a relatively strong relationship between the American-boundary index and patriotism ($r = 0.42$) but a weak relationship between the perception of boundaries and political conservatism ($r = 0.16$). A similar pattern is evident for Latinos, but political ideology is more strongly related to the perception of boundaries than for African American respondents.

Taken together, this analysis of the Twenty-First Century data shows important differences in the patterns of perceptions of belonging among Americans classified by race. Recognition of peripheral membership status is most clearly apparent in the responses Asian Americans, Latinos, and African Americans gave to the battery of questions asking people to delineate the characteristics that define an American. All Americans have strong positive affect for their nation, but the intensity and the form of that attachment is structured by their experiences as either core or peripheral members of the polity. Whites, who enjoy a status as core members, conceive of their nation as a primary social-group identity and show positive affect because they are included as a typical member of the nation. Confident in their inclusion in and belonging to nation, whites do not assert as rigid a set of group boundaries on Americanness and instead perceive the group to be inclusive and egalitarian. Those Americans who experience peripheral membership with the nation as a function of their status as racial minorities report different forms of American national identity from whites. African Americans and Latinos are more likely to perceive stricter boundaries of Americanness than either whites or Asian Americans. The racialized construction of Asian Americans and Latinos as foreigners makes members of these two groups feel like atypical members of the nation. Nevertheless, peripheral members embrace their status as members of the nation while simultaneously recognizing that the degree of inclusion they experience is not the same as it is for core members of the American polity.

Exclusion from the Nation: Racial-Group Identity

As the above analysis of national identity indicates, racial groups vary in their levels and perceptions of inclusion in the nation. These experiences of core membership versus peripheral membership also influence patterns of identification with others who share a similar position on the racial hierarchy. Members of the same racial group experience similar opportunities and constraints as a function of their position in the American racial order. Identification with one's racial group, feelings of closeness to others with the same racial classification, and recognition that one's individual fate is linked to that of the racial group are three ways racial-group identity has been measured by scholars. They measure different things, however, and in this section we review the existing scholarship on racial identity in order to make an argument for the concept of linked fate as the measure of racial-group identity that best captures racial-group position and exclusion from the nation. The measure of racial-group identity that should have relevance to political attitudes on immigration is one that is not only an individual choice but a structural feature of the American racial hierarchy. This form of racial-group identity chooses the individual as much as the person chooses it by structuring individual life choices as a function of racial categorization. The literature suggests that those who express a sense of linked fate with their racial group recognize that they share structural constraint as a function of their group membership. The aspect of racial identity that is relevant to political attitudes on immigration thus goes beyond perceptions of commonality (in terms of culture, interest, or family background) and closeness. Racial identity as perceived linked fate signifies awareness of one's structural racial position.

Marginalization and racial-group identification

The scholarship on racial-group identity has shown that experiences of marginalization and exclusion are key characteristics that lead to racial-identity development. Early research on racial-group identity focused on the formation of a politicized racial consciousness that grew out of perceptions of economic deprivation (Conover 1981; McAdam 1982; Miller et al. 1981; Shingles 1981). Social science at the time was heavily influenced by the civil rights movement, in which blacks not only fought for a common political cause but also successfully persuaded the national government to enact policies aimed at correcting persistent economic inequalities. Even political behavior studies explained blacks' unique participatory patterns as a product of their perceived deprivation (Verba and Nie 1972).

But economic deprivation alone could not explain the persistent racial divides in attitudes, particularly as African Americans were afforded greater opportunities in the post–civil rights era (Wilson 2009). Race was generally assumed to be a proxy for disadvantage and low socioeconomic status, and blacks' political agenda was argued to emanate from frustration with these economic disparities. Yet, even as African Americans became more socially mobile and the size of the black middle class increased, African Americans still maintained significant political cohesion and demonstrated collectively distinct political opinions from the mainstream white population. These observations influenced a shift in analysis of racial-group identity among African Americans, and strong levels of group identification could not be attributed solely to shared lower class status. Michael Dawson's (1994) theory of linked fate described black political cohesion as a product of rational action and a sense of shared racial disadvantage. African Americans are more aware than whites that the treatment of the racial group has a direct impact on the opportunities made available for individuals. This collective perception among African Americans developed from the discrimination they continue to experience even with increasing levels of social mobility (Dawson 2001). Linked fate describes the perception that the life chances of the individual are inherently linked with those chances afforded to the group and acts as a mechanism for cohesive and distinctive black attitudes.

Although Dawson's linked-fate theory is most applicable to blacks, he presents a number of ideas that can be used to generalize about the role of racial identity in politics. First, awareness of one's racial-group status and recognition that group status has implications for one's own personal opportunities are key attributes of racial-group identification. Simply being classified as a racial minority does not imply that one is automatically aware of his or her racial status. Second, racial identity can also explain when and why more constrained and uniform attitudes are observed within a racial group. Groups with a larger proportion of members who perceive stronger racial-group identity in linked fate demonstrate more cohesive political attitudes. Members of groups with weaker perceived linked fate are more heterogeneous in political attitudes because as attachments to the racial group weaken, it is more likely individuals will consider their own fate ahead of that of the group. For those who rely on individual preferences over perceived benefits to the group, other factors attributed to the individual such as ideology, education level, and age better explain political choices.

Racial background influences how one experiences the world and thus shapes an individual's worldview. Because racial groups experience race in unique ways and vary in how they see their race's level of opportunity, racial groups do not all share the same perceptions about how society operates. There is an important distinction between the strength of racial identity and the content of that identity. When individuals have a strong sense of linked fate, racial identity will be significantly related to their position on political issues, and this relationship should exist across all racial groups. Alternatively, the content of the racial identity is informed by the position of groups in the hierarchy and is specific to the placement, historical context, and political circumstances for each racial group. Thus the content of racial identity may not have the same effect for all groups. For example, because African Americans are located at the bottom of the racial hierarchy while whites are ranked at the top, a strong black racial-group identity informs different substantive political interests than a strong white racial-group identity. This leads to the expectation that blacks with a strong racial identity will have distinct political attitudes from whites with a strong racial identity. In terms of attitudes toward immigration, we anticipate that the strength of racial-group identification determines the magnitude of effect identity has on a dependent variable, while the content of racial identity determines the direction of that effect.

Variation in strength of racial-group identification across groups

Existing research has documented the strength of racial-group attachments vary across groups. Although this finding appears to be well-accepted in recent literature, the reasons behind divergence are under-specified. Why should we expect some groups to demonstrate stronger racial-group identities than others? As the theories we have reviewed on black racial identity suggest, racial-group identification cannot simply be described as a social-group identity. Race does not designate a personal characteristic or preference but a particular social category imposed on individuals. Therefore we cannot expect all racial groups to report similar levels of racial-group identification and consciousness given that individual attachment to the racial group cannot be explained as simply a personal sense of in-group affect. Rather, the power of the racial hierarchy makes some groups more reliant on their racial categorization than others. Recognizing the role of the racial hierarchy is important for understanding observed variation in racial-group attachment across groups.

African Americans have the highest degree of racial-group identity of all racial groups. Their placement at the bottom of the hierarchy reflects not only the long-standing status of blacks as second-class citizens but also the relatively modest individual-level resources in wealth, education, and social connections among African Americans. An important dimension of Dawson's linked-fate theory is that racial solidarity among blacks is the product of rational action to rely on their group identity because they realize it is a more effective strategy. Without collective action, individual success is more difficult to achieve. While scholars have documented racial-group identity among Asian Americans and Latinos, perception of linked fate is weaker among those populations (e.g., de la Garza et al. 1992; Jones-Correa and Leal 1996; Lien, Conway, and Wong 2004; Masuoka 2006; 2008; Wong et al. 2011; García Bedolla 2005; Bowler and Segura 2011).[28] Most explain the lower rates of racial-group identification among Asian Americans and Latinos as the result of the high degree of ethnic or national-origin diversity within these two groups. Because people have the option to identify with their national-origin group over the pan-ethnic racial group, perceived linked fate for Asian Americans and Latinos is weaker than that observed for blacks (for example, see DeSipio 1996). Important as these explanations are, they neglect the structural role of the racial hierarchy in group identity formation (see Lee 2008). The black racial category is also ethnically diverse, but the opportunity to identify as a distinctive national-origin group is highlighted only in the literature on Asian American and Latino racial identity.[29]

A more generalizable theory to explain varying rates of racial-group identification across racial minority groups must consider individual identity choice as well as take into consideration the structural nature of race. We concur with Chong and Kim's (2006) "theory of opportunities," which posits that the development of racial-group consciousness varies across racial minority groups because each faces a different set of social and economic opportunities. Chong and Kim's theory encourages us to see racial-group consciousness as a product of how members of racial groups experience the barriers and opportunities imposed by racial classification in social and political context. Groups experiencing quicker socioeconomic success are more likely to view society as open and accepting rather than excluding on the basis of race. Chong and Kim find that blacks, who have experienced the slowest rates of social mobility over time, are more likely to view society as closed and exclusive and so are more likely to support racially redistributive public policies. The authors show that Asian Americans, who on average hold relatively high levels of education and family income, experience higher rates of residential integration with whites, and have higher rates of interracial marriage,[30] are likely to believe society offers more opportunities. Latinos may mirror blacks in their relatively low economic status, but they have experienced relatively faster inroads into mainstream society as evidenced by their relative speed of integration into the electorate and other indicators of assimilation (Alba and Nee 2005). As a result of more numerous social and economic opportunities they experience compared with blacks, Asian Americans and Latinos both develop relatively weaker perceptions of racial solidarity and lower levels of support for racially redistributive policies.

Finally, it is important to recognize that whites also perceive racial-group identity (Wong and Cho 2005). Whites can be aware of the racial hierarchy and understand the implications of their racial status on their personal life chances.[31] Yet because white racial identity in the post–civil rights era has been most commonly linked with white supremacist ideals often normatively framed as both racist and extremist (Green, Abelson and Garnett 1999; Swain 2002), it may seem socially inappropriate for whites to publicly assert a white racial identity. This may represent one important reason why whites are the least likely of the four racial groups to report racial-group identity. At the same time, low levels of white racial-group identification may also be the result of the fact that, unlike racial identity among minorities, white racial identity is not as closely linked to perceived opportunities or structural constraints because whites occupy the top spot on the racial hierarchy. In this respect, whites are less constrained by their race and therefore less likely to develop awareness of how their race structures life chances.

Content of racial identity: informing group interests

If racial-group identity is a form of social-group identity, then classic theories would assume that strong racial-group identities lead to protection of one's own group's interests. Indeed, the theory of ethnocentrism states that humans are inherently predisposed to hold strong positive in-group affect as well as strong out-group prejudices (Kinder and Kam 2009; Sumner [1906] 2002). Research on racial-group contact provides evidence that ethnocentric ideas are outcomes of strong racial-group identities for all groups. For example, studies that focus on black-Latino and black-Asian conflicts reveal that the desire to protect one's own group interests leads to conflict with other racial groups, particularly in urban areas characterized by limited space and resources. For example, Vaca (2004) argues that African Americans' concerns about diminished political power in historically black neighborhoods make them one of the strongest opponents of bilingual policies, which they perceive as placing higher priority on Latino and Asian American immigrants' needs rather than their own. Studies on white racial resentment also document that discriminatory views arise when whites believe blacks receive undeserving benefits (Kinder and Sanders 1990; Sears, Sidanius, and Bobo 2000).

Yet the evidence from Kinder and Kam (2009) shows that racial groups vary in their levels of in-group favoritism. The racial stereotypes data summarized in chapter 3 show that members of all racial groups attribute positive traits to their own group, but racial minority groups rate whites more positively than their own group, and whites were the only group to show positive in-group favoritism when stereotyping other groups. Kinder and Kam found that although members of each racial group gave the highest favorable rating to their own group, racial minorities gave higher favorability ratings to other groups compared to those reported by whites. Since the literature shows that racial minority groups in general express strong racial identities, the fact that racial minorities at the same time report weaker forms of ethnocentrism against out-groups does not correspond to most expectations of how social-group identity functions. Furthermore, case studies on racial-group contact reveal that conflict is not necessarily the only product of interracial interaction. The pioneering work by Browning, Marshall, and Tabb (1986) on minority political incorporation in cities in California documented the successful development of cross-racial minority political coalitions.

Taken together, the evidence suggests that racial identities among African Americans, Latinos, and Asian Americans cannot be characterized as simple social-group identities. Instead, racial minorities develop racial-group identities as a result of the constraints they experience, and group solidarity is not cultivated solely out of in-group favoritism. Strong group identities develop from the recognition of how race structures their individual agency. Shared racial-group identification for minorities emanates from the shared experience of constraint based in categorization as a race other than white. The literature supports the position that strong racial-group identities reflect in-group favoritism as well as awareness of racial hierarchy. This explains why racial minorities, who are more likely to hold strong racial-group identities than whites, more easily perceive the privileged status of whites in the racial hierarchy. This same awareness of American racial order provides the basis for seeing individual interests based on minorities' position in the racial hierarchy.

As a result of their placement on the top of the hierarchy, whites' racial-group identity is based not on a shared disadvantaged status but instead structured by their experiences as a member of the most privileged group. We anticipate that those whites who perceive a high degree of racial-group identity are both aware of their privileged ranking and recognize their interest in preserving the racial order. In contrast, we expect whites with weak racial-group identities are those who oppose the hierarchy of the racial order. Whites with weak racial-group identity are therefore more likely to report progressive racial attitudes and are more willing to recognize the existence of discrimination against racial minority groups. We expect racial minorities with strong racial-group identities recognize that the racial hierarchy exists and are aware of their own group's position on the racial hierarchy. The relationship between strong racial-group identities and support for the hierarchy among minorities is exactly the opposite of that among whites. Strong racial-group identity among Asian Americans, Latinos, and African Americans reflect awareness of marginalized status, while weak racial-group identities reflect perceptions of racial equality. Racial minorities with strong racial-group identities are those who recognize the existence of discrimination and so will support measures to combat inequality. Since racial minorities with weak racial identities lack awareness of inequality, they are less likely to challenge the hierarchy and may actually embrace actions that seek to uphold that hierarchy.

Because relative position in the racial hierarchy structures the content of racial-group identity, we continue to anticipate differences across racial minority groups. Blacks, who occupy the lowest position on the hierarchy, are those who should report the greatest awareness of racial inequality regardless of their level of racial-group attachment. Asian

Americans, who currently occupy the highest place in the racial hierarchy among minorities, will be less concerned about racial inequality.
Asian Americans with strong racial-group identities also perceive discrimination, but the influence of racial identity will be weaker among
Asian Americans than African Americans. Since Latinos represent a
position between blacks and Asian Americans, we anticipate racial identity among Latinos to have a stronger impact on racial attitudes than
it has among Asian Americans but a weaker impact than it has among
blacks.

Racial-Group Attachment and Perceived Linked Fate

To compare rates of racial-group attachments across each of the four racial groups, we analyze data from the 2004 National Politics Study (NPS).
This was a nationally representative telephone survey of adults including
919 whites, 756 African Americans, 503 Asian Americans, and 757 Latinos.[32] The study included extensive measures on racial attitudes and
racial-group identity, and the design allows researchers to make direct
comparisons across groups. Given the expectations articulated in the
previous section, we focus on perceived linked fate, a measure capturing
the extent to which respondents believe their individual fate is connected
to that of others in their racial group.[33] This was measured by a two-part
question: "Do you think what happens to [respondent's race] people in
this country will have something to do with what happens in your life?"
If a respondent answered yes, he or she was further asked, "Will it affect you a lot, some or not very much?" We combined these two questions and operationalized the variable as a four-point ordinal scale with
a range of 0 to 1. This measure of perceived linked fate both captures the
perception of connection with one's racial group and incorporates the
recognition that racial categorization has political consequences.

Scholars have also conceptualized racial identity based in positive affective attachment to one's racial group. A survey question consistently
asked in public opinion surveys is a measure of group closeness, operationalized by this wording: "How close do you feel to [respondent's racial group] in your ideas, interests and feelings about things? Very close,
fairly close, not too close or not close at all?" We examine the group
closeness measure with a variable constructed out of a four-point ordinal
scale with a range of 0 to 1. While the measures of both perceived linked

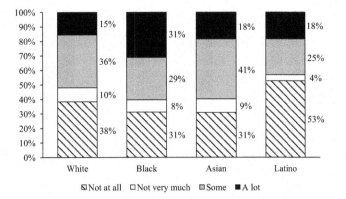

⊠ Not at all   □ Not very much   ▨ Some   ■ A lot

FIGURE 4.1. Distribution of responses on linked-fate measure by race. *Source*: National Politics Survey.

fate and group closeness capture a sense of group identity, we expect the linked-fate measure to be a stronger explanatory factor in predicting racial attitudes.

To assess variation in racial identity by racial group, we first present the distribution of responses on both racial-group-identity measures for Latinos, Asian Americans, whites, and African Americans in figure 4.1. Blacks report the highest levels of perceived linked fate, with nearly one-third (31%) reporting strong levels of perceived linked fate, and the average score on the linked-fate scale for African Americans was 0.53 (on a scale of 0 to 1). While Asian Americans score higher (0.49) than whites (0.43) on the linked-fate scale, the distribution of responses for these two racial groups was similar. Latinos reported the lowest levels of perceived linked fate, with an average score of 0.36. Regression analyses accounting for differences in age, gender, socioeconomic status, foreign-born status, and political ideology across groups confirm that, even when all of these factors are held constant, blacks hold the highest levels of perceived linked fate and Latinos hold the lowest of all four groups. There is no significant difference in perceptions of linked fate between whites and Asian Americans.

Illustrating the measure of closeness to racial group, figure 4.2 shows low variance across the distribution of the measure across racial groups. Everyone has positive affect for his or her own racial group, and overwhelming majorities report feeling either "fairly close" or "very close" to their group. Responses on this measure comport with the expectation

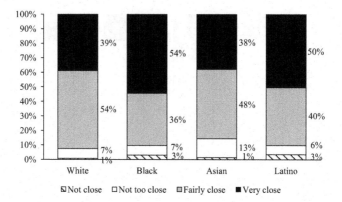

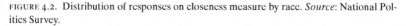

FIGURE 4.2. Distribution of responses on closeness measure by race. *Source*: National Politics Survey.

of social identity theory that members will feel close to their group. The data do reveal differences by race. At least half of Latinos and African Americans report feeling "very" close to their group, while white and Asian American respondents were most likely to say they feel "fairly" close to their group. Results from regression analyses confirm that, accounting for demographic variation, blacks and Latinos have the strongest feelings of racial-group closeness, while Asian Americans feel the weakest level of closeness.

While both the linked-fate and group closeness measures capture racial-group identity, each emphasizes different aspects of solidarity, and the correlation between the two measures is positive but modest across all four groups. The correlation between the two measures of racial identity is lowest for Latinos ($r = 0.13$) and highest for Asian Americans ($r = 0.22$) and African Americans ($r = .20$), with whites ($r = 0.17$) in between.[34]

To confirm that perception of linked fate is a better reflection of a respondent's recognition of the placement of his or her group in the racial hierarchy than is the measure of group closeness, we examined the relationship between these two group-identity measures and perceptions of racial discrimination. Figures 4.3 and 4.4 show that perceived linked fate has a stronger relationship to perceptions of discrimination against one's racial than the measure of group closeness. Those with high levels of perceived linked fate are more likely to report "a lot" of discrimination against their own racial group than those with low perceived linked fate. For example, 71% of blacks with high perceived linked fate perceive a lot of discrimination against African Americans, compared with 38% of those with low perceived linked fate. There are similar patterns of perceptions of discrimination among Asian Americans and Latinos with high perceived linked fate, but the relationship between feelings of group closeness and perceptions of discrimination is inconsistent for these two groups. Perceptions of discrimination are generally weaker among respondents who report strong group closeness compared with those with high perceived linked fate. In addition, respondents who feel close to others in their racial group are not necessarily more likely to perceive more discrimination than those with low group closeness. Among Latinos, 45% who feel strong closeness to their group perceive racial discrimination, while 48% of Latinos with weak closeness perceive a lot of discrimination against the group.[35]

Perceptions of linked fate and group closeness are also apparent among white respondents, though there is a weak connection between racial-group identity and perceived discrimination. In contrast to the patterns for minority Americans, only 7% of whites with high levels of perceived linked fate say there is "a lot" of discrimination against their group, and 2% of whites with strong group closeness report "a lot" of discrimination against whites. Perceived linked fate and group closeness are therefore distinct in terms of relationship to perceptions of discrimination for whites compared to the pattern of relationship among Latinos, Asian Americans, and African Americans. These distinctions are expected given the placement of whites at the top of the racial hierarchy.

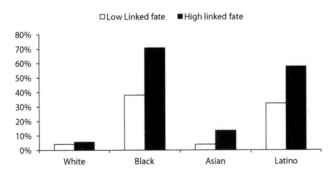

FIGURE 4.3. Proportion perceiving "A lot" of discrimination by perceived linked fate and race. *Source*: National Politics Survey.

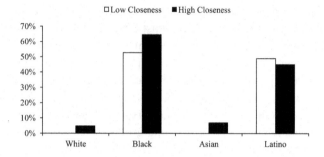

FIGURE 4.4. Proportion perceiving "A lot" of discrimination by closeness to group and race. *Source*: National Politics Survey.

Racial classification for this group signifies advantage rather than marginalization and discrimination.

The NPS also included racial attitude items often described as "racial resentment" questions.[36] We examined the relationship of these measures and perceived linked fate for all racial groups in order to further confirm the appropriateness of perceived linked fate as the best measure of awareness of racial position. We used responses for level of agreement with the following statement: "If racial and ethnic minorities don't do well in life they have no one to blame but themselves." This is a measure commonly employed in studies on racial resentment and reflects emphasis on individual merit rather than structural disadvantage.[37] In addition, we included two measures of support for policies of affirmative action and racial profiling. All measures were operationalized on an ordinal scale with the highest value reflecting disagreement with the statement on blame, support for affirmative action, and rejection of racial profiling. We expect that racial minorities with strong perceived linked fate to hold political attitudes consistent with enhancing equality and reducing the negative influence of the racial hierarchy because they recognize the connection between the racial order and their group's marginalization. Whites with strong racial identities should be committed to preserving their status and the racial hierarchy.

To estimate the importance of perceived linked fate on these racial attitudes, we ran separate regression models on each of the items by racial group while accounting for individual-level differences in age, gender, socioeconomic status, foreign-born status, and political ideology.[38] Table 4.3 summarizes the results of the analysis by showing the direc-

TABLE 4.3. **Summary of Direction and Significance of Influence of Perceived Linked Fate on Racial Resentment Items by Race**

	Whites	Blacks	Asians	Latinos
Believe minorities should *not* only blame themselves for failure		pos.	pos.	
Oppose racial profiling	neg.	pos.		
Support affirmative action	neg.	pos.	pos.	

Source: National Politics Study

tion of the estimated coefficient on the measure of perceived linked fate, and only coefficients significant at the $p < 0.1$ level are reported. The results support our hypotheses, and we find that strong perceptions of linked fate predict support for racial profiling and rejection of affirmative action among white respondents, though white perceived linked fate is unrelated to the perception that racial minorities should blame themselves for failure. The results are the opposite among racial minorities. For both Asian American and African American respondents, the estimated coefficient on the measure of linked fate coefficient is positive and significant. For blacks, strong perceptions of linked fate are related to the belief that minorities cannot only blame themselves for failures and to opposition to racial profiling and support for affirmative action. Likewise, high perceived linked fate among Asian Americans encourages support of affirmative action and reduces emphasis on personal failure. While there were no statistically significant results for Latinos, the direction of the coefficient on the linked-fate measures was nevertheless positive for all three measures of individual blame for lack of progress, affirmative action, and racial profiling.

Finally, we examined the relationship between racial-group identity as perceived linked fate and perceptions of discrimination against racial groups. If racial identity reflects general awareness of a hierarchy, then respondents with strong perceived linked fate should not only recognize their own group's position on the hierarchy but also that all groups ranked in lower positions than whites experience discrimination. We conducted a similar analysis employed for the racial attitude analysis but estimated the effect of perceived linked fate along with a series of individual-level factors to predict perceived discrimination against Latinos, African Americans, whites, and Asian Americans. The measures of perceptions of discrimination were coded as an ordinal scale with perceptions of "a lot" of discrimination as the highest value.[39] Table 4.4

TABLE 4.4. **Summary of Direction and Significance of Influence of Perceived Linked Fate on Perceptions of Discrimination against Racial Group by Race**

	Direction of effect of perceived linked fate			
Perceived target of discrimination	Whites	Blacks	Asians	Latino
Whites		neg.		
Blacks		pos.		pos.
Asians			pos.	pos.
Latinos		pos.		pos.

Source: National Politics Study

presents the data by showing the direction of statistically significant estimated coefficients on the linked-fate variable.

While the results for perceptions of discrimination differ slightly from the racial attitudes analysis, the pattern nevertheless conforms to our expectations. For white respondents, perceived linked fate is unrelated to perceptions of discrimination for any racial group, and characteristics such as education and political ideology are the strongest predictors of perceptions of racial discrimination. For racial minorities, perception of linked fate is a significant predictor, but the findings vary depending on the target of discrimination. Among Asian Americans, perceived linked fate is relevant only for perceptions of discrimination against their own group and not other minority groups. For African American and Latino respondents, perceived linked fate has a significant effect across models in the expected direction. While perceived linked fate has the strongest impact among Asian Americans in terms of more progressive racial attitudes, the same measure of racial-group identity increases perceptions of racial discrimination among Latinos. But for blacks, perceived linked fate has a consistent and significant impact on both their racial attitudes and perceptions of racial discrimination, confirming the recognition among African Americans of their position in the American racial hierarchy. The relatively weaker racial constraints experienced by minority groups placed higher in the racial order are reflected in the more modest influence of perceived linked fate among Asian Americans and Latinos on racial attitudes and perceptions of discrimination. Taken together, these findings from the 2004 NPS confirm that the measure of perceived linked fate most closely mirrors the refractive mechanism specified in the Racial Prism of Group Identity model.

Group Identity as American Boundaries and
Perceived Linked Fate

In perceptions of political belonging, racial categorization structures the contours of group membership through national identity and racial-group consciousness. While measuring distinct dimensions of identity, perceptions of American boundaries and racial-group-linked fate are nevertheless deeply intertwined. As we have argued throughout, the American racial hierarchy structures perceptions of national belonging through its systematic influence on both of these aspects of group identity. In contrast to much of the literature in social psychology and political psychology, our analysis of data from two important US national surveys conducted in 2004 documents systematic divergence between whites and minority Americans in their perceptions of political belonging, as well as the simultaneous existence of group identity in terms of national boundaries and racial-group-linked fate (e.g., Gaertner and Dovidio 2000; Transue 2007). Contrary to the assumption that one identity must be more important than others, the analysis confirms our hypotheses that the relationship between racial-group identity and national identity are not the same for everyone.[40] Instead, the relationship between race and nation varies systematically by position in the American racial order.

The data demonstrate that only among white respondents do boundaries of Americanness and racial-group-linked fate overlap neatly. Privileged as the default racial category of American, the alignment between race and nation is an indicator of the relatively wide agency white Americans experience. Among whites, racial-linked fate is correlated with national identity, but given norms of social desirability, white respondents may underreport their sense of racial-group identity and instead express their group identity in terms of the nation. In contrast, people classified in racial categories ranked lower in the hierarchy experience more constraints on their agency as conditional members of the polity. Their American identity exists in tension with their racial-group identity. Data from African Americans, Asian Americans, and Latinos reveal a pattern of group consciousness moderated by their marginalization as peripheral members of the American in-group. As a result, racial minorities are more likely to see their national identity and their racial identity as two important but distinctive identities. A final analysis of data from the NPS study supports these conclusions. The NPS included a question about identity prioritization: "Which would you say is more important to you: being American, being [respondent's race] or are both equally important to you?" When forced to choose, white respondents overwhelmingly respond that their national identity is more important to them than their racial identity (70%).[41] In stark contrast, just the opposite pattern is apparent for all racial minorities who privilege their national and racial identity equally. Seventy-seven percent of Latinos and 72% of both African American and Asian American respondents say being American and being a member of their race are equally important.

Our analysis of survey data confirms that the legacy and persistence of the American racial hierarchy is reflected in divergent experiences of political belonging across racial groups. Their position at the top of the hierarchy and the presumption of legitimate membership among whites allows them to embrace their identification with the nation as core members. National identity among whites functions like a social-group identity. The normative privileging of whiteness for citizenship in the United States provides the context in which whites can easily perceive their racial-group identity and national identity as overlapping. In contrast, racial minorities are peripheral members who have experienced incomplete membership and a conditional welcome in the nation. African Americans, Latinos, and Asian Americans therefore embrace their national identity as America in a systematically differently way from whites by developing attachments to the categories that mark their difference from core members. For minority Americans group identity as American and perceived linked fate are aligned but not fully overlapping.

The distinctive patterns in the relationship between the measures of American boundaries and racial-linked fate among Americans classified by race have important implications for how we will interpret the findings from the Racial Prism of Group Identity model in the next chapter. Questions on immigration policy invoke issues of political belonging. Whites demonstrate significant overlap between expressions of their national and racial-group identities, and we expect that perceptions of stricter boundaries on Americanness and stronger perceived linked fate will influence white attitudes on immigration in a restrictive direction. Consistent with social identity theory, in-group members will seek to protect the boundaries of their group. As peripheral in-group members of the nation, African Americans may see more rigid group boundaries that define the nation than either whites or Asian Americans and Latinos, who are ranked higher in the hierarchy. For all minorities, however, the perception of stricter group boundaries should also predict more restrictive attitudes on immigration because despite their status as peripheral members, they are nevertheless members of the American in-group. In contrast, because racial identity as perceived linked fate among African Americans, Asian Americans, and Latinos is developed out of an awareness of their relative position in the racial order, higher perceived linked fate reflects greater recognition among minority Americans of the exclusionary practices implicit in immigration and naturalization policies. In this way, stronger perception of linked fate among Asian Americans, African Americans, and Latinos will predict less restrictive attitudes on immigration.

CHAPTER FIVE

The Racial Prism of Group Identity

Antecedents to Attitudes on Immigration

T he preface to John Higham's classic work, *Strangers in the Land: Patterns of American Nativism, 1860–1925* ([1955] 2002), includes a humorous summary of the topic: "Fundamentally, this remains a study of public opinion, but I have sought to follow the movement of opinion wherever it led, relating it to political pressures, social organization, economic changes and intellectual interests. It is not, therefore, a book about crackpots, though there are crackpots in it; it deals with the American people" (xi). Higham's study chronicled Americans' reactions to immigrants during the height of foreign migration to the United States in the late nineteenth and early twentieth centuries, and many of his insights about American nativism remain relevant today. The fable of America as a nation of immigrants with arms open in welcome embrace of newcomers stands in stark contrast to the protectionist stance against immigration held by most Americans. Nativism is a long-standing and persistent feature of public opinion in the United States, and despite the liberalizing aspects of the 1965 Immigration and Nationality Act passed during the height of civil rights reform, the public has generally been most supportive of keeping constant or decreasing the number of new immigrants to the nation.[1] Demarcating and enforcing national boundaries is a consistent feature of nation-state behavior across the world. National immigration policy governing entry and abode differentiates between newcomers who are welcome and those who are excluded from the national group. Thus the impulse to protect national group boundaries is rooted in the same imperatives that drive the dynamics of social identity for other social groups, and this sentiment is reflected in public opinion on immigration.

The "public" in public opinion, however, has become increasingly racially diverse in America since the mid-twentieth century. Data on racial stereotypes and group identity analyzed in the previous chapters reveal systematic differences in perceptions of belonging, the recognition of one's status as a peripheral rather than a core-group member of the American polity, and the intensity of perceived racial-group-linked fate among Americans classified by race. These patterns are consistent with expectations generated from the Racial Prism of Group Identity (RPGI) model for differences between Latinos, Asian Americans, whites, and African Americans in political attitudes on immigration.

The distinctions in public opinion are visible in the responses to survey questions querying general stance toward increasing or decreasing the number of immigrants allowed into the United States and to questions about specific policies governing the treatment of newcomers once they have arrived. In response to the question "Do you think that the number of immigrants to America nowadays should be increased, decreased or remain the same?" asked of the nationally representative sample of Americans in the Faces of Immigration Survey, the distribution of attitudes varies significantly between racial groups. Whites hold the strongest preferences for decreasing immigration: 44% of whites want immigration reduced a lot, and 33% say they prefer immigration to be reduced a little, for a total of 77% in favor of restrictionist immigration policy. African Americans also prefer decreased immigration but to a lesser degree than whites, with a total of 67% in favor of further restrictions, comprising 34% preferring that immigration be reduced by a lot and 33% saying it should be reduced by a little. In contrast, much smaller shares of Asian American and Latino respondents favor further restricting immigration. Half of Latinos support the restrictionist position, and those within this group are evenly divided about reducing immigration by a lot or a little. Asian Americans are the weakest supporters of restrictionist immigration policy, with only 9% favoring reducing immigration a lot and 30% saying immigration should be reduced by a little. Taken together, the data show that all Americans, including racial minorities, support reducing immigration. Increasing immigration to the United States is favored by very small proportions of white and African American respondents (3% and 2%, respectively), but there is more support for increasing immigration among Latinos (14%) and Asian Americans (21%). Those in favor of keeping immigration numbers the same are led in proportion by Asian Americans (40%), followed by Latinos (34%), African Americans (27%), and then whites (20%).

Existing research in public opinion has developed multiple theories and identified factors relevant to explaining immigration attitudes, particularly among white Americans. As comprehensive as is this impressive collection of research, the model specifications cannot explain the reasons behind racial-group-level variation in public opinion on immigration. As the literature suggests, attitudes are influenced by individual-level factors such as partisanship and personality predispositions such as authoritarianism, but racial-group differences persist even after accounting for these factors. Furthermore, analyzing data collected from the US population and specifying a model with control variables for racial minority status forecloses the possibility of observing whether or not political attitudes on immigration among whites and minority Americans are influenced by the same or unique configurations of antecedents. Behind this common construction of inferential models to explain political attitudes is an assumption that explanatory measures will have the same effect on political attitudes among all Americans. While usually not explicitly stated, the assumption is nevertheless apparent in a common strategy employed by political scientists of specifying one multivariate explanatory model that includes dummy variables for minority status and analyzing the effect of other individual-level traits when race is assumed to be held constant. This approach of using control variables for race ignores the structuring of individual-level characteristics by racial categorization.

Because race imposes differential constraint on agency, the influence of factors such as partisanship, group identity, and economic outlook may have distinctive effects on political attitudes on immigration. It is plausible that one factor may explain more negative attitudes toward immigrants for members of one racial group while at the same time driving more positive attitudes for members of a different group. In order to observe these patterns, we use a method of comparative relational analysis and estimate explanatory models separately for each racial group. This strategy enables us to identify the unique intercepts and slopes of the coefficients on explanatory variables and in thus demonstrate the distinctive structural relationships between individual-level explanatory variables and political attitudes on immigration.

We test the RPGI model in this chapter with data from the 2006 Faces of Immigration Survey. We analyze the antecedents to immigration attitudes on a general measure about increasing or decreasing the number of immigrants to the United States as well as two specific questions governing immigrant abode policies. A key feature of the RPGI model is the specification of the moderating effect of group identity on political attitudes on immigration. The model specifies two aspects of group identity elaborated in chapter 4, the measures of American boundaries and perceived racial-linked fate. In the first part of the chapter, we analyze a general question on decreasing or increasing immigration that is commonly analyzed by public opinion scholars and test the influence of these aspects of group identity on attitudes on immigration. We agree with scholars on immigration opinion such as Kinder and Kam (2009) who argue that restrictionist attitudes are driven largely by group identity, especially the desire to protect the nation. Those who perceive strong national-group boundaries are more likely to support restriction, and the direction of the effect of national identity on attitudes toward immigrant admissions should be the same for all racial groups.

We first consider the results of the analysis of the RPGI model for the effect of the group identity variables among white respondents. We expect that whites with a strong sense of both American boundaries and racial-linked fate will hold more restrictive attitudes about immigration. Whites with a high degree of group identity see as obvious the group-based differences between themselves and immigrants. Theories of ethnocentrism apply to whites because of their status as core members of the nation and the most privileged racial group. The moderating influence of group identity for whites for both American boundaries and perceived linked fate should be consistent and positive. At the same time, other individual-level characteristics of partisanship and ideology among whites can either attenuate or enhance restrictionist attitudes on immigration.

In contrast, we expect racial minorities who are strongly aware of their racial position will support greater inclusion of immigrants. Given the use of race to exclude those classified as nonwhite from equal membership in the nation, minorities who are aware of the hierarchy are more sensitive to the injustices caused by exclusion. Thus, we hypothesize that stronger perception of linked fate among Asian Americans, Latinos, and African Americans will dampen support for restricting immigration. While the relationship between the racial-linked-fate measure and attitudes on restricting immigration should be negative for minorities, the relationship between the measure of national-group identity and opinion should be positive, as it is for whites. Despite their status as peripheral members of the in-group, Latinos, blacks, and Asian Americans still see themselves as members of the American polity. Viewing stricter boundaries of what it means to be an American should have a positive effect on support for decreasing immigration. Thus the second expectation for the results of the RPGI model is that the estimations should yield positive coefficients on the American-boundary measure and negative coefficients on the linked-fate measure for minority respondents.

Finally, while these two types of identity are crucial for explaining variation between racial groups, the influence of race on attitude formation cannot be fully explained by sense of racial-linked fate and American boundaries. Existing research has identified the importance of other individual-level characteristics for political attitudes. These factors should also be related to immigration attitudes, but because racial categorization structures agency, not all individual-level factors will function in the same way for all racial groups. Thus, our third expectation is that the results of the comparative relational analysis of the RPGI model will reveal distinctive sets of antecedents predicting immigration attitudes for African Americans, Latinos, whites, and Asian Americans.

Identifying Antecedents to the Formation of Political Attitudes

Political attitudes are assumed to form as a product of a complex set of perceptions, preferences, and psychological predispositions. As a general objective, most public opinion scholarship seeks to identify the unique antecedents that drive attitudes. The goal in this research field is to identify a causal mechanism that has its own distinct impact on the formation of opinion. Scholarship has successfully identified and empirically verified those key factors that explain attitudes on political issues. The factors that have repeatedly influenced attitude formation on different dependent variables now constitute what we term the "established model" for explaining public opinion. This model includes standard variables assumed to be included in any explanatory model of political attitudes. The established model includes a number of distinct variables that can be classified into four basic categories: demographics, cognitive sophistication, personality, and political context. We begin this review of the literature in public opinion by discussing the variables included in the established model. Next, we review the less voluminous research on public opinion on immigration. There are additional antecedents specific to attitudes on immigration.

Variables included in the established model

The first set of variables always included in a model of political attitudes are the demographic characteristics of age, gender, race and class. The inclusion of these measures reflects the hypothesis that one's life position and the experiences that occur as a result of it influence the formation of attitudes. For example, age is identified as an important factor because of life-cycle and generational effects. Older people hold different attitudes than the young because of accumulated wisdom and life experience. Major events that occurred during a person's "coming of age," such as war or an economic depression, may influence one's political outlook for the rest of one's life (Jennings and Niemi 1975; Miller 1992). Other characteristics such as gender, race, and class are also assumed to account for a different perspective on politics because of the distinct experiences and interactions with others among people in these groups.[2] Repeated findings have verified that men and women, wealthy and poor, and whites and blacks hold systematically different attitudes from one another on a variety of issues. Traditionally, these variables have been accounted for in public opinion studies as control variables.[3]

Once systematic differences across the population are controlled for, the key aim of researchers is to identify a specific characteristic or trait that has its own impact on attitude formation. The second dimension of variables included in the established model represents what we label as cognitive sophistication. This dimension includes one of the most influential variables for political behavior and attitudes: education. A person's educational level reflects many things and is not necessarily a proxy for intelligence. Those with higher levels of education have been exposed to more ideas, concepts, and relationships than those with lower levels of education, which makes highly educated individuals better able to recognize more alternatives (Delli Carpini and Keeter 1996).[4] While the cognitive skills developed through education have been important to explaining political behavior, education can also inform how individuals perceive others and social values. For our purposes of explaining immigration attitudes, the literature suggests that education will encourage more inclusive perspectives toward immigrants. The literature on the effects of education has found that because students are given increased exposure to democratic norms, education will create a more enlightened and tolerant population (Bobo and Licari 1989; Nie, Junn, and Stehlik-Barry 1996; Stouffer 1955).

The dimension of cognitive sophistication is not limited simply to outcomes of education but also includes variables that account for one's awareness of events. Developing a position on a political issue presumes that individuals hold an adequate level of awareness about the topic to make a reasoned assessment and develop a position that is consistent with one's values and interests. Indeed, it is unlikely that respondents will report stable or ideologically consistent opinions on issues they have little exposure to. Because Americans receive their news from media sources, the amount of time spent reading and listening to the news is one proxy for the amount of information gathered. Of course, attention to media is not the only way to measure awareness of events. For example, Delli Carpini and Keeter (1996) argue that awareness can also be measured through a test of the respondent's level of political knowledge. However, while awareness of an issue does impact the substantive answer provided by a respondent, high attention to media sources and political events may also indicate extensive exposure to elite messages. Indeed, politically aware individuals may know the issues but are also more likely to develop similar positions as those political elites they follow in the media (Stimson 2004; Zaller 1992). Since the media can control the kinds of narratives provided to audiences, research shows that they are highly influential in molding how viewers develop attitudes about an event or issue (Baumgartner and Jones 1993; Druckman 2010). Assessments of media content on immigration show that news stories are disproportionately more likely to target Latino immigrants and portray immigrants in a negative light (Branton and Dunaway 2009; Chavez 2008; Dunaway, Branton, and Abrajano 2010).

Variables accounting for the third dimension, personality, are increasingly being included in the established model in order to account for some traits that explain inherent differences between individuals. Personality theories focus on psychological predispositions. Although individual behaviors are generally understood as responses to one's environment, how one is predisposed to react is assumed to be a key factor that dictates response. Not all personality traits are relevant to politics, but some such as authoritarianism have long been of interest to political and social scientists. The authoritarian personality was originally used to explain why individuals were willing to commit violence against other human beings during World War II (Adorno et al. 1950). Those with in authoritarian personalities are high on submissiveness, glorify superiors, and place strong emphasis on obedience and so are more supportive of punishment for deviant behavior. As a result, highly authoritarian persons are more likely to have strongly positive views of the in-group and to be highly prejudiced toward out-groups (Feldman 2003; Hetherington and Weiler 2009). Because authoritarianism places emphasis on group protection, this trait has a particularly strong influence in determining one's political preferences on issues pertaining to social and cultural threat (Feldman and Stenner 1997). Hetherington and Weiler (2009) found that, in addition to other factors, high levels of authoritarianism lead to stronger restrictionist attitudes toward immigration.

Finally, although personal preferences are clearly outcomes of both psychological and experiential processes, political context is an important consideration in determining the positions individuals choose to take on an issue. Political elites and parties are those who ultimately have the most influence on decision making in the policy process and consequently have a clear interest in convincing the public to support their policy positions. The influence of elite opinion and party identification serve as useful cues for individuals to use when formulating an opinion. In particular, partisanship has been found to be one of the most important factors that predict the direction and magnitude of individual opinion (Stimson 2004). Political parties not only help establish positions on issues for the general public but also represent important social groups with which individuals can feel a sense of membership and trust (Green, Palmquist, and Schickler 2004).

One of the challenges in studying the role of partisanship in immigration attitudes among the general public is that elite positions on the issue have been historically inconsistent (but see Neiman, Johnson, and Bowler 2006). Tichenor (2002) documents the unusual political coalitions formed around immigration reform legislation throughout American history. In the contemporary period, libertarians and pro-business Republicans who would normally be closely associated with conservative politics have aligned with liberals to support more progressive policies on Mexican migration to the United States. As they have on many other issues, parties have over time changed positions on immigration depending on the historical context and which party identified new immigrant voters as most central to winning new coalitions of voters. Since the major changes of the 1965 Immigration and Nationality Act, both Democratic and Republican elites have supported policies to reduce immigration, including legislating employer sanctions and increasing border control on the US-Mexico border. However, since the mid-1990s Republicans have publicly represented themselves as the restrictionist party and are more likely to be attached to restrictive policies than Democrats (Nevins 2010; Newton 2008). The party divide on the immigration issue has been most prevalent during election years, especially as the Republican party has catered to conservative white voters (R. Jacobson 2008; Schrag 2011).

Antecedents unique to attitudes on immigration policy

Variables in the established model are commonly included in multivariate models used to explain attitude formation on all political issues. Given that there are unique properties to the issue of immigration, scholars have theorized the importance of other individual-level factors. The first is ethnocentrism, or strong preference for one's in-group. Since immigrants are by definition outsiders to the nation, Kinder and Kam (2009) argue that we must take into account the general human tendency to by wary of out-groups. Social psychologists have argued that all humans have the predisposition to be ethnocentric and quickly divide others into members of either their own in-group or an out-group. Ethnocentric values can be a powerful predictor of one's response to outsiders. However, while most scholars agree that the concept of ethnocentrism is relevant to the study of immigration attitudes, a point of disagreement is how individuals determine what constitutes the in-group. Because immigrants differ from Americans by nationality, some scholars have focused on the role of national identity in immigration attitudes. Americans who feel strong attachments to the nation will view immigrants negatively because they were born in a country outside the United States (Schildkraut 2011; C. Wong 2010). In this way, the group boundary is divided between Americans and non-Americans. Alternatively, Burns and Gimpel (2000) suggest that race is another way respondents can define the out-group: "Of course it is well known that the term 'immigrant' is increasingly associated with 'ethnic minority' in both the United States and Europe" (204). They found that among white respondents, antipathy toward racial minorities, which they defined as racial prejudice, drives negative attitudes toward immigrants (see also Kinder and Kam 2009). But regardless of which group boundary is emphasized, those who report strong positive affect for their own group will also report strong negative affect for out-groups. Work by Sniderman and colleagues on immigration attitudes in Europe show similar effects of in-group bias among respondents in the Netherlands and Italy (Sniderman and Hagendoorn 2007; Sniderman et al. 2000).

A second theory applied to the study of immigration attitudes is group-contact theory (Ha 2010; Hopkins 2010).[5] Group-contact theory is related to ethnocentrism because it states that a person's surrounding context strongly shapes reactions to out-groups. There are two contradicting hypotheses that have developed out of contact theory. From one perspective, contact with out-groups is expected to make an individual more tolerant of those groups (Oliver and Wong 2003; Welch et al. 2001). This position posits that lack of contact encourages negative and dehumanized portrayals of out-groups, while more intimate contact increases positive affect. The contrasting hypothesis argues that increased contact encourages stronger negative perceptions of out-groups (Blalock 1967; Blumer 1958). Contact with out-groups is argued to increase awareness of that group, and negative experiences with members of an out-group can also be used to substantiate existing negative stereotypes. Application of group-contact theory to public opinion on immigration has yielded mixed findings. Morris's (2000) study on African American attitudes toward California's Proposition 187 found that interminority contact between blacks and other minority groups had no effect on black political attitudes. However, Hopkins (2010) found that while those white Americans historically exposed to large immigrant populations are no more anti-immigrant than others, whites living in areas with growing new immigrant populations are more likely to feel a sense of threat. Scholars continue to test whether contact with immigrants plays a role in political attitudes on immigration, but the evidence from applications of group-contact theory remains inconclusive.

The last factor tested on a model of immigration attitudes is concern about economic prosperity. Rational-actor theories, which emphasize the motive of protecting material interests, claim that individual political preferences are driven largely by economic interests. Theories on candidate preference have long argued that individual vote choice is largely determined by respondents' perceptions of the economy (Vavreck 2009). Macropolitical theories on immigration flow point to the economic health of both the sending and receiving country as a main cause of migration (Cornelius and Rosenblum 2005). In terms of public opinion, a key hypothesis is that negative attitudes toward immigrants are rooted in more general concerns about national economic health (Espenshade and Hempstead 1996). Although data demonstrating immigrants hurt the economy is mixed (Borjas 1991; Card 1990), it is a common American perception that immigrants are detrimental to the national economy. Those who feel that the economy is faltering are more likely to have negative perceptions about new immigrants (Citrin et al. 1997).[6] Economists such as Borjas (1991) suggest that groups who struggle the most economically are most likely to support restrictive immigration policies.[7]

Minority Public Opinion: Structural Constraints on Attitude Formation

Existing studies of political attitudes described above have identified relevant antecedents to opinion formation on immigration. However, in-depth analyses on specific racial groups also suggest that while the standard factors used in public opinion models are relevant to minority opinion formation, they do not always operate the same for racial minorities as they do for whites. The research in minority politics demonstrates that racial categorization has a powerful impact in moderating the effect of even the standard individual-level factors such as age, education, and partisanship on political attitudes. The most important theoretical development offered in the minority public opinion and behavior literature is that racial background has more influence on political attitudes than was accounted for in the public opinion literature focusing primarily on white Americans. This led to two insights about minority public opinion. The first is that racial considerations are more chronically accessible to minorities than they are to whites. Race is intimately interconnected with how minorities experience the world. Therefore racial minorities more quickly perceive racial undertones in policy debates without the influence of elite framing or priming (White 2007; Hutchings et al. 2006).

Second, because race is more likely to influence minority life chances, group-based identities are just as relevant to political attitudes than other individual-level characteristics if not more so. In multivariate models, racial identification, particularly those measures that capture a sense of politicized group identity, are found to be powerful predictors of political attitudes, particularly on issues pertaining to racial equality (Bobo and Gilliam 1990; Barreto 2007; DeSipio 1996; Jones-Correa and Leal 1996; Junn and Masuoka 2008a; Sanchez 2006). Other scholars focus on specific perceptions of alienation or marginalization to account for the unique experiences of racial minorities. From this perspective racial-group identification represents a social-group identity that is separate from perceptions of marginalization, and perceptions of discrimination are used as measures to account for the recognition of racial-group alienation (García Bedolla 2005; Lien 2001; Schildkraut 2005; Chong and Kim 2006).

Direct measures of the effects of racial categorization such as racial identification and discrimination are well studied in the literature, while research on the relationship of other antecedents to opinion is more limited. Nevertheless, existing research helps inform distinctive hypotheses for each racial group. Resource-based characteristics such as economic class are not distributed equally across racial minority groups, and African Americans are disproportionately clustered at the lower end of measures of income and wealth and have historically represented one of the most economically disadvantaged groups in American society. For example, blacks are disproportionately more likely to drop out of high school, become imprisoned, and suffer from serious health conditions.[8] Similar structural problems are faced by Latinos, and discriminatory practices have also influenced the economic progress of Latinos (Massey 2007).

The variation in economic challenges for racial groups led Chong and Kim (2006) to develop their theory of opportunities reviewed in the last chapter. As they argue, systematic exclusion from the economic market not only mobilizes racial-group consciousness but also informs the general look among members of racial groups. Persistent economic and social inequality has been used to explain higher support among African Americans for government intervention while simultaneously influencing relatively low levels of trust in government (Nunnally 2012).[9] Dawson's (1994) theory of linked fate is rooted in the unique effects of social mobility on the political outlook of African Americans. Blacks who experience mobility are more aware of discrimination than other blacks. Although some economists argue that African Americans feel the most economically threatened by new immigrants (Borjas 1991), blacks' greater awareness of systematic discrimination may make economic outlook less relevant to their political attitudes than to those of others who have experienced less discrimination. In contrast, while systematic exclusions also disadvantage Latinos in the economic market, some immigration scholars claim that Latinos are experiencing slow but steady movement in social mobility over generations (Alba and Nee 2006; Perlmann 2005). As the economic market allows opportunity for Latinos, their outlook may be better characterized by classic rational-actor theories than that of African Americans.

Structural perspectives can also help explain why demographics have unique effects on Asian American political attitudes on immigration. As discussed previously, federal immigration policies privileging high-skilled workers and family reunification have created a selection bias for highly educated Asian immigrants who come to the United States legally. High levels of immigration from Asian countries since the 1965 Immigration and Nationality Act have resulted in an Asian American population that is more than three-quarters foreign-born. Not only have many of these Asian Americans been educated outside of the United States, but their experience in economic and social life as relatively high-status workers distinguishes them from native-born Asian Americans with a potentially greater range of discriminatory experiences resulting from their race (Wong et al. 2011). Generation of migration will therefore be an important predictor of variation in attitudes on immigration among Asian American.

In terms of cognitive sophistication, existing research provides evidence that political awareness varies between racial minorities and whites as a function of foreign-language media sources for Latinos and Asian Americans in particular. The black press has been historically recognized as a distinctive source of news highlighting black interests (Clawson, Strine, and Waltenburg 2003). Similarly, scholars have shown that non-English media sources present political news in the United States differently than the mainstream media in terms of the stories highlighted, frames used to present information, and the analyses provided by broadcasters. For example, Abrajano and Singh (2009) find that mainstream media outlets are more likely to frame immigrants negatively, while Spanish-language media outlets are more likely to present immigrants in a positive light. Therefore, racial minorities who use varied media sources are exposed to a broader set of viewpoints than Americans who rely only on mainstream media sources for political news. While exposure to mainstream media sources may encourage negative attitudes on immigration given the frames most commonly employed by broadcasters, exposure to other sources may not have the same negative effect.

Political party identification is widely recognized to be an important determinant of political attitudes, and attitudes about race are an important dividing line between Republicans and Democrats. Carmines and Stimson's influential theory of issue evolution posits that racial policy issues, particularly policy concerns over inequality between whites and African Americans, have structured the divide between the two parties, with the Democratic Party's decision to support civil rights in the 1960s ensuring the support of that party by black voters for most of the rest of the century. The position of the Republican Party on civil rights and equality leaves African Americans with no viable alternative to the Democratic Party (Frymer 1999; Philpot 2007). As a result, African Americans are not evenly distributed across the party identification spectrum, and data from the American National Election Studies indicate that at least 75% of black respondents self-identify as Democrat and nearly all (95%) voted Democratic in the 2008 election.[10] Although party identification is found to be an important political cleavage that splits white Americans, who are well-distributed between Democrats, Republicans, and independents, partisanship will not have the same predictive power for African Americans in distinguishing attitudes on immigration.[11]

Research on party identification among Asian Americans and Latinos also suggests that partisan choices for these two groups are also subject to attitude constraint on the basis of race. Both of these populations are closer to the immigrant experience than either whites or African Americans, and the development of the civic skills necessary for participation as well as the ways in which they perceive their political positions may be systematically different from Americans whose families have been in the United States for generations (Fraga et al. 2010; Wong et al. 2011). As a result, the role of partisanship and party identification for political attitudes among Asian Americans and Latinos is less clear. Hajnal and Lee (2011) find higher rates of independent and unaffiliated responses among Latinos and Asian Americans. Political partisanship has been treated as an indicator of political incorporation and assimilation (Hajnal and Lee, 2011; McConnaughy et al. 2010; Tam Cho 1999). Similarly, because immigrant voters are often perceived as unnecessary for a winning coalition, political parties have not attempted to mobilize their voters to the same degree as other groups of voters. This diminishes the role of party attachment among Asian Americans and Latinos (J. Wong 2006).

The growing field of research on minority public opinion extends beyond the studies reviewed here, and this is not an exhaustive discussion of expectations for Latinos, African Americans, and Latinos. But, taken together, the findings of these selected studies highlight the systematic variation between whites and minority Americans and underscore the structural influence of racial classification on the antecedents to political attitudes. Racial differences and their impact on public opinion cannot simply be accounted for by a control variable. Even factors such as authoritarianism have different underlying dynamics for different racial groups (Hetherington and Perez 2010). While authoritarianism encourages stronger ethnocentrism among whites, it is not a strong predictor of attitudes among blacks, suggesting that this personality trait may not indicate the same predispositions for all racial groups. These findings underscore the desirability of analyzing the dynamics of the antecedents to immigration attitudes separately by racial group.

Explaining Immigration Attitudes with the Racial Prism of Group Identity Model

We use data from the 2006 Faces of Immigration Survey to estimate the RPGI model and test the effects of antecedents to immigration attitudes on the question of whether respondents think the number of immigrants coming to the United States should be increased or decreased or remain the same.[12] This measure is widely used in the public opinion literature. To explain the formation of restrictive attitudes toward immigration policy, we specified a multivariate regression model that included the two measures of group identity described in chapter 4. These are the scale-measuring characteristics respondents perceive to demarcate the boundaries of being an American and the racial-group-consciousness measure of perceived linked fate. Respondents who perceive stricter boundaries are most likely to support decreasing the number of immigrants. A stronger sense of linked fate with others in one's racial group indicates awareness of the racial hierarchy and its consequences. Higher group consciousness among minority respondents should attenuate support for restrictionist policy, but stronger perceived linked fate among white respondents should mirror the effect of the national-group-identity measure and enhance support for decreasing immigration.

In addition to these two measures of group identity, we also included measures of characteristics identified in prior research that have been shown to be relevant to political attitudes on immigration. The first set is demographic characteristics of the respondent, including age, gender, and family income. Because the share of foreign-born immigrants varies within each racial group, we also account for whether or not respondents are foreign born. The next set of antecedents are indicators cognitive sophistication, and the two variables of education and media attention were measured as number of years of educational attainment and amount of attention to national news and politics. We also included a measure of authoritarianism with responses to agreement with the statement "It is better to live in an orderly society in which the laws are vigorously enforced than to give people too much freedom." Those with a stronger authoritarian orientation are those who strongly agree with this statement.[13] Finally, we included a measure of political party identification operationalized on an ordinal scale with those who identify as strongly Republican representing the highest value.[14]

The RPGI model also includes indicators that account for factors specifically hypothesized to influence public opinion on immigration. Although studies on intergroup contact have found conflicting results, contact is a relevant antecedent to attitudes about immigration policy. Scholarly research has shown that how Americans view racial diversity is different from the actual level of diversity in the population, and individuals most often overreport the size of the racial minority population (Sigelman and Niemi 2001; C. Wong 2007).[15] Researchers also use objective measures of racial diversity with census data matched to respondent zip code. We included two indicators of the context of racial diversity. The first measures whether or not the respondent lives in a high-immigration state (i.e., among those with the largest immigrant populations in 2006).[16] A second measure of the context of racial diversity is the response to a question asking respondents to report the diversity level of their neighborhood. This variable is coded as a dichotomous measure of whether or not respondents report living in a racially diverse neighborhood.[17] Finally, to account for the potential significance of economic interests on immigration attitude formation, we included a measure of economic outlook about personal finances. The highest value on this measure represents those respondents who believe that their finances will be worse off in the next two years. We estimated the model predicting support for decreasing immigration, with ordered logit analysis, and the results are discussed in detail below.[18]

Effects of group identity on preference for decreasing immigration

Table 5.1 summarizes the results for our two key group-identity variables, perceived American boundaries and linked fate. The estimates of the logit coefficients reported in the table are all significant at the .10 level. After accounting for all other factors identified by public opinion scholars to explain attitudes about decreasing immigration, both group-identity variables are significant for all racial groups. The American-boundary measure has a consistent and positive effect on preferences among whites, African Americans, Latinos, and Asian Americans for decreasing immigration. Regardless of whether one is a core or peripheral member of the United States, strong national identity has a positive impact on restrictionist attitudes on immigration.

The regression results for the RPGI model also confirm that perception of racial-group-linked fate is a significant predictor of immigration attitudes for all Americans as well. In contrast to the results for the identity measure of American boundaries, perceived linked fate has a positive impact on white attitudes on decreasing immigration and a negative estimated coefficient for all racial minority groups. Whites with stronger perceived linked fate with other whites are more likely to support decreasing immigration, while blacks, Asians, and Latinos with a high degree of perceived linked fate are less likely to support restrictionist immigration policy. These findings are consistent with the expectations of the RPGI model and confirm the positive and overlapping relationship between national- and racial-group identity among whites on attitudes on immigration. Perception of racial-group-linked fate works in

TABLE 5.1. **Summary of Effect of Group Identity on Preference for Decreased Immigration (Estimated with Logit)**

	Decrease immigration			
	Whites	Blacks	Asians	Latino
Linked fate	.26 (.15)	−.35 (.13)	−.39 (.18)	−.67 (.14)
American boundary	.32 (.05)	.08 (.04)	.20 (.05)	.15 (.04)
N	401	386	349	376

Source: Faces of Immigration Study

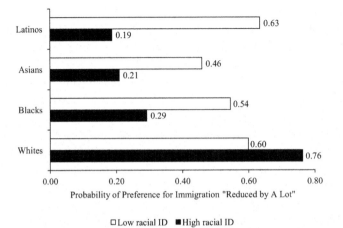

FIGURE 5.1. Probability of preferring immigration "reduced by a lot" for strong boundaries. *Source*: Faces of Immigration Survey.

the opposite direction for Americans ranked below whites on the racial hierarchy and stronger awareness of their group's position has a negative impact on preferences for decreasing immigration to the United States.

The coefficients produced by logit estimations provide precise information about what factors are statistically significant and the direction of the effect, but the magnitudes of the effect of the antecedents are difficult to interpret without calculating predicted probabilities. Thus, to aid in visualizing the effect of group identity on preference for decreased immigration, we simulated particular types of respondents, each with varying levels of national identity. For each hypothetical respondent, we then calculated the probability that the person wants immigration "reduced a lot." Figure 5.1 displays the calculations of the predicted probabilities for a respondent who perceives strong national boundaries.[19] The first striking finding is that, among respondents who emphasize rigid national boundaries, the likelihood of a white respondent supporting decreasing immigration is high. The probability that a white respondent with strong perceived racial-linked fate and who perceives rigid national boundaries strongly agrees with decreasing immigration is 0.76.

In contrast, the probability of Asian Americans and Latinos with strong perceived linked fate and strict American boundaries supporting decreasing immigration is comparatively low, predicted at 0.21 and 0.19, respectively. African Americans with a strong sense of linked fate and

strict group boundaries are also less likely than whites to support decreasing the number of immigrants, though the probability of their supporting restriction is slightly higher than among strongly identifying Latinos and Asian Americans. Figure 5.1 also shows that, in general, the
probability that racial minorities will support reducing the number of
immigrants a lot is lower than even whites with weak perceived racial-
group-linked fate. The only exception to this is for Latinos with strong
national identities but weak perceived linked fate, whose probability of
favoring decreasing the number of immigrants a lot is 0.63. These predicted probabilities show that even though racial minorities, especially
African Americans and Latinos, are the groups that perceive the most
rigid American boundaries, the effect of this identity on restrictive immigration attitudes is nevertheless weaker than the effect for whites.

The predicted probabilities show that racial minorities are less likely
to favor reducing the number of immigrants than whites and that the
level of perceived racial-group-linked fate alters the probability that a
respondent will support a restrictionist position. For whites, perceived
racial-group-linked fate increases support for immigration restriction,
and whites with high perceived linked fate are 16% more likely to support decreasing immigration than whites with weak racial-group identities. Exactly the opposite pattern is apparent for racial minorities.
Among those perceiving strong American boundaries, high perceived
linked fate reduces support for restricting immigration. This finding
adds further support for the distinctive moderating effect of group identity on attitudes by race. Perception of racial-group-linked fate has the
opposite effect for the group at the top of the racial hierarchy than it
does for minority groups ranked lower on the hierarchy. For whites, perceived racial-linked fate enhances preferences for reducing the number
of immigrants and enhancing exclusion. In contrast, greater awareness of
the racial hierarchy and strong perceived racial-group-linked fate among
African Americans, Latinos, and Asian Americans attenuates the restrictionist impulse and promotes attitudes of greater inclusion among
members of racial groups ranked lower in the hierarchy. Not only do the
results reveal opposite patterns for the effect of racial-group identity on
restrictionist preferences among whites and minorities, but the findings
also demonstrate that the impact of perceived linked fate on Latinos',
Asian Americans', and blacks' opinions on immigration is stronger than
it is for whites. The change in support for reducing the number of immigration from strong to weak identities is 16% for whites but 25% among

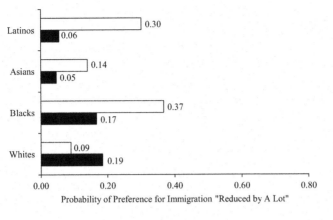

FIGURE 5.2. Probability of preferring immigration "reduced by a lot" for weak boundaries.
Source: Faces of Immigration Survey.

African American respondents. Asian Americans with a strong sense of racial-linked fate are also 25% less likely to support decreasing immigration than those with a weak racial identity. The effect of the movement from weak to strong perceived racial-group-linked fate is strongest for Latinos at 44%.

For the national-group-identity measure, differences between perceptions of American boundaries have a strong influence on immigration attitudes. Figure 5.2 displays the calculations of the predicted probabilities for respondents who perceive weak American boundaries.[20] Comparing the results presented in figures 5.1 and 5.2 shows that perception of strong American boundaries explains much of the variance on the dependent variable among whites. The probability that whites with strong racial identities who perceive *strong* national boundaries will support reducing the number of immigrants by a lot is 76%, while the probability that whites with strong racial identities who perceive *weak* national boundaries will support reducing the number of immigrants by a lot is only 19%. Thus, as we expected, the most important group-identity measure for attitudes on immigration among whites is the American boundaries scale of national identity.

For racial minorities, the likelihood that Asian Americans, blacks, and Latinos with strong perceptions of American boundaries support the number of immigrants being reduced by a lot is lower than among those with weak perceptions of national boundaries. However, for African Americans and Latinos who perceive more porous boundaries, the moderating role of racial-linked fate is greater than it is for whites and Asian Americans. The difference between the probability of strong racial identifiers and weak racial identifiers for African Americans and Latinos is twice what it is for Asian Americans and whites. This pattern suggests that those ranked at the bottom of the hierarchy who experience the most exclusion hold attitudes on immigration consistent with their recognition of their relatively low group position. In contrast, Asian American attitudes on immigration are influenced more strongly by their perception of American boundaries than their sense of racial-linked fate, a result predicted by their position above blacks and Latinos in the racial order.

Structuring by race: antecedents to immigration attitudes by racial group

The results discussed above support our claim that the same factor can have different effects on attitudes across racial groups. There are other important individual-level characteristics in addition to the measures of group identity that help explain support for reducing the number of immigrants to the United States. The full results of estimates of the models are displayed in Table 5.2 and show a distinctive pattern of results for Americans classified by race. The first column in the table presents the results for white respondents. The measures of group identity are most important to explaining support for decreased immigration, and only one other variable in this model reaches statistical significance. Those living in racially diverse neighborhoods are more likely to support reducing the number of immigrants than are whites from racially homogenous neighborhoods. While existing scholarship has highlighted the importance of characteristics such as economic outlook, personality, and partisanship on immigration attitudes, few have included national-group identity and perceived racial-linked fate for whites. The significance of the American boundary and perceived racial-group-linked fate measures for whites overwhelm the effect of these other characteristics in the model estimated among white respondents. While not statistically significant, the direction of the estimated coefficients nevertheless comports with expectations generated from previous research. Excluding American boundaries and perceived linked fate from the models results in statistically significant estimates of coefficients on the measures

TABLE 5.2. **Antecedents to Preference for Decreased Immigration by Race (Estimated with Logit)**

	Whites	Blacks	Asians	Latino
	β (se)	β (se)	β (se)	β (se)
Group boundaries				
Linked fate	.26 (.15)*	−.35 (.13)***	−.39 (.18)**	−.67 (.14)**
Amer boundary	.32 (.05)***	.08 (.04)**	.20 (.05)***	.15 (.04)***
Demographics				
Age	−.003 (.07)	.01 (.07)	.17 (.08)**	.15 (.07)**
Income	−.03 (.03)	.04 (.03)	.06 (.03)**	.01 (.03)
Female	−.02 (.20)	−.10 (.20)	.61 (.21)***	−.06 (.20)
Foreign born	−.81 (.50)	−2.1 (.56)***	−.57 (.22)**	−.86 (.26)***
Sophistication and attention				
Education	−.10 (.09)	.05 (.10)	−.21 (.11)*	−.14 (.09)
Attention to media	.01 (.10)	−.07 (.09)	−.02 (.11)	−.03 (.10)
Personality				
Authoritarianism	.18 (.12)	.10 (.12)	.04 (.14)	.09 (.12)
Politics				
Party ID (Republican)	.11 (.12)	−.62 (.19)***	.15 (.14)	.16 (.13)
Context				
Diverse neighborhood	.49 (.24)**	−.03 (.20)	−.34 (.21)	−.03 (.21)
Immigration state	−.08 (.22)	.10 (.21)	−.35 (.21)	.19 (.20)
Economics				
Economic outlook	.15 (.16)	−.08 (.16)	.13 (.17)	.04 (.16)
N	401	386	349	376
Log likelihood	118.25	42.44	83.39	87.59
Percent predict correct	.514	.438	.424	.481
PRE	.174	.159	.034	.220

Source: Faces of Immigration Survey

*p < 0.10

**p < 0.05

***p < 0.01

of age, foreign-born status, education, partisanship, and authoritarianism.[21] These individual-level traits among whites are therefore substantively relevant to attitudes on immigration, but the results of our estimation of the RPGI model demonstrate that group identity is a stronger moderating force on public opinion on immigration among whites.

The second column in table 5.2 presents the results for African American respondents. In addition to the strong results for both measures of group identity, this estimate shows that foreign-born status and partisanship are significantly related to black attitudes on decreasing the number of immigrants. There is a statistically significant coefficient on the measure of Republican Party identification, but given the small size of this group (3% of black respondents in the sample), the finding might best be interpreted as the result of extreme marginality of this category. At the same time, black Republicans hold more libertarian stances on immigration than typical Republicans and therefore oppose decreasing the number of immigrants to the United States. All told, the results of the estimation of the RPGI model for African American respondents confirm that attitudes about immigration are explained largely by perception of strong American boundaries and racial-group-linked fate. In contrast to what was found for whites, results of the estimation of a model excluding the group-identity measures shows that the results do not change. Other factors commonly identified as antecedent to immigration attitudes such as authoritarianism or education remain insignificant for blacks. This suggests that current theories of political attitudes are better suited to explaining variation in opinion among whites than among African Americans.

Turning to the third column of table 5.2, showing results for Asian American respondents, we find important variation across demographic groups and education, even when including the two measures of group identity. Foreign-born Asian Americans have more inclusive attitudes toward increasing immigration. But older, wealthier, and female Asian Americans are more likely to support decreasing immigration when perceptions of American boundaries and racial-group-linked fate are considered. Higher levels of education significantly attenuate restrictionist attitudes on immigration. The results for Asian Americans show that demographic characteristics and education explain more variation on immigration attitudes than either the personality or contextual variables.

The far-right column of table 5.2 shows results for Latinos. The estimation of the RPGI model shows that antecedents other than the American boundaries and linked-fate measures reach statistical significance as predictors of preference for reducing the number of immigrants among Latinos. Only age and foreign-born status are significantly related to restrictionist attitudes, with older Latinos more likely to support decreasing immigration and foreign-born Latinos more likely to support increasing immigration. When the model is specified to exclude the two group-identity variables, the results are different. Political partisanship and education reach statistical significance, albeit marginally, and the direction of partisanship and education are consistent with expectations, with higher levels of education encouraging more inclusive attitudes and those who identify as Republican holding more restrictive attitudes.

The range of results presented in table 5.2 underscores an important point about the distinctive antecedents to immigration attitudes by racial group. The substantive conclusion that individual-level factors such as partisanship, personality and even education function the same for whites as they do for African Americans or Latinos or Asian Americans is not supported by the data. Instead, attitudes on immigration are generated out of different sets of antecedents for each group. Only national identity and perceived racial-linked fate are statistically significant across all of the models, while the direction of the coefficient varies by core versus peripheral American group status.

Immigration Abode Policy

The analysis of attitudes on immigration thus far has focused on the antecedents to preferences for reducing or increasing the number of immigrants to the United States. Most studies of public opinion on immigration focus on this overall policy position not only because of the standardization of the question wording but because the issue of immigration admissions is among the more visible aspects of national immigration policy. Issues of political belonging cover who is allowed to enter but also the conditions under which newcomers are allowed to stay. Policies about immigrant incorporation and the question of which rights are afforded to immigrants fall under the rubric of abode policies—actions by government to regulate the conditions under which immigrants live in the United States and interact with its people and government.

In this section, we analyze the extent to which the same antecedents predicting attitudes on decreasing or increasing immigration affect Americans' views on two abode policies, involving English as the official national language and the provision of social services to all immigrants. Immigration admission and abode policies both target newcomers and are therefore likely to correlate with one another, but given the variety of immigrant incorporation policies proposed in recent years, ranging from social welfare to educational services to racial profiling, attitudes about this diverse set of policies may not be governed by the same set of concerns (Schneider and Ingram 1997). Thus we do not assume that immigration attitudes are one-dimensional. More important, the RPGI model predicts that position on the racial hierarchy informs the interests of members of any given group. Groups at the bottom of the racial hierarchy are more aware of social inequality and exclusion and so are more sensitive to policies that maintain or exacerbate inequality. Similarly, as discussed in chapter 3, groups at the bottom of the racial hierarchy are more likely to ascribe more positive stereotype traits to lower-ranked groups, while groups higher in the hierarchy only awarded positive traits to their own group and those ranked higher than their own group. We therefore anticipate that groups ranked lower on the racial hierarchy will generally be more willing to support policies that favor disadvantaged groups and help reduce social inequalities involving redistribution of resources and services while rejecting policies that reinforce group racialization such as policies of racial profiling. In contrast, groups higher in the racial hierarchy will seek to protect the maintenance of order and defend the status quo by support policies that keep the hierarchy intact.

The 2006 Faces of Immigration Survey included other questions on immigrant abode policies, including a question asking whether all immigrants should be eligible or ineligible for social services provided by government. A second question asked respondents whether they favored making English the official language of the United States.[22] The choice to analyze these two immigration abode policy questions is intended as a representation of two dimensions normally used to classify immigrant incorporation policies around economic and cultural concerns (Cornelius and Rosenblum 2005). Economic concerns emanate from perceptions that immigrants will compete for low-wage jobs with native-born Americans and that immigrants are likely to use government assistance in the form of welfare, public schooling, and other social services. Culturally, because immigrants arrive from different nations, their distinctive languages, practices, and religions are seen as conflicting with those of native-born Americans. Symbolic concerns about immigrants eroding national identity and culture have been famously articulated (Huntington 2004). As a result, Americans have witnessed proposals for immigrant abode policies such as outlawing bilingual services by public schools, dictating the languages used on commercial signs, or monitoring the type of clothing styles people may wear. Although the classification of economic versus cultural threat is a basic dichotomy used to describe a policy area that is growing increasingly more complex, these two categories help us consider how cultural and economic concerns reflect group-based interests.

These two questions on the provision of social services and English as the official language of the United States also tap into national and racial-group identities in distinctive ways. Policies providing social services to immigrants address the equitable distribution of resources among members of a community, and racial-group identities may be more important in opinions on redistributive policies (Gilens 1999; Hancock 2004; Kinder and Sanders 1996). Policies addressing cultural concerns such as the normative goal that all Americans speak English are likely to be influenced by stronger perceptions of American boundaries. So while racial-group identities should influence attitudes on the social services measure, national identity may be a more important factor in explaining attitudes on English-language policies.

To examine how racial groups vary in their positions on immigrant abode policies, we used the same strategy of comparative relational analysis and estimated each of the equations separately by racial group. The same antecedents as in the models predicting attitudes on immigration restriction are specified in these models, and a method of logistic regression is used to estimate the coefficients. The social services question is a dichotomous variable, and the English-language policy question is a four-point ordinal measure, so ordered logit was used to estimate these models.

White attitudes on immigration abode policy

Similar to the results for the analysis of the question about decreasing the number of immigrants, the measure of American boundaries has a strong influence on white attitudes favoring policies making English the official language of the United States and whites' preference for not providing social services to all immigrants. The results for the two dependent variables are displayed in table 5.3. Whites who perceive rigid national boundaries are significantly more likely to prefer that social services not be provided to immigrants and to support a constitutional amendment to make English the official national language. For whites, responses to immigrants, both in terms of admissions and incorporation, are strongly influenced by how they view national boundaries. Comparing the configuration of statistically significant antecedents between the social services and English-language models, each immigrant abode policy taps into different concerns. Attitudes on the English-language policy are driven largely by ethnocentrism, and perceived racial-linked fate also had a significant effect in favor of the policy. Education and party identification are also significant in this model, with education producing more tolerant responses against an English-only amendment.

In contrast, support for providing social services to immigrants is influenced strongly by the measure of American boundaries and political

TABLE 5.3. **Antecedents to Attitudes on Social Services and English-Only Policy among Whites (Estimated with Logit and Ordered Logit)**

	Social services	English only
	β (se)	β (se)
Group boundaries		
Linked fate	.21 (.21)	.39 (.19)**
Amer boundary	.29 (.07)***	.36 (.06)***
Demographics		
Age	.15 (.10)	.002 (.09)
Income	−.02 (.04)	−.00 (.03)
Female	−.33 (.29)	.17 (.25)
Foreign born	−.37 (.63)	−.28 (.60)
Sophistication and attention		
Education	−.13 (.13)	−.36 (.12)***
Attention to media	.13 (.14)	.25 (.12)**
Personality		
Authoritarianism	−.15 (.19)	.26 (.16)*
Politics		
Party ID (Republican)	.49 (.19)**	.32 (.16)*
Context		
Diverse neighborhood	.11 (.34)	−.22 (.28)
Immigration state	−.01 (.31)	.30 (.28)
Economics		
Economic outlook	−.35 (.23)	−.01 (.20)
Constant	−2.0 (1.2)*	—
N	398	401
Log likelihood	61.82	124.47
Percent predict correct	.804	.693
PRE	.000	−.042

Source: Faces of Immigration Survey

*p < 0.10

**p < 0.05

***p < 0.01

party identification. The fact that party identification is a statistically significant predictor for both of the immigrant abode policies but not the measure of preference for decreased immigration may speak to the relative clarity of Democratic and Republican parties' positions on immigrant abode versus admission policies. Republicans have been most successful in spearheading major anti-immigrant abode policies, including initiatives at the state level such as California's Proposition 187 and major reductions in federal services to immigrants such as the Illegal Immigration Reform and Immigrant Responsibility Act of 1996.[23] Furthermore, studies on racial attitudes of economic redistribution policies such as welfare show that conservative ideology is a strong predictor of white preferences. Although scholars disagree over the extent to which conservative ideology is a proxy for white racism, research has documented a distinctive relationship between ideology and racial attitudes among whites (Sears et al. 1997). Our findings on the social services question are consistent with these studies.

African American attitudes on immigration abode policy

For black respondents, the results show that attitudes on immigrant abode are not significantly influenced by group identity. The results, detailed in table 5.4, reveal neither perception of racial-group-linked fate nor the perception of strict American boundaries is a significant predic-

TABLE 5.4. **Antecedents to Attitudes on Social Services and English-Only Policy among Blacks (Estimated with Logit and Ordered Logit)**

	Social services	English only
	β (se)	β (se)
Group boundaries		
Linked fate	−.10 (.15)	.39 (.14)***
Amer boundary	.04 (.04)	.16 (.04)***
Demographics		
Age	.03 (.08)	.07 (.08)
Income	.12 (.03)***	.05 (.03)*
Female	.10 (.24)	−.003 (.23)
Foreign born	−.11 (.69)	−1.2 (.60)**
Sophistication and attention		
Education	−.22 (.13)*	−.04 (.13)
Attention to media	−.02 (.11)	.12 (11)
Personality		
Authoritarianism	−.11 (.13)	.11 (.13)
Politics		
Party ID (Republican)	−.16 (.22)	−.09 (.21)
Context		
Diverse neighborhood	.31 (.24)	.38 (.24)
Immigration state	.05 (.25)	.76 (.26)***
Economics		
Economic outlook	.15 (.19)	.24 (.19)
Constant	.49 (.93)	—
N	385	387
Log likelihood	23.57	61.98
Percent predict correct	.686	.649
PRE	.040	.035

Source: Faces of Immigration Survey
*p < 0.10
**p < 0.05
***p < 0.01

tor of support for social services for immigrants. In this model, class and education predict support for providing all immigrants with social services. The lack of a significant finding for the group-identity measures is inconsistent with the expectation that recognition of the racial hierarchy through group position and perceived linked fate would influence attitudes on redistributive and egalitarian policies.

In contrast, African American support for English as the official language policy is driven primarily by group-based interests. Here both perceived linked fate and American boundaries influence attitudes on a policy designed to be an antidote to a cultural threat of immigration. Although racial-group identity reduces support for restrictive immigration policies for blacks, perceived linked fate increases support for an English-only amendment. The results for the English-only model show that there are cases in which race and nation align for blacks, and symbolic concerns of protecting certain characteristics as American do not appear to conflict with blacks' perceptions of their racialized status. African American attitudes on the English-language policy are also influenced by contact with immigrants, and the results show a significant effect of living in a high-immigration state. Across the three measures of attitudes on immigration—decreasing the number of immigrants, providing social services to all immigrants, and making English the official language of the United States—the pair of group-identity measures have different effects for black respondents. African Americans' status as peripheral in-group members in combination with their status as the lowest-ranked group on the hierarchy structures this set of relationships.

Asian American attitudes on immigration abode policy

Table 5.5 displays the results from the estimation of the models for Asian American respondents. Attitudes on both the social services and English-language policies are influenced by the measure of American boundaries. Asian Americans who perceive rigid national boundaries are more likely to agree that all immigrants should not be eligible for social services. Similarly, the national-identity measure also predicts stronger support for an English-only amendment. In contrast, perceived racial-group-linked fate is not a statistically significant antecedent for either of these immigrant abode policies.

While this finding may be surprising at first glance, the pattern of results from the other predictors explains why perceived racial-group-

TABLE 5.5. **Antecedents to Attitudes on Social Services and English-Only Policy among Asian Americans (Estimated with Logit and Ordered Logit)**

	Social services	English only
	β (se)	β (se)
Group boundaries		
Linked fate	−.25 (.20)	.23 (.20)
Amer boundary	.15 (.05)***	.23 (.05)***
Demographics		
Age	.19 (.09)**	.04 (.09)
Income	.01 (.03)	−.02 (.03)
Female	.42 (.24)*	.48 (.23)**
Foreign born	−.27 (.25)	.42 (.24)*
Sophistication and attention		
Education	.06 (.13)	−.05 (.13)
Attention to media	.01 (.12)	.05 (.12)
Personality		
Authoritarianism	−.14 (.16)	.68 (.16)***
Politics		
Party ID (Republican)	.28 (.16)*	.45 (.16)***
Context		
Diverse neighborhood	−.78 (.25)***	.04 (.24)
Immigration state	−.03 (.24)	.02 (.23)
Economics		
Economic outlook	−.09 (.19)	.07 (.19)
Constant	−1.8 (1.1)	—
N	346	350
Log likelihood	39.59	87.85
Percent predict correct	.633	.609
PRE	.244	.105

Source: Faces of Immigration Survey

*$p < 0.10$

**$p < 0.05$

***$p < 0.01$

linked fate is not a significant indicator of perspectives on either of the abode policies. Support for more intolerant incorporation policies among Asian American are driven by factors indicating support for assimilation. For example, foreign-born Asian Americans are more supportive of the English-language policy than their native-born counterparts because those who are foreign born feel a greater need to demonstrate their Americanness. Partisan attachment is also a significant determinant of Asian American positions on both policies, with those who identify as Republican more likely to say immigrants should be ineligible for social services and to support an English-only amendment. These results are consistent with findings on political party attachment among white respondents. At the same time, Hajnal and Lee (2011) found strong partisan affiliation to be indicative of an assimilationist perspective among Latinos and Asian Americans. They found Asian Americans with weak racial attachments to be more likely to identify as Republicans, while those with stronger awareness of their racialized status were found to be more likely to identify as Democrats.

Latino attitudes on immigration policy

The results of the estimation of the models predicting attitudes on immigrant abode policies among Latino respondents are detailed in table 5.6. Both national identity and perceived racial-group-linked fate influence opinions on providing social services to all immigrants and having En-

TABLE 5.6. **Antecedents to Attitudes on Social Services and English-Only Policy among Latinos (Estimated with Logit and Ordered Logit)**

	Social services β (se)	English only β (se)
Group boundaries		
Linked fate	−.54 (.17)***	−.47 (.15)***
Amer boundary	.14 (.05)***	.22 (.04)***
Demographics		
Age	.24 (.09)***	.06 (.07)
Income	.03 (.03)	.03 (.03)
Female	−.28 (.26)	.01 (.22)
Foreign born	−1.0 (.31)***	.08 (.27)
Sophistication and attention		
Education	−.26 (.12)**	−.26 (.10)***
Attention to media	−.21 (.12)*	−.15 (.10)
Personality		
Authoritarianism	.03 (.16)	.38 (.14)***
Politics		
Party ID (Republican)	.66 (.18)***	.47 (.15)***
Context		
Diverse neighborhood	.37 (.28)	−.005 (.23)
Immigration state	.28 (.26)	.03 (.22)
Economics		
Economic outlook	−.07 (.20)	.01 (.16)
Constant	−.26 (1.0)	—
N	372	374
Log likelihood	82.44	94.37
Percent predict correct	.747	.586
PRE	.190	.055

Source: Faces of Immigration Survey
*$p < 0.10$
**$p < 0.05$
***$p < 0.01$

glish as the official language of the nation. Latinos with strong perceived racial-linked fate are significantly more likely to support social services for immigrants and to reject an English-only amendment. Latinos with strong national identities prefer the opposite. Based on the consistent role of group identity on Latinos' positions on all three immigration questions we analyze in this chapter, immigration is a question of Latino group identity. Latinos who emphasize the importance of their racial group are more likely to support more inclusive and generous policies toward new immigrants, while Latinos who emphasize national group boundaries are more likely to hold restrictive attitudes toward immigrants.

Other predictors of attitudes on immigration among Latinos demonstrates that, as among Asian American respondents, Latinos who support assimilationist viewpoints are more likely to hold restrictive attitudes toward immigration. The results of these models show that Republican partisan identification is a significant predictor of restrictive immigration attitudes on both abode policy items for Latinos. Like Asian Americans, partisan affiliation for Latinos is an indicator of both party loyalty and assimilationist preferences. Since the racialization of Latinos is also strongly characterized by their foreigner status, Latinos like Asian Americans may try to escape this racialized trope by demonstrating restrictive preferences toward new immigrants.

The Constraint of Race on Public Opinion

In the foregoing chapters, we document the ways in which racial categorization and position in the hierarchy structure the way Americans view themselves and others in society. Racial-group classification is not simply an individual-level characteristic to be controlled for in inferential models of public opinion. Instead, race is a powerful social structural force that, along with institutional and historical processes of racialization, systematically influences the degree of agency among whites, African Americans, Latinos, and Asian Americans. The significance of race for political attitudes on immigration is not the same for Americans of different races, and important group-based differences are apparent in the analysis of results from the RPGI model. In this chapter, we have tested the influence of the two measures of group identity theorized to best capture the moderating force between race and political attitudes on immigration.

The results from the analysis demonstrate that the role of national identity measured by perceptions of boundaries defining American-ness was consistent across all Americans in increasing support for re-strictionist policy. Americans are choosy about whom they let in to the polity, and individuals of all races do not support admitting any and all newcomers. Consistent with social identity theory, stronger national-group identity as Americans enhances the impulse to exclude outsiders. Among both core and peripheral in-group members of the nation, the analysis showed that stronger group identity at the national level encour-aged perceptions of immigrants as outsiders and predicted support of policies of restriction. Despite the consistent and positive influence of the American-boundaries measure of national-group identity on pref-erences for immigration restriction, a strong sense of American bound-aries was most important for attitudes on immigration among whites compared with the magnitude of the effect among racial-minority re-spondents. Similarly, white attitudes on the immigrant abode policies of denying social services to all immigrants and supporting a constitutional amendment to make English the official language of the United States were influenced positively and significantly by national-group identity. These patterns of the effect of national identity on immigrant abode pol-icies among whites were mirrored in the estimates of the models for both Asian Americans and Latinos but to a more modest degree. Among Af-rican Americans, stricter perceptions of group boundaries influenced support for making English the official language of the United States but did not significantly affect support for a policy of denying social services to all immigrants.

In contrast, perceived racial-group-linked fate was shown to work in distinctive ways for groups positioned at different places in the racial hi-erarchy. Whites, at the top of the hierarchy, are the anomalous group. A stronger sense of perceived racial-linked fate among whites predicts more restrictive opinion on decreasing immigration. Both of the measures of group identity for whites predict restrictionist attitudes on immigration, and the influence of national identity and racial-group identity overlap. Among minority Americans, national identity and racial-group identity work at cross-purposes, one encouraging a preference for decreasing im-migration, and the other attenuating restrictionist sentiment. The effect of perceived racial-linked fate on preference for decreasing the number of immigrants among African Americans, Latinos, and Asian Ameri-cans is negative. Minority racial groups ranked lower in the hierarchy recognize their relative disadvantage, and stronger perceptions of linked fate predict positions on immigration policy that are more inclusive of immigrants. For the specific immigrant abode policy questions, Latinos are the only group for which strong perception of racial-linked fate consistently and significantly predicted opposition to policies of denying all immigrants social services and making English the official language of the United States. Latinos with high perceived racial-linked fate recognize the stereotypes of Latinos as unwanted and "illegal" immigrants along with their relatively low position in the racial hierarchy. The results for the impact of strong perceived racial-group-linked fate and opposition to denying social services to immigrants was negative for both African Americans and Asian Americans, but the estimated coefficients were not statistically significant. For the policy of making English the official language of the United States, the impact of perceived racial-linked fate among blacks and Asian Americans was positive, as it was for whites, but statistically significant only for African Americans.

Taken together, the results from the estimations of the RPGI model provide strong support for our claim of the structural significance of racial classification, group position, and the racial hierarchy for political attitudes about immigration. Equally as important, the distinct patterns in the results estimated separately for Latinos, African Americans, whites, and Asian Americans attest to the importance of using a strategy of comparative relational analysis to understand the contours and dynamics of American public opinion on immigration. A finding that racial classification matters must be accompanied by an explanation of why distinctions are observed in political attitudes among Americans of different races. The stakes for understanding the dynamics of public opinion on immigration among racial groups are most obvious when one considers the framing of immigration in political communications and the ways in which target groups are primed in political elites' discourse on immigration policy reform. This is the task of the next chapter, on the role of political communication in framing immigration for the American public.

CHAPTER SIX

Framing Immigration

*"Illegality" and the Role of
Political Communication*

During the 1994 California gubernatorial race, Republican Pete
Wilson sought to revive what appeared to be a failing bid for reelection by taking a tough stance against illegal immigration. Ironically,
when Wilson was a US senator from California, he had fought to preserve farmers' easy access to immigrant labor during congressional deliberation on the 1986 Immigration Reform and Control Act (Newton
2008). In 1994, however, amid growing public concern over rising levels
of immigration, Wilson supported the ballot initiative Proposition 187,
which would deny public services to unauthorized immigrants, including
public-school education for children. To mobilize voter support for his
reelection, Wilson ran television advertisements highlighting immigration. One of the ads showed a grainy video of people running across the
US-Mexico border checkpoint with the ominous voice-over "They keep
coming." Political communications such as these and Governor Wilson's
support of Proposition 187 have been argued to have been important factors in his successful reelection (Nicholson 2005).

As concern over immigration has moved onto the national agenda,
political candidates across the country are expected to take positions on
immigration. In 2008 immigration was considered a powerful issue to
mobilize voters, so much so that most candidates vying for their party's
nomination, including then senator Barack Obama, made immigration a
core policy issue. Colorado congressman Tom Tancredo centered his bid

for the Republican nomination on the issue of immigration and border security. In a campaign advertisement later dubbed "Someone Needs to Say It," the self-described "border hawk" linked immigration and terrorism.[1] In this ad, a hooded figure with a backpack is seen walking, with the sound of a clock ticking loudly in the background. The ad ends with a black screen reading, "Before it's too late," accompanied by the sound of a bomb exploding.

In this chapter, we consider how public opinion on immigration is influenced by political elites and political communication. How competing candidates frame issues and the images they use to prime voters can drastically change the contours of debate over policy. Political campaigns are in many ways battles over creating the most convincing message (Chong and Druckman 2007). Political scientists know that individuals' attitudes on issues are based on their experiences and personal predispositions, but people are also systematically influenced by political communications. To motivate fear or threat, politicians can make linkages between immigration and national security. Alternatively, activists can emphasize fairness and opportunity in order to mobilize support for more open immigration policies. Individual attitudes toward immigration policy can be strongly influenced by competing messages that encourage individuals to prioritize some values over others.

In the contemporary debate over immigration policy reform, two characteristics of immigrants are often highlighted: residency status and racial background. Concerns about these issues are not new to the nation, and they continue to stir controversy in American politics. Unauthorized immigration has been identified as a national problem ever since the United States began placing numeric quotas on the number of immigrants allowed into the country, starting with the 1882 Chinese Exclusion Act (Ngai 2004). Moreover, the process of racial othering has been applied to all waves of immigrants, including those from southern and eastern Europe in the early twentieth century (M. Jacobson 1999; Roediger 2005). In particular, these two factors have been hypothesized to mobilize restrictive attitudes toward immigration, as they are assumed to challenge American assumptions about national membership and belonging (Brader, Valentino, and Suhay 2006; Burns and Gimpel 2000; Nevins 2002; Ngai 2004). However, the view that illegal residence and nonwhite race are perceived as a violation of American values presumes that all Americans hold the same assumptions about national belonging.

Based on the evidence presented the foregoing chapters, we posit that racial groups will respond very differently to political messages on immigration policy.

The evidence presented in this chapter shows that whites and racial minorities do respond to messages that highlight illegality or race in systematically different ways. This further demonstrates how consequential the racial hierarchy is in individual attitude formation. The racial hierarchy leads members of racial groups to develop their own views and assumptions about membership in the United States polity. Because racial groups differ in their baseline assumptions, the relevant considerations that are triggered by a political appeal will vary systematically. We thus cannot assume that a given political message will activate consistent responses across groups. In order to make reliable predictions of how a political communication strategy will work, social-scientific theories must first acknowledge how the racial hierarchy structures the baseline assumptions that are implicitly communicated in a political appeal. Theories on the role of political communication must provide a more exact match between the message of the political appeal and who constitutes the targeted audience.

Communication Strategies and the Formation of Public Opinion

In our everyday lives we witness how others make firm decisions or confidently express an opinion about a particular event. In this way, we expect a person's political attitudes to reflect a clear and consistent set of preferences. However, as any review of American elections would suggest, American preferences can change. Political leaders, public laws, and governing processes change with shifts in American attitudes. Political scientists know that, in reality, individual opinion about a political issue is malleable. This is because an individual's political position on an issue is often influenced by external sources of information or by a convincing argument. As John Zaller (1992) explains, there are two important components to attitude formation: the "information to form a mental picture of the given issue, and predisposition to motivate some conclusion about it" (6). This perspective leads us, on the one hand, to be optimistic about the human capacity to learn and compromise: political attitudes can change for the better when there is new information that leads a person to reconsider his or her position. However, on the other hand, it also means that opinion can be shaped by a convincing message that has been strategically developed to generate support for a particular political cause. It is in reference to this second perspective that we develop the ideas in this chapter.

"Politics in a democratic society," as succinctly described by Sniderman and Theriault (2004), "is distinctively the domain in which choices are contestable legitimately . . . [and] political preferences are contestable because choices necessarily must be made between competing values" (140). All public policies, including issues related to immigration, can generate competing interests. Some individuals see that they may benefit from a new policy, and others will immediately see what they can lose. Since governing decisions ultimately require the support of the public, competing interest groups, political parties, and elected officials all engage in political campaigns to generate support among voters for their own position. Because of this, the public is exposed to many different ways of looking at a policy. Because voters are not experts on every proposed policy, messages produced to mobilize support for a particular position can strongly influence individual opinion formation.

In general, scholars have identified two primary communications strategies employed by political elites and the media to mold public opinion, which have been labeled as "framing" and "priming." The distinction between framing and priming is subtle but important. Politicians employ framing by emphasizing those values or perceptions deemed most important to evaluating a policy (Druckman 2010). An issue frame is powerful because it provides "a central organizing idea or story line that provides meaning to an unfolding strip of events, weaving a connection among them. The frame suggests what the controversy is about, the essence of the issue" (Gamson and Modigliani 1987, 143). Framing is a useful tool for political elites because it helps direct focus to a particular value that makes a particular position more compelling. A common frame in today's immigration debate is the emphasis on "illegal" immigration. As we outline below, by emphasizing the distinction between "legal" and "illegal," politicians direct attention to the values of fairness, importance of law, and protection of national identity as justification for more punitive immigration policies.

Priming, on the other hand, occurs when politicians or media call "attention to some matters while ignoring others" (Kinder and Iyengar 1989, 63; see also Valentino 1999). Priming encourages individuals to think of certain characteristics or attributes as more relevant than others. Priming is often most powerful because it can activate what is considered implicit thinking or the more subtle and sometimes subconscious thoughts held by individuals. Social characteristics are connected to certain values, ideas, or emotions (Conover 1984). When an individual is primed to think about a particular characteristic, certain responses are also activated, such as positive or negative affect or an emotional response such as fear. Through priming, elites can activate predictable responses by emphasizing characteristics that they know will generate other implicit responses. To be sure, there are many individual-level characteristics such as age or occupation that affect Americans' evaluation of immigrants. However, immigrants' racial background is arguably more politically consequential to the formation of attitudes about immigration, given the controversies and tensions surrounding race in the United States. By providing cues evoking immigrants' racial background, politicians seek to make race one of the first considerations the public relies upon when making decisions about immigration policy.

Although framing and priming are distinct processes, evidence has found that both have similar effects on the formation of political attitudes in that they do become incorporated into how individuals think and talk about issues. Studies on framing show that people will adopt and employ frames presented by political elites (Gamson 1992; Druckman and Nelson 2003; Druckman et al. 2010). Gamson and Modigliani's (1987) study on affirmative action shows that frames emphasizing undeserved advantage and reverse discrimination today are commonly used to reject the policy. Furthermore, the classic study on the media by Iyengar and Kinder (1987) shows close correspondence between issues primed by the media and issues listed by viewers as extremely important. Recent studies also confirm that in addition to influencing the public's stance on an issue, politicians can also mobilize emotions, predispositions, or concerns through the use of priming. For example, research on implicit racial appeals show that white racial resentment is activated when whites are exposed to political appeals that prime the audience to think about blacks (Mendelberg 2001; Henry and Sears 2002).[2]

The Racial Hierarchy and Political Appeals

While the influence of framing and priming on the formation of public opinion is well documented, the reliability of framing and priming effects across the entire voting public has come into question. One of the perceived strengths of framing and priming is the ability of both strategies to influence attitudes across the electorate in predictable directions. Evidence tells us, however, that racial groups vary in their responses to political appeals. One reason differences in the effect of framing and priming on different races have been overlooked is that these communication strategies are traditionally assumed to function at a basic cognitive level by constraining the possible choices made available to individuals. As such, variation in how individuals respond to framing and priming is explained primarily by theories of cognition. But what is often overlooked is that the choices offered by these strategies are strongly informed by political culture and surrounding context. How a respondent chooses to interpret those choices is thus not only a matter of cognition but is also influenced by the cultural assumptions highlighted by a political appeal. This is most apparent in cross-national comparisons. As a simple example, say a message alludes to party competition. In the United States, Americans will automatically refer to their two-party system. In contrast, Western Europeans will likely assume a more complex multiparty system.

Thus, even if all cognitive factors are held constant, individuals from different groups may systematically respond differently to a political message because they hold different assumptions about their social world. These assumptions lead individuals to interpret the intent of a political message in unique ways. Individuals' assumptions vary because they exist in different contexts. This means that, aside from cognition, another key factor that moderates how individuals respond to framing and priming is social context. But while context is widely recognized to vary across nations, we argue that social hierarchies also lead members of the same nation to occupy unique contexts (see Philpot and White 2010). When individuals are ordered along a social hierarchy, social status determines how each person experiences social interactions and other processes. Indeed, in previous chapters we demonstrate the systematically distinct assumptions each racial group holds. The context informed by each group's placement in the racial hierarchy strongly informs perceptions of national membership and group identity. Placement in the hierarchy also informs how groups view others. Our analysis of stereotyping shows that in-group favoritism is exercised the strongest by those ranked at the top of the hierarchy.

Although we may expect racial groups to respond differently to communication strategies, studies testing the varying effects of framing and priming across racial groups are limited in number. Most studies in both political science and psychology test only white respondents. However, Ismail White's (2007) analysis of the different effects of racial appeals on white and black respondents is particularly informative about the moderating role of the racial hierarchy.[3] Racial appeals include political strategies that employ "the race card" and messages that highlight racial differences in order to generate perceptions of threat. However, as White indicates, racial appeals primarily highlight the deficiencies of blacks with the intent of generating white racial resentment. White's experimental tests showed that explicit racial appeals that directly connected blacks with a political issue were found to activate positive ingroup identification among black respondents. But, consistent with previous findings, White found that implicit racial appeals activated racial resentment among whites.

These opposing results between white and black respondents found by White encourage us to develop two important perspectives for developing a more detailed theory about the effects of framing and priming. First, before generating hypotheses about the effects of a message, scholars must pay attention to the intended audience of the message. Political elites and the media generate communication strategies to mobilize particular groups. Political appeals attempt to tap into deeply held assumptions and values of the targeted audience. Second, scholars must be aware that, because racial groups hold different assumptions about how society operates, a political appeal may have the unintended effect of mobilizing the opposite response among racial populations other than the targeted group. These unintended effects may have severe political consequences. Take, for example, the political landscape of California, which is now a majority "minority" population. While Wilson's 1994 advertisements described in the introduction of this chapter worked as expected on the native-born white electorate, they were interpreted quite differently by the Latino population. Latinos became staunchly Democratic in the state after 1994, and the California Republican Party has been unable to reverse that trend since. Today, Latinos make up nearly one-third of the California population, which may further doom Republican political power in the state (Pantoja, Ramirez, and Segura 2001).

We should expect there to be differences in framing and priming effects on different races in some instances but not all. It is not an inherent rule that racial groups will respond differently to political messages. White's attention to racial appeals was purposeful because the particular values and assumptions highlighted in racial appeals represent those that will cause racial-group responses to diverge. Racial appeals work because they imply to the targeted audience that certain groups are deviating from what are considered important values and behaviors. But while the values and behaviors held in esteem by one group might be assumed to be shared by all, they are in reality strongly affected by the racial hierarchy. The racial hierarchy informs the desirability of many values and behaviors. Behaviors understood to be socially desirable are assumed to be practiced by the dominant group in the racial hierarchy. For example, laziness is assumed to be a trait of low-ranked groups in the hierarchy, while hard work is an assumed trait of those ranked at the top of the hierarchy. Secondly, many of the most esteemed American norms, such as individualism, disregard the existence of a racial hierarchy. These norms tend to assume that there is equality in individual agency. Personal success, for example, is assumed to be a direct result of self-sufficiency and industriousness because there are no identified structural barriers that restrain action. This is true for those ranked at the top of the hierarchy, but for those ranked at the bottom of the racial hierarchy, individual lives are heavily structured. So while individualism may be perceived as important, racial minorities personally witness that it does not apply equally to all. Those who recognize the inequalities that exist in these norms are less likely to feel threatened or disappointed if those norms are violated.

Therefore, to understand the influence of political messages on individual attitude formation, we must recognize the role of racial hierarchy on both sides of communication. In messages employed by elites to mold public opinion, we find that the structure of the racial hierarchy is strongly implied in the content of a message. Elites often attempt to mobilize feelings of outrage, resentment, or threat by highlighting how a certain group violates cherished values embraced by the target audience. However, those implied norms are often used to uphold the existing social hierarchy. We must remember that political communications serve strategic purposes, and political elites draft their messages so that they resonate most among the target audience. Often the target audience is not the entire public but a very specific subpopulation. On the receiving end of the message, the racial hierarchy informs individuals' perceptions about society and politics. A political message will be consumed differently by each racial group because each group's perspective is structured by that group's position in the racial order.

As the examples in the introduction of this chapter suggest, framing and priming are often used to mobilize restrictive responses to immigration. In the remainder of this chapter, we examine two common communications strategies that have been employed in recent years: framing immigrants as "illegal" as opposed to "legal" and priming respondents to pay attention to the (nonwhite) racial background of new immigrants. Each strategy is assumed to have strong and predictable effects on mobilizing negative attitudes toward immigrants. Narratives that emphasize illegality in their framing direct attention away from considering immigrants as productive and desirable new members of the nation and toward thinking about immigrants as criminals. Illegal immigrants are presented as individuals who violate American norms of what is fair and lawful. As an example of priming, highlighting the nonwhite backgrounds of new immigrants is a strategy used to activate ethnocentrism or racism. By priming respondents to think of immigrants as nonwhite, political appeals remind respondents that they are inherently different and of an undesirable race.

In the two studies described below, we aim to demonstrate that political messages intended to generate restrictive attitudes toward immigration are not effective for influencing the opinion of all racial groups. We posit that communication strategies that seek to mobilize restrictive attitudes about immigration are explicitly lobbying for maintenance of the status quo. Immigrants cause changes to existing society that are perceived to be undesirable. To tap into this, communication strategies highlight why or how immigrants change society by implicating the racial hierarchy. Therefore, we expect to find that the group who enjoys the most benefits from that hierarchy, whites, are those most easily influenced by these strategies. White respondents will report more restrictive attitudes toward immigration in response to frames of illegality and to racial priming. In contrast, racial minorities, whose status remains marginalized because of the hierarchy, are all less subject to these strategies.

Framing: Examining Differences in Attitudes toward "Illegal" Immigration

The choice to use the term "illegal" to frame those immigrants who arrive without visas is an explicit political attempt to conjure specific norms of fairness, legal justice, and equality (Nevins 2002).[4] These norms at first glance may appear to be universally desirable and race-neutral values. If all Americans are assumed to value these norms, then the illegal-immigration frame could be expected to effectively mobilize restrictive immigration attitudes among all Americans, regardless of their race. However, the assumption that American law has been and continues to be color-blind is far from the truth. Legal historians have long pointed out that preferences to maintain white supremacy serve as clear motivations in codified law. Examples ranging from the early framers' decision to continue slavery to the modern legal decisions upholding racial segregation demonstrate how the law has not equally protected all Americans. Like other sectors of law, immigration policy and rules governing entry and abode have been created to help maintain the racial hierarchy in the United States. Before turning to our analysis of survey data, we first review how "illegality" has been constructed in the United States. This review will help inform our expectations of how racial groups will react to frames emphasizing illegal immigration.

The Construction of the "Illegal Alien"

The legal-illegal distinction is a relatively modern one for Americans. It began when the US government first placed quotas on the number of immigrants entering the country after the 1924 National Origins Act.[5] Over the last century, the distinction between legal and illegal immigration has arguably become a dominant one in the minds of Americans. Public outcry against illegal immigration is thought to have peaked in the early 1990s (Newton 2008). It was in this period that the federal government began to implement new policies targeting illegal immigration such as Operation Gatekeeper in 1994 and the Illegal Immigration Reform and Immigrant Responsibility Act in 1996. In this cultural movement toward a legal-illegal distinction, legal immigrants are often assumed to be an acceptable and welcomed subset of immigrants. Legal immigrants are "lawful" residents because they were officially authorized to enter the country. Illegal immigrants are "lawbreakers" who have entered without government authorization and thus do not deserve to be present in the country (see Bosniak 2006; Nevins 2010; Schrag 2011).

Because illegality is the result of immigration restrictions, we must remember that there was a clear racial component to how quotas were assigned in these policies. All the major restrictionist measures implemented through the twentieth century sought to exclude specific racial or national-origin groups from entering the country. Indeed, immigration restriction was used by the federal government to maintain a particular Anglo-Saxon racial makeup of the United States. Immigrants who were unauthorized to enter the United States were defined by their racial and ethnic background. Thus, from the beginning, the American construction of illegality involved obvious concerns about race. Any illegal immigrant who resided in the United States was, by definition of the law, racially undesirable. Even eastern and southern Europeans who were excluded through immigration restriction were deemed to derive from white races inferior to that of the Anglo-Saxon white majority (M. Jacobson 1998; Roediger 2005).

However, the strongly negative reactions we often find encouraged against illegal immigration are not simply rooted in the racial dimension of immigration policy. The term "illegal" is used to denote those engaging in criminal behavior. Ngai (2004) argues that it is through the *implementation* of restrictionist immigration policies that the state cultivates a correspondence between illegal immigration and criminal behavior in general. Once immigration restrictions were outlined, they required surveillance and policing in order to uphold the policy. At first, immigration officers were required to maintain quotas by denying entry to those without a visa. But as the number of migrants who failed to follow quota procedures increased, efforts to capture and deport those migrants also expanded. Patrolling that originally occurred along the border began to spread into the interior of the country as agents began to search for illegal immigrants who had already entered the country. Persistent media portrayals of policing activities that culminate in the apprehension and arrest of illegal immigrants have effectively encoded a clear correspondence between illegal immigrants and other criminals, such as thieves and murderers, within the minds of Americans (Abrajano and Singh 2009). As a result, illegal immigrants are likely to induce the same negative affect that most Americans feel toward violent criminals (see Ono and Sloop 2002).

Rising public concern about illegal immigration also corresponds with changing American norms about race. Early restrictionist policies were explicitly racialized through the national-origin quotas. However, immigration and citizenship law changed in the wake of civil rights policies that sought to combat racial inequities. Changes made in the 1965 Immigration and Nationality Act shifted restriction from being based on national origin to a preference system based on merit and the immigrant's perceived economic contribution. These changes in immigration law aligned with the new race-neutral message American officials sought to promote. Today, immigrants cannot be excluded on the basis of their race but because they do not meet the educational and economic requirements set by law. Legal immigrants thus are deemed as deserving because they hold what Americans have deemed desirable characteristics, but illegal immigrants are not because they have been denied a legal visa. Thus illegal immigration provides a socially acceptable and race-neutral context in which to discuss immigration restrictions.

It should also be noted that while policy makers attempted to make the 1965 norms racially neutral, contemporary immigration policy continues to create racial biases in migration patterns. Those who are deemed meritorious because they meet the educational and economic requirements are eligible for a legal visa. Most commonly, these migrants who are eligible for a legal visa reside in developed nations such as Canada as well as areas in Europe and Asia (Department of Homeland Security 2011; see also Junn 2007). Those who do not meet the high socioeconomic status requirements for legal entry must turn to other strategies in order to enter the United States. Today's immigration law, in conjunction with existing American economic demands, has created a growing illegal Latino (or more specifically Mexican) labor class in the country. The Department of Homeland Security estimates that most unauthorized migrants today arrive from Mexico (Hoefer, Rytina, and Baker 2012). As a result, many would argue that in the contemporary era, illegal immigration is publicly perceived to be Latino. Today, research has demonstrated that the concepts "Latino," "illegal," and "criminal" are strongly interconnected in the American mind (Perez 2010).

Expected racial-group differences on
restrictiveness toward illegal immigration

Relatively little systematic research has been conducted on the legal-illegal distinction in the context of contemporary American public opinion. However, public opinion surveys that do include questions on the difference between illegal and legal immigration demonstrate overwhelming rejection of illegal immigration. Figure 6.1 compares trends we collected for three versions of the question on decreasing immigration: attitudes about legal immigration, attitudes about illegal immigration, and

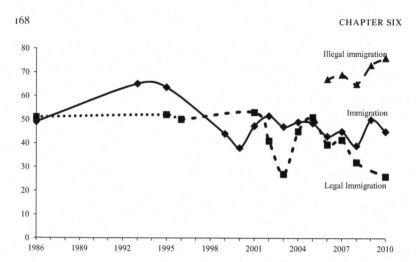

FIGURE 6.1. Proportion supporting decrease immigration by type of immigrants, 1986–2010. *Source*: Gallup iPOLL database.

the standard wording that asks about overall immigration (in which the question makes no distinction between legal and illegal immigration).[6] This figure shows that preference for decreased illegal immigration is the strongest among preferences for decrease legal, illegal, or legally unspecified immigration. Attitudes about overall and legal immigration demonstrate similar trends, with national support for decreasing overall immigration hovering around 50% since 2000. National trends, however, mask any diversity found within the general population.

We expect that the normative distinctions between legal and illegal immigration will be more important to whites than racial minority groups. The creation of what we know now as "illegal" immigration is the result of restrictive immigration policies that originally sought to exclude those perceived as racially undesirable from entering the United States. Illegal status has historically been applied to groups considered nonwhite (Ngai 2005). More important, the link between illegal immigration and criminality has effectively framed illegal immigration as a violation of cherished American norms of respect for institutions and fairness. As discussed above, those ranked at the top of the racial hierarchy are those who benefit the most from established laws and norms. Therefore, whites have the strongest desire to uphold those norms. The distinction between illegal and legal immigration will not only matter most to whites, but we expect whites to be the group that responds most negatively to illegal immigration.

We anticipate that the distinction between legal and illegal immigration will matter less to racial minority groups. The illegality frame, which implies a violation of norms, will not resonate as strongly among groups who recognize that many American laws and values do not equally apply to them. We argue that if a racial minority holds restrictive attitudes toward immigration, their level of restrictiveness is not influenced by the distinction between legal and illegal immigration. Rather, for racial minorities, restrictive immigration attitudes are generally applied to all types of immigrants. However, given our theory that those minority groups ranked at relatively higher levels on the hierarchy hold stronger desires to uphold the status quo than those groups ranked at the bottom, we expect that illegal-immigration frames will also have varying effects across minority groups. Asian Americans, who are ranked toward the top of the hierarchy, will be more likely influenced by a legal-illegal distinction, since they are more likely to uphold the status quo. In contrast, blacks, who have a historical memory of racially biased laws, are least likely to see a difference between legal and illegal immigration.

Finally, we must take into account the fact that modern frames of illegal immigration have been used primarily to attack Latino immigration. The association between "Latino" and "illegal" may be obvious enough that frames that emphasize illegal immigration likely appear to Latinos as an attack on their racial group. The mechanism that explains Latino response to illegal immigration will be distinct from that which explains responses of other racial groups. Following White's (2007) hypothesis on racial appeals, those appeals that activate an in-group identity will mobilize positive attitudes toward the message. Therefore we expect that illegal-immigration frames may activate Latino identity and that Latinos are likely to respond more positively to illegal immigration than other groups.

Examining attitudes toward legal and illegal immigration

In this data analysis, we take the first step toward examining the effect of the illegality frame on public opinion about immigration by examining survey items from the 2006 Pew Immigration Survey (Kohut et al. 2006).[7] This survey included a large battery of questions regarding illegal immigration as well as questions about immigration in general. This survey included a nationally representative sample with oversamples of black and Latino respondents. Unfortunately, the sample size of Asian

American respondents ($n = 30$) was too small for us to assess here. But, to our knowledge, this 2006 Pew study represents the only publicly available survey that offers systematic analysis of attitudes on illegal immigrant among nonwhite respondents. The 2006 Pew study offers the opportunity to assess attitudes toward illegal immigrant restriction as well as support for various policy proposals involving illegal immigration.

Because we are examining responses to survey questions on illegal immigration, we cannot identify a direct causal relationship between communication strategies and immigration attitudes in this study. Rather, since our data for this study is a cross-sectional public opinion poll, our analysis can only capture the respondents' immediate or "top of the head" response to illegal immigration. Given the range of survey items available in the 2006 Pew study, we can compare support for relatively lenient policies toward illegal immigrants, such as social welfare provisions, and support for more punitive policies, such as denying birthright citizenship to children of illegal immigrants, in order to compare the degree of restrictiveness toward illegal immigration preferred by different racial groups. Assessing survey responses to illegal immigration in this manner provides us with the baseline attitudes held by the public before manipulation by political communications. More extensive analyses using alternative strategies such as embedded experiments will be required in order to assess how restrictive attitudes might change in response to political communication strategies.[8]

Attitudes about illegal immigration

Respondents in the Pew study were first asked to think about illegal immigration when they were asked by interviewers to compare the problems associated with legal and illegal immigration. When asked what type of immigrants are a bigger problem for the United States, legal or illegal, few respondents believed legal immigration to be the bigger problem. The majority of all respondents believed that illegal immigration was the bigger problem. This is consistent with the growing national attention to the legal-illegal divide that has occurred over the last few decades. The data here confirm that the persistent political frames that emphasize the legal-illegal distinction in immigration have been embraced by the American public. Yet, when comparing responses to this question across racial groups, we do find group differences, as shown in figure 6.2.[9] Whites were overwhelmingly (66%) concerned about illegal

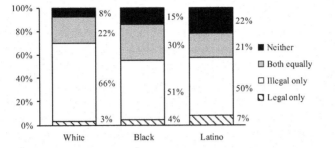

FIGURE 6.2. Distribution of responses on type of immigration as bigger problem by race.
Source: Pew Immigration Survey.

immigrants, whereas approximately half of black and Latino adults were most concerned with illegal immigration. A larger share of black respondents than white respondents perceived both legal and illegal immigration to be a problem, suggesting that the legal-illegal distinction may not resonate as strongly among blacks as it does for other groups. Latinos represent the group with the largest share of respondents who perceive neither legal nor illegal immigration to be a problem.

It is plausible that the group-level differences in responses to this question may be the result of some biases in the sample population. Racial-group differences on this survey item may not be attributed to race but rather to some other variation between groups, such as educational level. To determine whether attitudes on this illegal-immigration question do, in fact, vary by race and not some other individual characteristic, we conducted multivariate analyses.[10] We found that, even when demographics such as age, education, gender and the respondent's political ideology are controlled for, there were significant differences by race.[11] Both blacks and Latinos are more likely than whites to perceive neither legal nor illegal immigration to be a problem. Blacks were also more likely than whites to believe both legal and illegal immigration are problems. Thus blacks are less likely than whites to emphasize a distinction between legal and illegal immigration. Latinos are also more likely than whites to perceive neither legal nor illegal immigration to be a problem. However, we find no significant differences between blacks and Latinos in response to this question.

To further investigate this finding, we compare racial-group response to various policy proposals addressing perceived problems related to illegal immigration. The list of policy proposals asked about by Pew is not exhaustive. The policies Pew does ask about, however, represent a realistic sample of those policies most commonly discussed by political leaders over the last few years. Our goal is not to assess perspectives about every dimension of illegal-immigration policy but rather to compare the degree of restrictiveness or willingness to support more punitive measures across racial groups. Table 6.1 presents the questions about

TABLE 6.1. **Distribution of Attitudes on Policies Addressing Illegal Immigration**

	% Favor		
	White	Black	Latino
Should illegal immigrants be required to go home, or should they be granted some kind of legal status that allows them to stay here?			
Required to go home	59	47	19
Allowed to stay	33	47	77
Would you favor or oppose creating a new government database of everyone eligible to work—both American citizens and legal immigrants—and requiring employers to check that database before hiring someone for ANY kind of work?	66	72	61
Would you favor or oppose requiring everyone seeking a new job to have a new kind of driver's license or Social Security card that proves they are US citizens or are in the country legally?	79	78	61
Should illegal immigrants who are in the US be eligible for social services provided by state and local governments?	20	43	64
Should the children of illegal immigrants who are in the US be permitted to attend public schools, or don't you think so?	67	79	93
Which of the following actions do you think would be MOST effective in reducing the number of illegal immigrants who come to the US across the Mexican border			
Increasing number of border patrol agents	33	32	34
Building more fences on the border	9	7	12
Increasing penalties on employers who hire illegal immigrants	52	51	28
Would you favor changing the Constitution so that the parents must be legal residents of the US in order for their newborn child to be a citizen, or should the Constitution be left as it is?	46	36	23

Source: Pew Immigration Survey

illegal-immigration policies asked by Pew. In general, most policy proposals involving illegal immigrants involve the removal of rights from those immigrants. However, we can also recognize that some are more retributive than others. Some policy proposals involve wrongdoing by nonimmigrants, such as employer sanctions. Others present extremely restrictive measures such as the denial of birthright citizenship to children of undocumented immigrants.

Responses to illegal-immigration policies are quite varied. While some policy proposals result in clear differences across all three racial groups, others do not. There do, however, appear to be clear differences in opinion between Latinos and the other two racial groups. For example, only 20% of white adults support providing social services to immigrants, and nearly half (46%) support changing the Constitution to deny citizenship status to children of illegal immigrants. By contrast, 64% of Latino adults support providing social services, and only 23% support changing the Constitution. Interestingly, when it comes to providing rights and social services, Blacks attitudes fall squarely in the middle between whites and Latinos. When it comes to verifying legal status, all three groups overwhelmingly support identification policies such as identification cards and eligible-worker databases. Whites and blacks also report similar opinions on the best method to reduce illegal immigrants: slightly over half of both white and black adults support employer sanctions, while Latinos appear to be split over the viability of the proposed options.

Because there were so many policies covered in the 2006 Pew study, we created an index variable that added together responses to the policy proposals presented in table 6.1.[12] For this index, we counted the total number of restrictive responses, or those that were directly aimed at restricting behavior of illegal immigrants. Those who were strongly opposed to illegal immigration are those more likely to take the restrictive position on more of these policies. Moreover, since the policies included in the survey represent a range of disciplinary measures, those with higher scores on the index variable reflect those who would be more likely to support more punitive actions toward illegal immigrants.

Since we seek to identify and compare the degree of restrictiveness against illegal immigrants across racial groups, we examine the distribution of responses on the illegal-immigration policy index. A comparison of the distributions for each of the three racial groups is displayed in figure 6.3. We find that the distributions of both white and black respon-

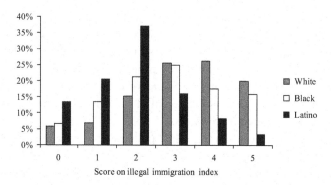

FIGURE 6.3. Distribution of responses on illegal immigration policy index by race. *Source*: Pew Immigration Survey.

dents are similar across the index. These two groups' responses were skewed toward the more restrictive end of the index. However, larger shares of whites hold extremely restrictive attitudes toward illegal immigrants (score of 4 or 5 on a scale of 5) than blacks. In contrast, Latino responses were more concentrated at the lower end of the index, or the more inclusive position. By calculating the mean scores on our illegal-immigration index, we find that, consistent with our hypothesis, whites' average score is the highest of all groups: 3.20 on a scale of 0 to 5 (standard deviation = 1.40). Latinos' average score is the lowest of the three groups: 1.95 (standard deviation = 1.26). Blacks' average score falls in the middle of the two groups: 2.81 (standard deviation = 1.46).

To again determine if the differences in these means are attributable directly to race and not to another factor such as education or ideology, we turned to multivariate analysis. We used ordinary least squares regression using our illegal-immigration index as the dependent variable and included race, age, education, income, gender, age, foreign-born status, and political ideology as independent variables.[13] We found that when these factors are taken into consideration, both blacks and Latinos report significantly lower scores on our illegal-immigration index than whites. In other words, whites are more likely to support restrictive and punitive measures against illegal immigrants than both blacks and Latinos. Furthermore, we found that Latinos also score significantly lower on the index than blacks. Our multivariate analysis does verify that even when we assume all else is equal, Latinos demonstrate the most inclusive attitudes toward illegal immigrants of the three racial groups studied here.

The data analysis presented here supports our expectation that the racial hierarchy moderates individual responses to illegal immigration. We find that the legal-illegal distinction is most likely to matter among white respondents. We also find that, while many blacks do see a problem with illegal immigration, blacks are more likely than whites to see no difference between legal and illegal immigration. This provides preliminary support for our claim that illegal-immigration frames, which encourage the belief that immigrants violate cherished norms, are less likely to resonate among blacks. Finally, the evidence does support the idea that illegal-immigration frames mobilize Latino in-group identity. Latinos as a group support the most inclusive policies toward illegal immigration. Latinos' positive responses to suggest that Latinos have positive views on those who are part of their racial group. But since this analysis is exploratory, a more detailed examination is needed in order to fully test this assertion.

Priming: The "Face" of Immigration

One issue dimension that has been used to engage the American public is race. Issues related to race have historically mobilized voting blocs to participate in politics in order to protect their interests. As we noted above, the racial-appeals hypothesis suggests that political elites can manipulate public opinion by linking social deviance of racial minorities to a particular issue or policy (Mendelberg 2001). By priming the audience to think about the racial background of those affected by the proposed policy, elites seek to activate racist thinking or resentment. Research has found that when resentment is activated, whites are more likely to support proposed punitive policy solutions to a problem (Entman and Rojecki 2000. Hurwitz and Peffley 2005; Valentino et al. 2002). As a result, racial appeals are assumed to have robust and predictable effects in mobilizing negative responses from white voters. The racial-appeals hypothesis has been applied recently to issues of immigration policy. Brader, Valentino, and Suhay's (2008) extensive test of the racial-appeals hypothesis on immigration attitudes confirmed that white respondents voice stronger opposition to immigration when primed to think about Latino immigrants than when they are primed to think about European immigrants.

Racial-appeals strategies are assumed to be powerful because they are believed to activate automatic stereotyping (Devine 1989). In controlled environments where individuals have enough time to process information, they can often control how they apply negative stereotypes and prejudice. However, since racial stereotypes are deeply embedded in society, people will be prone to apply those stereotypes in relevant situations. Racial appeals present negative stereotypes in such convincing ways that these messages encourage unintended reliance on those stereotypes. However, as we demonstrate in chapter 3, the tendency to apply stereotypes is determined by one's position in the racial hierarchy. Those at the top of the hierarchy are likely to apply only positive traits to one's own in-group and primarily negative traits to out-groups. In contrast, those groups at the bottom of the hierarchy are less likely to engage in negative stereotyping of out-groups. Thus, it is questionable whether priming racial minorities to think about nonwhite groups will activate automatic negative stereotyping. As White (2007) notes, if the recipient matches the race of the target in a racial appeal, then those appeals can have the opposite effect. Racial appeals may prime positive in-group identities if the appeal primes the respondent to think of his or her own racial group.

Expected differences in priming effects across racial groups

We argue that racial appeals can have predictable effects on activating negative thinking about race, but only for those in the targeted audience for which that appeal was designed. The racial-appeals hypothesis requires more explicit recognition of the match between the racial group used in the appeal and the race of the audience. Priming the audience to think about a nonwhite group will likely generate negative racial thinking only among whites. The same appeal should be expected to have systematically different effects on racial minorities.

In the context of immigration, we expect that priming the audience to think about nonwhite groups entering the United States will encourage more restrictive views among whites. The finding of Brader, Valentino, and Suhay (2008) will thus be replicable in other studies. Based on theories connecting power and stereotyping reviewed in chapter 3 (Fiske 1993), we argue that because whites rank at the top of the hierarchy, they are prone to negatively stereotype lower-ranked racial groups. Whites' stereotyping is directly attributed to their structural position at the top of the hierarchy: as the most powerful and high-status group, they can be more reliant on schematic thinking, as there are few incentives to pay detailed attention to lower-status groups. Whites' ranking at the top of the hierarchy also means that they are most invested in maintaining the racial hierarchy. Therefore, whites are most likely to attribute positive stereotypes to the higher-ranked groups and negative stereotypes to lower-ranked groups.

For the group ranked at the bottom of the hierarchy, blacks, racial primes that highlight the nonwhite background of immigrants will not automatically mobilize restrictive immigration attitudes. Consistent with our discussion of stereotyping, blacks are less likely to apply negative traits to out-groups. Thus, priming blacks to think about nonwhite groups will not necessarily trigger negative stereotyping. Because blacks are ranked at the bottom of the hierarchy, they are encouraged to pay greater attention to detail rather than be reliant on schematic thinking. For blacks, it is unlikely that race alone will mobilize restrictive attitudes. More information about those immigrant groups will be needed in order to generate perceptions of group threat among blacks.

The effect of racial priming on Asian American and Latino attitudes is expected to correspond to each group's relative position on the racial hierarchy. Since Asian Americans are ranked closer to the top of the hierarchy, racial priming will have an effect on Asian American attitudes on immigration as similar to its effect on white attitudes. We anticipate that because the racial hierarchy gives advantage to Asian Americans, they will seek to uphold that hierarchy. We can expect that, like whites, Asian Americans will attribute positive stereotypes to higher-ranked groups and negative stereotypes to lower-ranked groups. In contrast, since Latinos rank closer to the bottom of the hierarchy, alongside blacks, we expect racial primes to have effects on Latino attitudes on immigration similar to its effect on black attitudes. However, because Asian Americans and Latinos share the same racial categories as the majority of today's new immigrants, it is also likely that racial priming in the context of immigration will highlight in-group racial identities for Asian Americans and Latinos. Therefore, we anticipate Asian and Latino respondents to report more positive attitudes toward immigrants when they are primed to think of their own group.

Experimental design: testing priming effects

To examine how priming the race of the immigrant may influence public opinion, we turn to experimental design. One of the difficulties of study-

ing how the race of the immigrant might affect attitudes is that researchers are uncertain whom a respondent is picturing when asked a question
about "immigrants." Experimental design, which controls the information offered to the respondent, provides us with the most effective way of
determining the direct connection between the specific race of the immigrant and a respondent's evaluation of immigration. In our 2006 Faces of
Immigration Survey, we included an embedded survey experiment that
allowed us to determine how the race of the immigrant may influence attitudes. In these experiments our goal was simply to prime respondents
to think about those immigrants as a particular racial group before responding to questions about immigration and immigration policy.

For this experiment, we employed a split-third design in which respondents were randomly assigned to receive one of three conditions. As part
of the treatment, all respondents were shown the caption: "The United
States is experiencing a significant wave of immigration, and more than
10 million people from other countries have entered the United States
since 1996." Those respondents assigned to the Asian-immigrant treatment group were shown a photograph of Asians along with the caption.
Those assigned to the Latino-immigrant treatment group were shown a
picture of Latinos along with the caption. Those assigned to the control
group were provided only the caption, without a photograph.[14] Our strategy was to provide a cue to race and ethnicity by presenting respondents
with photographs of immigrants rather than explicitly asking about a
particular immigrant ethnic group.[15] We selected photographs designed
to prime the respondent to think about a specific racial or ethnic group
but did not communicate a specific negative or positive stereotype about
that group. The immigrants portrayed in our experimental treatment
were not pictured as particularly menacing or aggressive; rather, the photographs depict immigrant families standing in public places. These pho-
tos represent the type of immigrants that native-born Americans would
encounter in their daily lives.[16] Our goal was to vary only the race of the
immigrants, not to encourage respondents to think of particular stereotypes. We selected these manipulations because our goal was not to activate automatic negative affect about immigrants but to see how attitudes
might shift if respondents were primed to think of particular groups entering the country.[17]

After viewing the treatment, respondents were then asked to share
their attitudes on immigration policy. Our dependent variable is the
standard question asked in a public opinion survey, which asks respon-

dents whether they felt the number of immigrants to the United States should be increased, reduced, or kept the same. We coded this measure on a range of 0 to 1, with the preference for reducing immigration "a lot" representing the highest value. To analyze the effect of the treatment, we calculated the average responses for each treatment group on our three dependent variables. Since respondents were randomly assigned to a treatment group, we can identify priming effects by comparing how the mean responses to the question differ across treatment groups and across racial groups.

With this design, we can test multiple comparisons. First, we can compare responses across treatment groups to examine how changing the face of the immigrant causes shifts in opinion on immigration. The first comparison is between those respondents who received the Asian treatment and those who received the Latino treatment. We chose an Asian and a Latino prime in an attempt to examine how the contemporary racial hierarchy influences evaluation of immigrants. Since Asians are ranked above Latinos on the racial hierarchy, the difference in responses to the two treatment groups will reveal dependence on hierarchical thinking. Second, our data offer us the opportunity to examine how racial priming may have different effects across racial groups. This allows us to test, for example, whether white respondents exposed to the Latino prime report more restrictive attitudes than black respondents exposed to the same prime.

Finally, this design also allows us to identify the racial "face" of the immigrant that respondents picture when asked to provide their assessments about immigration more broadly. Respondents assigned to the control group were not provided a picture of immigrants and were simply asked to provide their attitudes about immigration. Answers provided by the control group thus likely mirror the attitudes found in other public opinion surveys (who are not primed by researchers to think about a particular racial group). Therefore, by comparing the responses of the treatment groups to the responses of the control group, we can make inferences about the assumptions respondents make about the race of the immigrant. If responses from one treatment are similar to those from the control group, then we can reason that the treatment did not cause respondents to alter their assumptions about the immigrants in question. A treatment that provides the expected image of immigrants will not force respondents to make new considerations that they would not have made otherwise. For example, if there are no significant differences between the responses of those who received the Asian treatment group and those who received the control group, then we can surmise that respondents are likely assuming that the immigrants are Asian when they answer questions about immigration. More likely, given the political emphasis on Latino immigration today, responses from the Latino treatment group will be similar to those in the control group.

Comparing priming effects across racial groups

Table 6.2 provides the mean responses from each treatment group to question about increasing, decreasing, or keeping immigration the same. In order to understand the effect of the treatment correctly, we first identify a baseline for immigration attitudes. To do this, we point to responses among those in the control group because these respondents were unprimed to think about a particular racial group. Focusing first on the results for whites, we find that whites in the control group strongly support decrease in immigration (mean of 0.8 on a scale of 0 to 1). Comparing means across treatment groups, we find that whites who received the Asian treatment report less restrictive attitudes toward immigration. However, mean responses among whites who received the Latino treatment are no different from those in the control group. There are also no significant differences in means between whites in the Asian treatment and those in the Latino treatment.

Like whites, black respondents in the control group strongly support a decrease in immigration (mean of .76 on a scale of 0 to 1). However, the racial primes had different results for black attitudes on immigration than we found for whites. Blacks who were primed to think about either

TABLE 6.2. **Mean Responses to Immigration Measures by Race and Treatment Group**

Race of respondent	Mean for Asian treatment (SD)	Mean for Latino treatment (SD)	Mean for control group (SD)	Diff. in means btwn Asian and control group	Diff. in means btwn Latino and control group	Diff. in means btwn Asian and Latino treatment
Whites	.73 (.24)	.76 (.24)	.8 (.24)	−.07**	−.03	−.03
Blacks	.71 (.24)	.70 (.22)	.76 (.22)	−.05*	−.06*	.01
Asians	.58 (.24)	.54 (.25)	.54 (.27)	.04	.01	.03
Latinos	.68 (.25)	.68 (.26)	.66 (.27)	.02	.02	.003

Source: 2006 Faces of Immigration Survey
*$p< 0.10$
**$p< 0.05$

Asians or Latinos reported less restrictive attitudes on the increase, decrease, or keep immigration the same measure. These experimental results for blacks suggest that racial primes may not have the anticipated effect on black attitudes on immigration. In fact, the results suggest that racial priming can encourage positive attitudes toward immigrants.

While we find priming effects for both white and black respondents, we find almost no priming effects for Asian American and Latino respondents.[18] Asian American respondents in the control group hold relatively inclusive attitudes toward immigration. Asian Americans' mean score on the increase, decrease, or keep immigration the same measure is near the median value, telling us that Asians are more likely to prefer immigration to stay the same rather than be decreased. Latino respondents in the control group also report relatively inclusive views toward immigrants. Latino respondents report slightly more restrictive responses to immigration (mean = 0.66) than Asian Americans (mean = 0.54), but Latinos' average score is still lower than that reported by both whites and blacks in the control group.[19] Interestingly, we find that the experimental treatments have no effect on altering immigration attitudes among either Asian American or Latino respondents. While we anticipated that Asian American and Latino respondents would respond more positively to immigrants of their shared racial group, our experiment shows that this is not the case. Our results suggest that Asian Americans and Latinos hold relatively firm and positive attitudes about immigration and are not influenced by racial priming.

Finally, to test whether racial priming causes higher-ranked racial groups to report more restrictive attitudes than lower-ranked groups, we compare mean differences across racial groups among those who received the same experimental treatment. Focusing first on those respondents who received the Asian immigrant treatment, we find that there are no significant differences between the mean scores of whites and blacks on the question about increasing, decreasing, or keeping immigration the same. However, whites' mean scores are significantly higher than both Asian Americans' and Latinos'.[20] This means that whites primed to think about Asians report more restrictive attitudes than Asian American and Latino respondents who received the same treatment. Asian American respondents who received the Asian treatment report the most positive attitudes toward immigration of all four groups who received the Asian immigrant treatment. However, we find significant differences between whites and blacks among those respondents who received the Latino treatment. We find that, of those who received the Latino treatment, whites' mean score is the highest of all four groups. In other words, whites primed to think about Latinos report the most restrictive attitudes. Interestingly, among those primed to think about Latinos, Asian American respondents report the most positive attitudes toward immigration.

In sum, our experiment confirms that racial priming has the most predictable effect on white attitude formation. Among whites, we found few differences in attitude between those who were primed to think about Latinos and those assigned to the control. This suggests that when whites are asked about immigration, without any reference to race, they assume that the immigrant is Latino. Thus, once we encourage whites to think about racial groups ranked highly on the racial hierarchy, such as Asian Americans, they are more likely to hold more open views toward immigration. Comparing mean responses across racial groups, we find that racial primes are likely to encourage whites to report more restrictive attitudes than racial minorities. Out of all racial groups, whites reported the most restrictive attitudes toward immigrants when primed to think about Latinos.

In contrast, we found evidence to support our hypothesis that for blacks, racial primes do not necessarily activate ethnocentrism or negative affect. We found that while blacks generally report more restrictive attitudes than Asian Americans or Latinos, their attitudes became more inclusive when they were primed to think about Latinos or Asian immigrants. It appears that instead of triggering negative responses, our racial primes humanized immigrants for black respondents. These results also tell us that for blacks, the ranking of the racial group is less likely to alter responses to immigration. For whites, we found different effects between those who received the Asian treatment and those who received the Latino treatment. But for blacks, both racial primes had the same effect.

Finally, our experiment yielded very few significant results from the Asian American and Latino respondents. Given that the two largest immigrant flows into the United States are from Asia and Latin America, we assumed that Asian and Latino respondents would rely on shared social-group identities when forming opinions. So we anticipated that, unlike whites and blacks, who do not perceive a shared racial identity with today's new immigrants, Asian Americans and Latinos would be more likely to respond positively to images of immigrants who share

their racial background. When examining general trends on immigration attitudes, we found that Asians and Latinos indeed hold more positive attitudes toward immigration than whites and blacks. However, we found no indication that racial primes activate positive in-group identity among Asian American or Latino respondents. This may be because of the fact that Asian Americans and Latinos hold generally positive views on immigration, so racial primes do not have an additive effect on their attitudes.

The Racial Prism and Political Communications

Overall, the findings summarized in this chapter tell us that members of different racial groups respond to political communications in different ways. When political elites design an advertisement or write a speech that employs a racial appeal, that appeal will not have the same effect on all audience members unless the audience is racially homogeneous. Members of racial groups hold different assumptions about their social world, which causes each group to respond differently to political stimuli. The findings discussed in this chapter are useful for moving forward in developing more complex theories on political psychology and communications.

Most important, our evidence demonstrates not only that race dictates the starting assumptions individuals hold but also that the racial hierarchy is deeply embedded in the content of those assumptions. The assumption that nonwhite groups activate negative affect assumes that there is a salient racial hierarchy in which whites represent the most desirable group and nonwhites represent the deviant and undesirable groups. Furthermore, cherished norms such as the assumed just nature of American law, merit, and fairness all presume that individuals are treated equally by governing institutions. In reality, many legal and governing institutions have disproportionately disadvantaged many different subpopulations in American society. Those who most desire to uphold the cherished laws and norms are those most protected by those institutions. We thus should expect that messages that directly implicate the racial hierarchy will be interpreted differently by each racial group.

The findings discussed in this chapter have implications not only for the development of academic research on political communications but also about the effectiveness of political ads and messages in American campaigns. These findings provide new insight for candidates running for office in increasingly diversifying districts. Although racial diversity once characterized only a few metropolitan areas, today most areas across the nation are no longer homogenous white districts. Growing minority populations mean that candidates must consider how their communication strategies will work on a diversifying population. Candidates must develop messages that, at minimum, will not explicitly offend these growing voting blocs. Furthermore, new communications technologies and the rise of the twenty-four-hour news cycle also mean that any racial appeal that may have been intended for a limited audience will likely be distributed to a nationwide audience within minutes. Candidates must then combat the counter-mobilization efforts that develop in response to their messages. The most effective strategies for campaigns in a diverse society thus cannot ignore race but rather should directly address the challenges created by the racial hierarchy.

Conclusion

The Politics of Belonging and the Future of US Immigration Policy

The contemporary hue and cry over the number and character of new-comers to the American polity—particularly those in the United States without government authorization—is based in the notion that the circumstances are both alarming and unprecedented. On the flip side, advocates of progressive immigration reform lament the increasing emphasis of federal legislation on border control, criminalization, and "illegality" as indicators of new and virulent racial antipathy. Most people think they live in exceptional times, and to some degree, their perception is correct; circumstances and events that seem extraordinary at a given time are being experienced as de novo. Thus in many ways the claims of a never-before-seen political context provide fertile ground for contemporary advocates of immigration policy reform on both the restrictionist and progressive sides to mobilize supporters by framing the issue in dire terms.

It is true that there were more unauthorized immigrants in the United States than ever before in the decade between 2000 and 2010, even compared to the last great wave of immigration a century ago. But this is only so because the concept of "illegal" immigrant had not yet been invented and codified by the government in the early twentieth century. The famous words of Emma Lazarus inscribed on a plaque at the Statue of Liberty signify a nation open to immigration:

> Give me your tired, your poor,
> Your huddled masses yearning to breathe free,

The wretched refuse of your teeming shore.
Send these, the homeless, tempest-tost to me,
I lift my lamp beside the golden door!
Emma Lazarus, "The New Colossus" (1883)

Hungry to expand westward and for labor to fuel the industrial revolution, the United States during this period had a European immigration
policy that was consistent with Lazarus's welcome of those tired, poor,
and huddled masses of "wretched refuse." Several decades hence, however, with what seemed to be too many immigrants crowding the nation's
cities, politicians cried foul and slammed the door shut to newcomers
with the National Origins Act of 1924. Contemporary characterization
of undesirable immigrants as unable or unwilling to assimilate to American culture, speaking the "language of the ghetto,"[1] or increasing crime
is reminiscent of the political rhetoric used a hundred years ago in support of immigrant restriction.

On the other side of the political spectrum, contemporary advocates
of progressive immigration reform point to the increasing emphasis of
existing federal law and proposed congressional legislation on targeting
immigrants from Latin America and Mexico. They are also correct in
noting that under Democratic president Barack Obama, the US government will deport a record number of people.[2] To advocates of immigrant
rights, this action feels unprecedented, particularly in comparison with
deportations under Obama's immediate predecessor, Republican president George W. Bush. During Bush's eight years in office an estimated
1.6 million people were deported. Acting under the 1996 Illegal Immigration Reform and Immigrant Responsibility Act and enforced by
an army of US Immigration and Customs Enforcement agents, deportation from the United States today is undertaken with explicit federal
statutory authority. While the magnitude of government deportation efforts may be greater today, the "repatriation" of Mexicans and other immigrants considered undesirable is a repeat of earlier government programs such as "Operation Wetback" during the 1950s that forcibly sent
Mexican nationals and US citizens of Mexican origin across the border.

While the American public and the political officials who represent
them may see the present circumstances of high levels of immigration,
large numbers of undocumented immigrants, and stinging racial antipathy against some immigrants as dire, they are certainly not unprecedented. Similar moments of welcome and then retreat into restriction

have characterized US immigration and naturalization policy throughout the history of the nation. Viewing the politics of belonging with a
longer lens reveals a cyclical relationship of welcome and expulsion,
where entrance to the American polity and the right to stay here are a
function of the political context of the time and are conditioned on the
racial categorization of newcomers. Despite the seemingly race-neutral
preference categories set forth in the 1965 Immigration and Nationality
Act, the politics of belonging in the United States today remains rooted
in group categorization and influenced by racial stereotypes.

This book makes the argument that the development of laws, legal
precedents, institutional practices, and the racial taxonomy in the United
States are critical to understanding the context in which the politics of
belonging takes place. Public opinion and political attitudes on immigration and naturalization policy in the United States today cannot be analyzed in the absence of this historical and institutional context. Looking backward to see forward allows analysts to better theorize how the
deeply embedded social structure of racial hierarchy influences individual choices and decisions. In the absence of perspectives accounting for
the systematic influence of social structure and context, explanations of
political behavior and attitudes rely too heavily on individual-level traits
to explain variation. Furthermore, disproportionate attention to the contours and dynamics of political attitudes among whites has narrowed the
vantage point from which one may view the dynamics of race in public
opinion. We take a different approach, explicitly highlighting the significance of the racial hierarchy in assessing individual-level agency. Americans of different races do not have equal agency and are instead systematically constrained by their position in the racial order. Public opinion
on immigration reflects this variation and is moderated at the individual
level through group identity with respect to perceptions of the boundaries of Americanness and a sense of linked fate.

Building on this perspective is our methodological position that analysis of contemporary public opinion in the United States must rely on systematic observation of all Americans. While separate studies of whites
or African Americans are useful in many ways, we argue that in order
to understand the dynamics—past, present, and future—of political attitudes on immigration, all racial groups should be analyzed comparatively
and in relation to one another. We have approached the empirical analysis in this book with these theoretical and methodological imperatives.
The main empirical findings presented in the book follow the progres-

sion in the chapters from the analysis of the development of the American racial hierarchy in chapter 2 through examination of individual-level survey data from the Multi-City Study of Urban Inequality, the Faces of Immigration Survey, the Twenty-First Century Americanism survey, the National Politics Survey, and the Pew 2006 Immigration Survey in chapters 3 through 6.

The historical analysis traces the development of the racial categories of black, white, Asian American, and Latino and emphasizes the institutional foundations of racial-group categorization in the United States. Building on the identification of the diamond shape of the American racial hierarchy as articulated in chapter 1, we review the links between US citizenship policy, territorial expansion, and economic development in the second chapter. Political belonging in America throughout much of the nation's history came with a racial prerequisite and a preference for whiteness. All nonwhite minority groups are not equal, however, and the analysis in chapter 2 highlights the distinct position and context of belonging for each of the four main racial groups today. The legacy of these dynamics of racial exclusion is apparent in the content and everyday application of racial-group stereotypes. In chapter 3, we document the contours of positive and negative group stereotypes for blacks, Latinos, Asian Americans, and whites. The survey data from two different studies confirm the position of the perception of whites at the top of the hierarchy, Asian Americans underneath but closer to whites, and Latinos and African Americans at the bottom of the racial order. While Americans of all racial backgrounds recognize the group stereotypes, there is important variation in the degree to which minority respondents apply them. We argue that stereotypes are the lingua franca by which the American racial hierarchy is expressed, and that group position is at the heart of perceptions of belonging and identification with groups. The analysis of data in chapter 4 confirms our hypotheses that whites—the default racial category defining Americanness—have the highest levels of national identity and relatively low levels of racial-group identity. In contrast, and reflecting their knowledge that they are conditional Americans whose full belonging is moderated by their nonwhite racial status, members of racial minority groups have stronger perceptions of linked fate with other members of their racial group.

The last two empirical chapters build on these foundations of group difference and analyze the contours of public opinion on immigration. In chapter 5 we test our hypotheses that whites, Asian Americans, blacks, and Latinos would exhibit different patterns of support for restrictive policies on immigration as a function of their position in the racial hierarchy and the distinctive moderating impact of group identity on attitudes. The data analysis provides strong support for our model of the Racial Prism of Group Identity. Stronger American identity, measured by the perception of tighter boundaries for characteristics of Americanness, is associated with more support for decreasing the number of immigrants to the United States among members of all racial groups. In contrast, stronger racial-group identity as measured by survey questions on linked fate has the effect of predicting more restrictionist sentiment among whites but more progressive attitudes on immigration among Latinos, Asian Americans, and African Americans. The distinctive moderating impact of racial-group identity on public opinion on immigration between whites and minorities, however, is not the only set of antecedents that vary systematically by race. Our analysis details a different set of both demographic and resource-based characteristics that explain attitude formation across racial groups. Finally, the analysis in chapter 6 supports our hypothesis that racial groups respond in different ways to political communication strategies. Our analysis of the 2006 Pew Immigration Survey data shows that the attitudes of white respondents are most susceptible to framing immigrants as "illegal" than either African American or Latino respondents. In addition, data from an embedded survey experiment designed to test the efficacy of priming attitudes on immigration by altering the race of immigrants show different effects across racial groups.

Analyzing public opinion through the prism of race yields three lessons for understanding the future of US immigration policy. First, immigration and naturalization policy define the context of political belonging experienced by Americans. Second, immigration is the central engine for racial formation in the United States, simultaneously accounting for the persistence of the racial hierarchy and serving as the mechanism behind the dynamism in both the shape of the racial order and the meaning of the racial categories themselves. Third, because race structures individual-level political attitudes, public opinion on immigration policy reform will depend on the both the demographic composition of the population and the ability of grassroots organizations, opinion leaders, and elites to mobilize Americans.

US Immigration Policy and the Context of Belonging

The contentious debate about immigration and naturalization policy in the United States is embedded in the politics of belonging. Immigration policy is much more complex than simply the control of borders, reflecting instead long-standing normative constructions of political membership. At the federal level, the tenor and content of immigration legislation since the mid-1980s is clear about the imperative to exclude and expel undesirable newcomers from the nation. The titles of federal legislation are telling, progressively increasing emphasis on restriction by the use of the words "control," "illegal," and "terrorism" since the neutrally named Immigration and Nationality Act (1965), evolving to the Immigration Reform and Control Act (1986), the Illegal Immigration Reform and Immigrant Responsibility Act (1996), and the Border Protection, Anti-Terrorism, and Illegal Immigration Control Act (also known as the "Sensenbrenner bill," 2005–2006), which passed in the US House of Representatives but failed in the Senate. Taken together, the growing focus of federal law on control and security of the southern US border, the criminalization of hiring unauthorized workers, and the enhancement of federal agencies' power to detain and deport immigrants sends a clear and strong signal to the American public that poor migrants from Latin America are undesirable.

The combination of greater racial and ethnic diversity and the overall growth in the size of the immigrant population—unintended consequences from the perspective of many of the original proponents of the 1965 Immigration and Nationality Act—provided the context in which the question facing policy makers and voters was no longer *Who should belong?* but *Who doesn't belong?* Despite the seemingly race-neutral preference categories of the 1965 act that continue to govern US entry policy, states and local governments affected by high levels of immigration began to enact abode policies aimed at defining the rights of immigrants and the conditions under which they would experience political and social life in the United States. California's Proposition 187 (1994), Arizona's SB 1070 (2010), and Alabama's HB 56 (2011), all of which sought to deny political and social rights to illegal immigrants, are examples of answers by states in response to the question of *who doesn't belong* as a member of the polity.

Long conditioned on a racial prerequisite, preferences for membership in the American polity have undergone important changes. From the first federal legislation on naturalization in 1790, through Asian exclusion laws of the late nineteenth and early twentieth centuries, and broadened in the 1924 National Origins Act, racial classification as white was a requirement for political membership in the United States. Three decades would pass under the restrictive 1924 law until the tentative reopening of the United States to newcomers with the 1952 McCarran-Walter Act. While this federal law eliminated racial and ethnic prerequisites to naturalization, existing quotas from the 1924 act remained largely intact. Not until the 1965 Immigration and Nationality Act did the United States fully institute a preference structure for lawful entry decoupled from racial and ethnic classification that was instead based primarily on occupational skills and family reunification. Formulated in an era dominated by the civil rights movement, scientific advances in space exploration, and the memory of Americans long separated from families in Europe, the 1965 law is considered the high watermark in nondiscriminatory citizenship policy.

The 1965 act was undeniably a radical break from the explicitly racialized conditions of belonging set forth in most US immigration law that preceded it. Nevertheless, the social and political context of the time in which the new policy specifying who should belong was crafted is critical to understanding both the sequence of subsequent immigration policy and the trajectory for future reform. In 1965, policy makers addressed the question of who should belong in a very different context from the members of Congress who crafted the exclusionary 1924 law four decades earlier. In the intervening time since closing the door almost completely to immigrants, the nation's population had grown and changed through internal dynamics rather than from the addition of new Americans from abroad. While nearly 15% of the US population were immigrants when the 1924 National Origins Act was signed into law, less than 4% of Americans were foreign-born forty years later. Irish, Italians, and Jews—groups of immigrants deemed inferior by the infamous Dillingham Commission and systematically excluded by law from entry—had over the course of time assimilated into the population of white Americans. Few new immigrants of these European ethnicities could come to repopulate the ethnic enclaves created by earlier waves of mass migration from southern and eastern Europe. Likewise, long-standing restrictions against Asian immigration and racially based abode policies such as alien land laws restricted both the size and mobility of the Asian American population. In 1965, policy makers and voters alike thought of immigrants as their parents and grandparents, and immigration policy was created in response to the question of "Who should belong?" with the image of the typical immigrant being that of those who had arrived from European shores in generations past.

The lesson to draw from explicit consideration of the context of the time in which immigration policy is formulated is the insight that public opinion and policy initiatives reflect prevailing conceptions of who should belong and who does not belong in America. Political time matters, as does the sequence of events and the extent to which policy choices are path-dependent. More sustained attention to the context of belonging provides greater comparative analytical leverage to understand how and why immigration policy has developed in the way that it has and what the future holds for public opinion on immigration.

Immigration as a Driving Force in Racial Formation

The image of the prototypical immigrant depends on the number and types of immigrants Americans see, and their mental images of immigrants varied substantially between the times in which the 1924 and 1965 acts were passed. Between the 1870s and the decades after the enactment of the 1924 National Origins Act, the percentage of immigrants in the US population declined precipitously. Few new immigrants were admitted into the United States in the era of exclusion before the 1965 Immigration and Nationality Act, and the proportion of foreign-born Americans reached an all-time low in 1970. Only 4% of Americans were immigrants at the time the door to immigration was reopened, and newcomers from abroad did not seem as threatening to policy makers and ordinary Americans in this context. But since the passage of the 1965 act, there has been a sharp increase in the percentage of immigrants in the total population. Immigration policy reform and the contemporary politics of belonging are now taking place in a demographic context much more similar to an earlier era characterized by immigrant exclusion and in contrast to the period of low immigrant visibility during the heyday of the civil rights movement.

While reliable data sources indicate that the largest share of unauthorized immigrants is from Mexico, Mexicans are not the only people residing in the United States without government authorization (Hoefer, Rytina, and Baker 2012). It is telling that there is no contemporary analog in the popular vernacular for those who cross the nation's northern border with Canada, and unauthorized immigrants from countries of origin all over the world reside in the United States today. The phrase "illegal immigrant" evokes a Latino immigrant in the mind's eye rather than a picture of the Irish national who has overstayed his tourist visa or the Ghanaian student whose visa has expired. Defined for the public by the focus of government policy, it is worth repeating Lippmann's (1922) observation: "For the most part we do not first see, and then define, we define first and then see. In the great blooming, buzzing confusion of the outer world we pick out what our culture has already defined for us, and we tend to perceive that which we have picked out in the form stereotyped for us by our culture" (81).

Among the ironies of the contemporary stereotype of "illegal alien" as being from Latin America is the fact that US immigration policy did not impose a quota limit on migrants from North America in the 1924 National Origins Act (Hattam 2007; Zolberg 2006; Tichenor 2002). Thus, Mexicans and Canadians had only to pay a tax and pass a literacy test to enter the United States legally between 1924 and 1965. With the small number of government officials at border crossings and the long-standing practice of moving to and from the United States and Mexico, authorized entry during this period was the exception. The same was true on the nation's northern border with Canada, where Europeans officially excluded from entry, including Jews during the interwar period, entered the United States without official authorization but not in violation of quota limits. The policy of porous borders and latent illegality was ideal for businesses in the American Southwest and West because these conditions provided an inexpensive and disposable labor force. The federal government was at the forefront of this arrangement, paving the way for the exploitation of foreign workers in its establishment of the Bracero Program (Rodriguez 2008; D. Cohen 2011; Ngai 2004) and its weak enforcement of protection of workers. Indeed, federal programs such as "Operation Wetback," instituted in 1954, only two years after the McCarran-Walter Act, were undertaken to "repatriate" workers who were deemed no longer useful.

Thus the stereotype of Latinos as "illegal aliens" undeserving of belonging has been a part of the national consciousness despite the absence of federal immigration law explicitly excluding Latin America migration (Ngai 2004). Over time, these policies and practices have resulted in the powerful negative stereotype of Latinos as unwanted outsiders. The studies described in chapter 6, along with systematic research by other scholars, demonstrate that voters of all political stripes are less supportive of progressive immigration policies when they are primed to think about Latinos (Perez 2011). Attitudes on immigration do indeed vary by political party identification, but Americans of all racial designations are influenced by the prevailing stereotype of Latinos as most likely to be in the United States without authorization.

Federal and state immigration laws have played a major role in defining the stereotype of "illegal alien" as Latino and, conversely, in defining stereotypes of the "model minority" as Asian American. In the contemporary period, California's Proposition 187, the ballot initiative passed by 56% of California voters in 1994 that prohibited unauthorized immigrants from eligibility for social services including public education for children, was and remains defined in the public imagination as an anti-Latino initiative. At the federal level, one of the main elements of the 2005 Sensenbrenner bill (HR 4437) was the construction of a seven-hundred-mile-long fence across the border the United States shares with Mexico. Subsequent mass protests during 2006 were identified as driven by Latinos in an effort to thwart passage of the law. Similarly, Arizona's 2010 law (SB 1070) requiring immigrant aliens to carry identification and empowering local law enforcement to stop, detain, and arrest potential lawbreakers is aimed specifically at Latino immigrants, as are similarly repressive laws such as Alabama's recent HB 56.

Immigration policy is also at the root of contemporary stereotypes of Asian Americans as desirable immigrants worthy of inclusion compared with Latinos. The 1952 McCarran-Walter Act outlawed the restrictions against Asian immigrants from becoming naturalized citizens that had been a defining element of federal laws supporting Asian exclusion since the 1870s. In the explicit terms of the Page Act of 1875, "undesirable immigrant" was defined to mean individuals from Asia whose intention was to engage in contract labor or prostitution, among other things. So effective was the United States policy of excluding racialized immigrants from Asia as undesirable and unworthy of belonging that by the time the 1965 Immigration and Nationality Act became law, there were fewer than 1 million Asian Americans in the United States, at a time recently following the admission to statehood of Alaska and Hawaii, both of whose populations included large numbers of Asians. The presence and power of the negative stereotypes of the nineteenth century that fueled Asian exclusion on the basis of their "coolie" status had receded along with their visibility and the perception that Asians were a dangerous influence on American society. Enter a new and different social class of Asian immigrants who came to the United States under the occupational-status preference system of the 1965 act, and the prevailing stereotypes of Asian Americans had changed dramatically from "coolie" to "model minority" (Junn 2007). At the same time, because of the persistent racialization of Asian Americans, buttressed by the racial classification taxonomy of the US government, the negative stereotype of "forever foreigner" along with the positive characterizations of high achievement, hard work, and self-reliance have become the prevailing stereotypes of Asian Americans (Rim 2007; Tuan 1998).

The lessons to draw from recognizing immigration as the driving force behind racial formulation is the insight that the placement of whites at the top of the racial hierarchy and minorities below remains stable, the result of a sequence of developments beginning with the justifications of slavery to the present-day vilification of Latino immigrants as "illegals." The shape of the hierarchy can and will change, along with the meaning of the racial categories, and the transformation of Asian American stereotypes and social standing is the best example of the dynamism of the politics of belonging rooted in immigration policy. One of the most important moving parts driving that dynamism are Americans themselves and the pressure they can exert on elected officials to alter government policy on immigration and naturalization.

Race—a critical organizer for stereotypes signifying complete or conditional belonging to the polity—is at once a social construction based in imaginary domains and a set of categorizations with enormous consequences for the daily lives of Americans. It may very well be that having "ethnicity without groups" (Brubaker 2004) is normatively preferable, as may be political equality for advocates of inclusive democracy. But the politics of belonging in the United States has proceeded along a path-dependent trajectory of group-based exclusion and discrimination that has thus far privileged political strategies of mobilization around racial-group consciousness and redress in order to reveal and overturn the privilege and dominance of the default category of whiteness. For Americans whose belonging is conditioned by their nonwhite status, race may indeed exist only in stereotypes in the mind's eye, but the consequences of racial classification are both palpable and politically exploitable.

Political Mobilization and US Immigration
Policy Reform in a Diverse Polity

With fully one-third of the nation classifying themselves as a race other than white, political leaders and candidates for office represent increasingly racially diverse constituencies, all of whom do not react similarly to the invocation of racial stereotypes. Minority voters will continue to be a growing force that politicians must recognize (Bowler and Segura 2012; García Bedolla and Michelson 2009; Ramirez 2005; J. Wong 2005). For proponents of stronger exclusion and restrictionist immigration policy, the prevalence and efficacy of racial stereotypes targeting newcomers who are construed as undesirable will be effective tools in forwarding their positions. For advocates of progressive immigration policy reform, the diversity, increasing minority electoral empowerment, and sensitivity of American voters to racial stereotyping will work in opposition to the goals of those attempting to restrict membership in the American polity. Understanding and foreseeing what the future holds for public opinion on immigration and immigration policy depend on analysts' ability to capture and discern the implications of the dynamism of race in the politics of belonging.

Experts in political communications, both inside politics in political campaigns and outside of politics in academic research, recognize the power of framing by subtle and often not-so-subtle racial-group stereotypes. Framing with negative racial stereotypes influences responses to policy questions on academic surveys and can also have real-world effects by changing the perceptions of candidates. The use of stereotypes in the infamous Willie Horton advertisements run by the Republican presidential campaign of George H. W. Bush in 1988 is emblematic of the power of race to prime individual attitudes and behavior (Mendelberg 2001). As the politics of immigration policy reform heats up, and to the extent that candidates for political office hold distinguishable positions on the welcome of new Americans, we should expect to continue seeing political communications strategies exploiting negative stereotypes of Latinos as undesirable immigrants unfit for belonging in the American polity. Negative portrayals of Latinos have been used by politicians such as Governor Pete Wilson during his 1994 campaign for reelection as California's chief executive and US Representative Tom Tancredo (R-CO) in his failed bid for the Republican nomination for president in

2008. The proven power of the negative stereotype of Latinos as "illegal aliens" portends more political communications in this vein. Nor are stereotypes of Asian Americans as foreigners being ignored by politicians. During the 2012 election cycle, candidates such as Pete Hoekstra (R-MI) ran advertisements featuring Asian stereotypes to energize negative sentiment among voters.[3]

But not all voters not react the same to communications based in racial stereotypes. The comparative relational analytical approach advocated in this book is based on the premise that all racial groups are not created equally in the politics of belonging. Instead, structural position in the American racial hierarchy creates systematically different perspectives at the individual level. Political context born of historically grounded contingencies for groups of Americans classified by race creates distinctive constraints and varying levels of agency in how individuals understand, interpret, and form opinion on immigration and naturalization policy. Racial-group consciousness of linked fate as well as conceptions of boundaries of what it means to be an American varies systematically among whites, African Americans, Latinos, and Asian Americans, and the moderating influence of these aspects of group identity constitute the mechanism that disperses observed preferences into an array of variation rather than a single unitary public opinion.

Viewed from this perspective, political advertisements such as Pete Wilson's portraying "illegals" running across California freeways near the border with Mexico, commercials conflating criminality and African Americans, and campaign communications emphasizing Asians as beneficiaries of outsourced American jobs will not have the same effect on minority voters as they will on whites. Minority candidates for office do not run a political communications campaign highlighting negative stereotypes of whites as inferior athletes or dancers lacking rhythm, especially when they are appealing to white voters. The same is true for political opportunists in a multiracial polity. While evoking negative racial stereotypes to win elections and enact restrictive immigration policies may be a short-term solution to mobilize fear and racial antipathy, it is also a strategy that can have long-term consequences. Perhaps the most prominent example is the legacy of the strong anti-immigrant positions taken by California Republicans and championed by Governor Pete Wilson in his 1994 reelection campaign (Pantoja, Ramirez, and Segura 2001). To the extent that California is an indicator of what is to come for the rest of the nation in terms of racial diversity in the population and eventually, the electorate, the legacy of immigration policies such as Proposition 187 to engender negative perceptions of the candidates who personify anti-immigrant policy provides pause for consideration. Will Latinos build political and electoral strength of sufficient magnitude to make political communications utilizing negative stereotypes untenable? Can immigrant Americans of all racial backgrounds work together to influence government policy on immigration and naturalization? What coalitions, if any, will African American political groups forge with other minority Americans? These questions remain for future analysts to tackle. The lesson from this insight is that the politics of immigration will be conducted in an increasingly racially diverse polity. How scholars and political commentators think about race will influence how well they will be able to anticipate and understand the future of immigration policy in the United States.

Notes

Appendixes referenced in this book can be found online at http://www .press.uchicago.edu/sites/masuoka/.

Introduction

1. Leland Stanford, inaugural address as governor of California, 1862: "To my mind it is clear, that the settlement among us of an inferior race is to be discouraged, by every legitimate means. Asia, with her numberless millions, sends to our shores the dregs of her population."

Chapter 1

1. Data are from the 2006 Faces of Immigration Survey, which was based on a national sample of Americans. The survey was designed by the authors and included large samples of African Americans, Asian Americans, and Latinos.

2. Pew Research Center for the People and the Press, "Public Supports Arizona Immigration Law," Pew Research Center Publications, May 12, 2010, accessed August 8, 2010, http://pewresearch.org/pubs/1591/public-support-arizona -immigration-law-poll.

3. Data are from the 2006 Faces of Immigration Survey. See appendix A online for details.

4. The Office of Management and Budget Statistical Policy Directive No. 15 of 1977 mandates five categories of race and ethnicity to be used for official data collection and reporting and includes "American Indian or Alaskan Native" in addition to the four categories of analysis discussed here (Hattam 2007). We do not explicitly address this fifth category primarily for reasons of data limitation, but we recognize the historical and political significance of the group.

5. The design and implementation of studies of public opinion rarely if ever consider this relatively small group in data collection and analysis. The data we analyze are unfortunately no exception, and we have insufficient empirical observations to develop and test our model for this racial group. See Wilkins and Stark (2010); Wilmer, Melody, and Murdock (1994).

6. A good visual representation of the RPGI model can be found on the cover of Pink Floyd's album *Dark Side of the Moon*.

7. *Lou Dobbs Tonight*, CNN, March 27, 2006, transcript at http://transcripts .cnn.com/TRANSCRIPTS/0603/27/ldt.01.html.

8. In most US population surveys, the sample sizes for Asian Americans or those of "other" races are too small to include in the analysis.

9. Political scientists have made important contributions to understanding the dynamics of public opinion through focused studies on explanatory or independent variables such as partisanship and ideology (e.g., Campbell et al. 1960; Converse 1964;Green, Palmquist, and Schickler 2004). Other work focuses on attitudinal or psychological variables such as authoritarianism (Hetherington and Weiler 2009). Kinder and Kam's (2009) exemplary work on the role of ethnocentrism in public opinion and Delli Carpini and Keeter's (1996) study on political knowledge consider other critical determinants of public opinion. While there is comparatively less research on the role of gender and class in public opinion, important work by Burns (2005) and Burns and Kinder (2012) analyze the significance of sex in structuring political behavior.

10. See Harris-Lacewell (2003) and Junn and Brown (2008) for critiques of the control variable within the context of explanations of African American politics and intersectionality. See Emirbayer (1997) for a critical assessment of assumptions underlying quantitative models in social science.

11. This perspective could apply to any characteristic involving social hierarchies such as gender. Similar practices of using a control variable to account for gender often assume male is the excluded category and key reference point.

12. Regression coefficients for each independent variable specified in a model reflect an averaging of all respondents in the sample. Because whites still make up two-thirds of the nation's population, national samples will mirror that distribution and be majority white. This automatic numerical majority is not the case in sampling designs such as MCSUI based in urban metropolitan areas or our 2006 Faces of Immigration Survey that was undertaken with a stratified sampling design.

13. George Lipsitz (1998) succinctly describes the hidden power of whiteness: "As the unmarked category against which difference is constructed, whiteness never has to speak its name, never has to acknowledge its role as an organizing principle in social and cultural relations" (1–2).

14. Scholarly work in gender and intersectionality provides important theo-

retical guidance and precedent for this analytic strategy. See Scola and García Bedolla 2006; Hancock 2007; McCall 2001.

Chapter 2

1. Nativists targeted the law as too generous given the relatively short period of residency of two years, and the residency period was changed in 1795. Further restrictions were made through the Alien and Sedition Acts of 1798, which extended the residency requirement to fourteen years (Tichenor 2002).

2. In 1855, the California state legislature passed the "Act to Discourage the Immigration to This State of Persons who Cannot Become Citizens." The act required shipmasters to pay a fee of fifty dollars for each passenger who could not be naturalized, but the law was later nullified by the state's supreme court in 1857 on the grounds that it violated the federal government's authority to establish uniform rules regarding foreign trade (H. Kim 1994). One year later, California responded with yet another "Act to Prevent the Further Immigration of Chinese or Mongolians to this State."

3. The racial motives of Congress were upheld by the Supreme Court, which ruled that immigration policy is not subject to the same strict scrutiny that it had applied to cases involving race and minorities (Neuman 1996; Chin 1998; Bosniak 2006). The Supreme Court explicitly stated that "no limits can be put by the courts upon the power of Congress to protect . . . the country from the advent of aliens whose race or habits render them unsuitable as citizens, or to expel such if they have already found their way into our land, and unlawfully remain therein" (*Wong Wing v. United States*, 1898), and the plenary power of the federal government in immigration policy was affirmed by the Supreme Court in *Arizona v. United States* (2012).

4. Congress did try to limit immigration multiple times between the passage of the 1882 Chinese Exclusion Act and the 1924 Johnson-Reed Act, notably with the Immigration Act of 1917, also known as the Asiatic Barred Zone Act, which barred the admission to the United States of all immigrants from Asia and the Middle East. The 1924 act was a revised version of an immigration bill passed in 1921, and the later version established stricter quotas and created the formula that prioritized immigration from western Europe (Daniels 2004a).

5. For example, in a case involving Native American tribes, *Elks v. Wilkins* (1884), the Supreme Court ruled that inhabitants of territories were not entitled to the same rights as natural born citizens.

6. Mexicans may have been legally considered as white, but in practice Mexicans came to be viewed as what has been termed "other-whites" (Gomez 2008, Gross 2008). Mexicans' whiteness was seen as not quite the same form of white

that was applied to Anglo Americans (Haney López 1996; Gross 2008). "Other-whiteness" or "off-whiteness" served as a pretext for political marginalization and social segregation at the state and local level.

7. Restrictive land covenants against Mexicans and Hispanics and Latinos in general were designed to exclude all nonwhites from white neighborhoods. According to Albert Camarillo (1984), in 1920 about 20% of municipalities in the Los Angeles had instituted such covenants; by 1946, more than 80% of them had passed relevant ordinances (see also Montejano 1986). For example, the 1855 California Vagrancy Act, also known as the "Greaser Act," specifically targeted the "idle Mexican" as a social threat while "greasers" were also perceived as the "treacherous Mexican male[s]" whose desire for white women was an explicit sexual threat to the Anglo populace (Bender, 2003).

8. It is also important to recognize that the legal association between Mexican and white did not go unchallenged. There were numerous attempts by both citizens and local governments to racialize Mexicans as nonwhite. Some political leaders attempted to classify the different racial stocks of Mexicans by applying the existing American racial categories of white, black and Indian to Mexican inhabitants (Menchaca 2002). Those easily classified as Indian and black were denied citizenship rights using existing American laws which then governed citizenship. Mexicans of the elite and landowner classes, however were better able to assert their "whiteness" and maintained political voting and property rights in the United States.

9. Ayala and Bernabé (2002) contrast Puerto Rico's incorporation as a territory to the nonincorporation of the Philippines, which was always expected to be given independence from the United States, as evidence of Americans' perception of Latinos as white. Puerto Ricans were perceived to be possible American citizens because they fit the appropriate racial mold, while Filipinos were too racially distinct to ever be included in the nation. Ngai (2004) notes that Filipino hostility toward the United States and their bitter war for independence with the United States that began immediately following the Spanish-American War fueled the American perception that the Philippines would not be incorporated into the Union.

10. These cases were *Ozawa v. United States* (1922) and *United States v. Thind* (1923), both of which resulted in judgment by the US Supreme Court that neither man was white (Haney López 2006).

11. Interestingly, while nonwhite classification appeared to be clear for immigrants arriving from East and Southeast Asia, the federal courts could not easily decide the whiteness of Syrians, Armenians, Arabs and Mexicans, and decisions on the racial classification of these groups contradicted one another (Haney López 2006; Gross 2008).

12. The federal courts upheld the curfew, exclusion and evacuation orders of citizens of Japanese descent citing national security and the need for martial law

(Daniels 2004a; Takaki 1998). See *Yasui v. United States* (1943), *Hirabayashi v. United States* (1943) and *Korematsu v. United States* (1944).

13. While we isolate these four racial groups, the increasing prevalence of "multiracial" Americans will present growing complexity for scholars of race and politics. Questions about which of the traditional racial categories multiracial Americans will select as identity choices and the political consequences of a multiracial identity are the subject of important of new research (Masuoka 2008b).

14. Mary Waters (1990) argues that whites today identify with their ethnic identity to assert individuality within the white population. In this respect, ethnicity can be perceived as a positive attribute that helps to maintain a level of distinctiveness. Waters suggests whites perceive ethnic identification as a personal choice that implies the option of individual agency and have difficulty understanding the structural barriers of race experienced by nonwhites.

Chapter 3

1. Biden's remarks can be found in Xuan Thai and Ted Barrett, "Biden's Description of Obama Draws Scrutiny," CNN Politics, January 31, 2007, http://articles.cnn.com/2007–01-31/politics/biden.obama_1_braun-and-al-sharpton-african-american-presidential-candidates-delaware-democrat?_s= PM:POLITICS.

2. See CNN Transcripts, http://archives.cnn.com/TRANSCRIPTS/1109/12/se.06.html.

3. Chua, "Why Chinese Mothers Are Superior," *Wall Street Journal*, January 8, 2011, http://online.wsj.com/article/SB10001424052748704111150457605971 3528698754.html.

4. For example, in response to Chua's editorial, *New York Times* columnist David Brooks wrote, "Chua plays into America's fear of national decline. Here's a Chinese parent working really hard (and, by the way, there are a billion more of her) and her kids are going to crush ours." Brooks argues that Americans perceive Chua and "Chinese parenting" as a foreign threat. "Amy Chua Is a Wimp," *New York Times*, January 17, 2011, http://www.nytimes.com/2011/01/18/opinion/18brooks.html.

5. For further discussions on whites and social desirability, see Berinsky (1999); Mendelberg (2001); and Schuman et al. (1997). Social desirability is not only a concern among whites, and as Jost, Banaji, and Nosek (2004) note, social desirability concerns actually encourage racial minorities to accentuate ingroup attachments as a result of social expectations that individuals will be loyal to their own group. Although racial minorities may believe that their own group is inferior, they also feel pressure to express positive in-group identity. Research

has found that black respondents are more likely to dampen their reported levels of support for racial policies when talking with white interviewers than when they are interviewed by a black interviewer (Anderson, Silver, and Abramson 1988).

6. This survey of Americans residing in metropolitan areas was designed by a team of scholars: Lawrence Bobo, James Johnson, Melvin Oliver, Reynolds Farley, Barry Bluestone, Irene Browne, Sheldon Danziger, Gary Green, Harry Holzer, Maria Krysan, Michael Massagli, Camille Zubrinsky Charles, Joleen Kirschenman, Philip Moss, and Chris Tilly. The data were collected from a sample of households and employers. We analyze only the household sample, which had a total sample size of 8,916. In total, 2,790 white, 3,111 black, 1,124 Asian, and 1,783 Latino respondents were interviewed for this portion of the study. Respondents were identified using a multistaged stratified clustered area probability design. Interviews were conducted face to face in respondents' homes in English, Spanish, and a variety of Asian languages. Respondents were surveyed where possible by an interviewer of the same race, and whites in Los Angeles and Latinos in Boston were least likely to be interviewed by a person of the same race.

7. The MCSUI represents Americans living in the selected metropolitan areas. The most racially diverse areas in the United States are in metropolitan areas. The MCSUI data represent observation of stereotype trait ratings among individuals who actually experience diversity and allow us to examine to what extent stereotypes are reflective of general societal narratives and personal experiences. All data reported were run both with and without weights, and any differences are documented.

8. Question wording and sample demographics are provided in appendix B, available online at http://www.press.uchicago.edu/sites/masuoka/.

9. For figures 3.1 through 3.4, sample sizes for whites are between 1,262 and 1,282, for blacks between 1,351 and 1,403, for Asian Americans between 305 and 325, and for Latinos between 577 and 615. for Figure 3.5, the sample sizes for each of the groups was as follows: whites = 615, blacks = 712, Asian Americans = 291, and Latinos = 543.

10. All differences of means are significant at the .01 level.

11. The Faces of Immigration Survey was conducted by Knowledge Networks of Palo Alto, California. Selection into the Knowledge Networks is by random digit dialing. Panel participants were adults and included individuals who do not have Internet access. Those without access are provided Internet access by Knowledge Networks. The study was conducted between December 20, 2006, and January 24, 2007, and the cooperation rate for the survey was 78.7%. In total, the sample included 433 white, 438 black, 385 Asian, and 410 Latino respondents. This study was conducted in English only. The share of foreign-born in the Asian sample is close to the proportion reported by the US Census Bureau, but the Latino sample is disproportionately native-born. Weighted data are pre-

sented, though the results remain consistent without weighting. This consistency reduces the possibility that the results for the Asian American and Latino respondents are influenced by a larger share of more assimilated Americans in these racial groups.

12. Question wording and sample demographics are provided in appendix A, available online at http://www.press.uchicago.edu/sites/masuoka/.

13. Sample sizes were 433 whites, 438 blacks, 385 Asian Americans, and 410 Latinos.

14. Sample sizes were 405 whites, 389 blacks, 351 Asian Americans, and 386 Latinos.

15. Mean difference between whites and all three racial minorities is significant at $p < 0.01$. There are no significant differences in average number of negative Latino stereotyping across racial minority groups.

16. Whites' mean positive rating of Latino immigrants is significantly lower than the mean ratings for both blacks and Latinos ($p < 0.01$) and no different from Asians' mean ratings.

17. There are no statistically significant differences between average trait ratings assigned by black and Latino respondents on any of these stereotype measures.

18. Instead of being asked to respond to specific stereotype pairs, respondents in the Faces of Immigration Survey were asked to choose the stereotypes they though applied to each immigrant group. This measurement technique makes it possible to count the number of positive and negative traits to each group and provides an indicator of hierarchical thinking.

19. Sample sizes were 405 whites, 389 blacks, 351 Asian Americans, and 386 Latinos.

20. Difference of means is significant at $p < 0.01$. For the multivariate results, we estimated two different models. The first model used higher negative stereotypes as the dependent variable, the second model used higher positive Asian stereotypes as the dependent variable, and both included race, age, education, income, gender, foreign-born status, and controls for an embedded experiment treatment employed in the survey as independent variables in the model. The model results are reported in appendix table A.2. In order to assess whether the antecedents to racial stereotyping differed by racial group, we estimated a set of regression models predicting total number of negative and positive stereotypes applied to Latino and Asian immigrants. Independent variables included socioeconomic status, age, gender, political partisanship, attention to media, living in a top-five immigration state (California, New York, New Jersey, Florida, or Texas), a measure of perceived racial-linked fate, and controls for an embedded experiment in the survey. The results are summarized in appendix table A.3, and the full results are documented in tables A.4 through A.7.

21. Communications and political science studies that track the use of ste-

reotypical images of racial minorities and immigrants tend to examine content presented in major media outlets such as national network and cable programs. However, research has found that not all media outlets present information in the same manner. Ethnic media outlets have been found to use alternative perspectives from traditional media providers when reporting the same event (see for example, Clawson, Strine, and Waltenburg 2003). Other research has also found that ethnic media often provide more positive frames about issues such as immigration compared to traditional media, which tend to frame such issues negatively (Abrajano and Singh 2009).

Chapter 4

1. Michele Obama made the original statement at a political rally on February 18, 2008. Cindy McCain made her statement on the same day while introducing her husband at a get-out-the-vote rally. CNN Political Ticker, February 19, 2008, http://politicalticker.blogs.cnn.com/2008/02/19/cindy-mccain-michelle-obama-in-patriotism-flap/. See also Michael Cooper, "Cindy McCain's Pride," The Caucus: The Politics and Government Blog of the *New York Times*, http://thecaucus.blogs.nytimes.com/2008/02/19/cindy-mccains-pride/.

2. For example, another important dimension to this interaction is gender. Gender has also been used as a characteristic to define full inclusion in the citizenry as citizens were originally defined exclusively as male. For discussions on the gendered traditions of American citizenship see Kerber (1998) and Pateman (1988). See Glenn (2002) for a discussion on race-gender intersectionality and citizenship.

3. Political controversy over the birthplace of President Obama continued several years into his presidency. Attacks on the veracity of Obama's official birth certificate are rooted in the perception that he is not a "true" American. Other claims, such as the notion that President Obama is a Muslim or a black nationalist are based in the perception that he does not represent a prototypical colorless American.

4. The Twenty-First Century Americanism survey was conducted in 2004 by principal investigator Deborah Schildkraut. A full discussion of the study and its findings are detailed in her 2011 book, *Americanism in the Twenty-First Century*. Appendix C, available online at http://www.press.uchicago.edu/sites/masuoka/, provides question wording and sample characteristics of the survey. The National Politics Study was also conducted in 2004 under the supervision of principal investigators James Jackson, Robert Brown, Vincent Hutchings and Cara Wong. Appendix D provides question wording and sample characteristics of the study.

5. *Patriotism* is commonly defined as a love of one's country (Huddy and Khatib 2007; Sidanius et al. 1997), whereas *nationalism* is typically described as the perception that one's own nation is superior to others. The nation is often conceptualized as a construct disassociated with the self where perceptions of one's nation are assumed to be separate from how one views personal identity. There has been significant scholarly attention to both constructs. For example, see Kosterman and Feshbach (1989); Li and Brewer (2004); Parker (2010); and Sullivan, Fried, and Dietz (1992).

6. Additional examples include findings by Schildkraut (2011) showing that experiences of racial discrimination weaken preference for the "American" identity label among Asians and Latinos but have no effect on identity preferences among blacks or whites. Sidanius et al. (1997) found that social dominance orientation influenced national attachments of whites and blacks but not Asian Americans and Latinos.

7. We note the important distinction between "excluded" members and "peripheral" members. Experimental research on social identity often uses manipulations to establish distinctions between group members. Because these distinctions are created in the laboratory, emphasis has been on excluded members rather than those who are peripheral in real life. Scholarship on racial minorities and marginalized populations such as women or the poor does focus on the experiences of peripheral members. See, for example, Steele's (2010) work on stereotype threat that examines the implications of negative stereotypes on individual behavior.

8. The existence of peripheral group members is consistent with theories of social dominance that explain the formation of group-based hierarchies based on categories such as age, race, and gender (Sidanius and Pratto 1999). Integrating social dominance theory with social-group identification theory reveals a predisposition to create hierarchies even within in-groups, which leads to a distinction between core and peripheral members.

9. The survey was collected using computer-assisted telephone interviews conducted between July and December of 2004. Respondents had the option of answering the survey in either English or Spanish. The response rate for this survey was 29.8%, and the sampling error was ±1.89. For additional information, see http://www.icpsr.umich.edu/icpsrweb/DSDR/studies/27601.

10. For each of the seven characteristics, respondents were given the following options for response: "Very important," "Somewhat important, "Somewhat unimportant," or "Very unimportant." Ratings for this analysis were coded on this ordinal scale: very important = 3, somewhat important = 2, somewhat unimportant = 1, and very unimportant = 0. We then created an index variable by adding together responses to all seven characteristics of Americanness. The index variable was a scale of 0 to 21 and standardized to a range of 0 to 1. The Cron-

NOTES TO PAGES 98-100

bach's alpha is 0.66. Appendix table C.2 shows the distribution of the American-boundary index by race of respondent. Sample sizes were 1,590 whites, 287 blacks, 173 Asian Americans, and 296 Latinos.

11. Schildkraut (2011) also makes an important argument that ascriptive boundaries are not the only way citizens define what it means to be American. She argues that Americans also hold onto important civic and republican ideals which are more egalitarian and therefore more strongly embraced by all Americans. Her results show that whites and racial minorities all share the perspective that American identity is defined by key political ideals such as being civically engaged and knowing about American political institutions.

12. Commendable studies on developing national-identity measures in surveys include Citrin, Reingold, and Green (1990); Huddy and Khatib (2007); Theiss-Morse (2009); Transue (2007); and C. Wong (2010). By using common measures of national identity in the Faces of Immigration Survey, we can add to the existing literature by directly addressing what we believe is the most significant weakness: generating a theoretical explanation for why there are racial-group differences across measures.

13. In order to eliminate the possibility of competing national loyalties, particularly among populations with high proportions of immigrants, data are presented only for respondents who are US citizens. Approximately 6% ($n = 103$) of the respondents were noncitizens. The sample sizes for citizen populations are 1,590 whites, 287 blacks, 173 Asian Americans, and 296 Latinos. Because oversampling was used to obtain large minority samples, frequencies and means presented in this section were weighted to reflect the national population.

14. Sample sizes for each question vary but are no smaller than 1,563 whites, 273 blacks, 167 Asian Americans, and 289 Latinos.

15. Difference-of-means tests confirm that African Americans report higher scores on "being born in America" and "being a Christian" than the three other groups ($p < 0.05$). Blacks are also significantly more likely than Asian American and Latino respondents to believe that "having American citizenship" is very important ($p < 0.05$).

16. Differences are significant at $p < 0.05$.

17. Studies on the role of education have found that more education increases ability to process more complex information (Nie, Junn, and Stehlik-Barry 1996). One possible explanation is that those with higher levels of education may be less likely to rely on basic assumptions such as ascriptive characteristics to define Americanness and instead emphasize more complex notions such as ideology or political norms.

18. See appendix C, available online at http://www.press.uchicago.edu/sites/masuoka/, for survey sample characteristics.

19. To assess the differences between whites and racial minorities, we used the following regression model: American boundary = β_1 (black) + β_2 (Asian) +

β_3 (Latino) + β_4 (other race) + β_5 (age) + β_6 (education) + β_7 (income) + β_8 (female) + β_9 (foreign born) + β_{10} (ideology). In this model, the category of white is excluded, which allows us to compare the effects of race assuming that whites are the reference group. To analyze the differences across racial minority groups, we used two regression models: American boundary = β_1 (white) + β_2 (Asian) + β_3 (Latino) + β_4 (other race) + β_5 (age) + β_6 (education) + β_7 (income) + β_8 (female) + β_9 (foreign born) + β_{10} (ideology) and American boundary = β_1 (white) + β_2 (black) + β_3 (Latino) + β_4 (other race) + β_5 (age) + β_6 (education) + β_7 (income) + β_8 (female) + β_9 (foreign born) + β_{10} (ideology). In the first of these two regression models, blacks are the excluded category, and in the second, Asian American is the excluded category. By excluding different racial groups, we can assess whether the coefficients may change when the reference group changes. Regression results are provided in Appendix table C.3.

20. While we advocate a methodological strategy of comparative relational analysis that specifies modeling racial group separately, we show here that the control-variable approach remains useful for answering questions such as this one. In this case, we evaluate the hypothesis that racial groups all perceive national boundaries in a similar manner. We need to first determine if there are actual differences attributed to race rather than some other systematic difference found across respondents. Most simply, the regression models here test the question of whether or not race matters. Once it is determined that race does matter, we propose that scholars continue to uncover, by engaging in comparative analysis, where there are differences. The regression analyses that follow disaggregate respondents by racial group and explain the distinct patterns by racial groups.

21. To ensure that our measures correspond with existing studies, we selected statements that most closely matched those used by Theiss-Morse (2009). Respondents reported if they "strongly agree," "somewhat agree," "somewhat disagree," or "strongly disagree" with each of the three statements. For each question on the index, we coded "strongly agree" as the highest value of 3 and "strongly disagree" at the lowest value of 0. The index was created by adding the scores for each of the three statements with a range of 0 to 9 and then standardized to a range of 0 to 1. The Cronbach's alpha for the index is 0.54. Appendix table C.4 presents the distribution of the typicality measure among US citizens only, and sample sizes were 1,590 whites, 287 blacks, 173 Asian Americans, and 296 Latinos.

22. While perceptions of typicality and affective national attachment are found to be positively correlated among whites, both Huddy and Khatib (2007) and Theiss-Morse (2009) show that these two scales measure distinct attitudes toward the nation. Similar to the strategy used for the typicality measures, we selected questions in the Twenty-First Century study that most closely matched those used by Theiss-Morse (2009) and Huddy and Khatib (2007). We used a similar operationalization strategy applied to the typicality index. The final vari-

able had a range of 0 to 6, and to assist in comparing across measures, we re-coded the variable to a range of 0 to 1. The Cronbach's alpha for the index is 0.56. Appendix table C.5 presents the distribution of the national identity measure among US citizens, and sample sizes were the same as for the typicality index as referenced in n. 21.

23. Appendix table C.6 documents the estimates of three models of the ante-cedents to perceptions of typicality. In model 1, white is the excluded category, which allows us to determine significant differences between whites and racial minority groups. Models 2 and 3 use blacks and Asian Americans, respectively, as the excluded category, which allows us to observe differences across racial mi-nority groups.

24. The differences were significant at $p < 0.05$ level.

25. A modeling strategy similar to that used for the typicality index was used, and the results of the estimation of the models are documented in Appendix ta-ble C.7. All differences reported are significant at $p < 0.05$.

26. All correlations (Pearson's r) shown in table 4.2 are significant at $p < 0.10$. Data include responses for US citizens only, and sample sizes are no smaller than 1,456 whites, 252 blacks, 158 Asian Americans, and 276 Latinos.

27. Patriotism is measured using the survey item: "Please tell me if you strongly agree, somewhat agree, somewhat disagree or strongly disagree: I am proud to be an American." We operationalized patriotism on a four-point or-dinal scale of 0 to 1 with a value of 1 equal to "strongly agree." Ideology was operationalized as an ordinal variable with the lowest value of 0 representing a respondent who is strongly liberal and the highest value of 1 representing a re-spondent who is strongly conservative.

28. Although scholars document the relatively weak racial-group attachment for Asian Americans and Latinos compared to African Americans, research still shows that racial-group identity is an important factor in explaining political attitudes and behavior. Group identity is related to distinctive political attitudes among Latinos and Asian Americans (Jones-Correa and Leal 1996; Lien, Con-way, and Wong 2004; Padilla 1985; Sanchez 2006; Stokes 2003; Wong et al. 2011). Studies also show that priming group identity can be used to mobilize Asian American and Latino voters (Abrajano 2010; Barreto 2010; Junn and Masuoka 2008a, 2008b; Leighley 2001).

29. There is a small but growing literature on expressions of black ethnicity in American political life (Waters 2000; Rogers 2006; Greer 2013).

30. Classic theories of immigrant assimilation, such as that proposed by Mil-ton Gordon (1964), suggested that interracial marriage was an effective indicator of immigrant incorporation into mainstream society. Gordon argued that mar-riage reflected positive racial interaction as well as intimate interactions between ethnic groups. Recent analysis of census data suggests that both Asian Ameri-

cans and Latinos out-marry with (non-Hispanic) whites at higher rates than African Americans (Lee and Edmonston 2005). Scholars interpret this as evidence
that Latinos and Asian Americans will assimilate quickly (Alba and Nee 2005).
There is growing argument that interracial marriage is not an appropriate indicator of weakening racial divisions, since there are racial and gender biases in selection of partners (Lee and Bean 2010; Qian 1997).

31. This is the assumption in theories about intergroup conflict and threat
that whites practice discrimination in order to maintain their group status (e.g.,
Blumer 1958; Bobo and Hutchings 1996; Key 1984; Sidanius and Pratto 1996).

32. The survey was conducted using computer-assisted telephone interviews.
Interviews were conducted between September 2004 and February 2005. The
American Association for Public Opinion Research response rate for this survey
was 30.63%. Minority respondents were selected using stratified sampling targeting high-density areas and surname lists. Interviews were conducted in English
and Spanish. This study also collected an oversample of Afro-Caribbeans ($n =$
404). Since this sample was over half foreign born and represents a relatively
small share of the black population in America, these respondents are excluded
from the analysis. For further information on the study, see http://www.icpsr
.umich.edu/icpsrweb/ICPSR/studies/24483.

33. Both the linked-fate and group commonality measures are used extensively in the political science literature. See, for example, Conover 1984; Leighley and Vedlitz 1999; Lien, Conway, and Wong 2004; Masuoka 2008; McClain
et al. 2006; Miller et al. 1981; Sanchez 2006; Sanchez and Masuoka 2010; Stokes
2003; J. Wong 2006. These measures have been tested extensively for validity
and reliability.

34. The correlations are all significantly different at the 0.01 level.

35. Regression analyses specifying perceptions of discrimination against the
respondent's racial group as the dependent variable demonstrate that perceived
linked fate is a positive and significant predictor for perceptions of discrimination among all minority respondents ($p < 0.05$), while group closeness is a significant predictor only among African Americans ($p < 0.01$). The significant effect of perceived linked fate among racial minority groups persists even after
accounting for age, gender, socioeconomic status, foreign-born status, and political ideology ($p < 0.05$).

36. Because of the controversial nature of the topic of race, research has
shown that respondents modify their responses in order to provide more socially desirable answers that do not appear to be racist. Berinsky (1999) found
that whites are more likely to abstain from answering a question on racial policies or questions about black Americans rather than providing an answer reflecting negative racial attitudes. Social acceptability concerns are discussed at
length in Dovidio and Gaertner (1986); Kinder and Sanders (1996); Mendelberg

(2001); Schuman et al. (1997); and Hatchett and Schuman 1975. Other scholars argue that whites reject racial policies advantaging minorities as a function of a principled political ideology rather than prejudice (Sniderman and Carmines 1999; Sniderman and Piazza 1993). Although research has demonstrated that blacks who complete surveys with black interviewers give different answers than those interviewed by white interviewers (Anderson, Silver, and Abramson 1988; D. Davis 1997b), it is unclear whether or not these race-of-interviewer effects encourage less truthful answers or greater comfort among black respondents to report their real attitudes (D. Davis 1997a). Jost and Banaji (1994) claim that racial minorities are less subject to social acceptability concerns because of the structure of the racial hierarchy.

37. We selected only questions that reference all racial and ethnic minorities rather than questions targeting a particular group in order to reduce potential confounding of in-group favoritism. See appendix D, available online at http://www.press.uchicago.edu/sites/masuoka/, for question wording.

38. The analysis earlier in the chapter confirmed that perceptions of linked fate vary significantly by race, and so for this analysis, we employ a method of comparative relational analysis. Equations were estimated separately by racial group in order to observe the effect of perceived linked fate for each dependent variable. The regression model was specified as racial attitude measure = β_1(linked fate) + β_2(age) + β_3(education) + β_4(income) + β_5(female) + β_6(foreign born) + β_7(ideology). Results of the estimations are documented in appendix tables D.2 through D.4. Sample sizes for each model vary depending on response rates but sizes are no smaller than 796 whites, 649 blacks, 429 Asian Americans, and 662 Latinos.

39. The regression models were specified as Perceptions of Discrimination = β_1 (linked fate) + β_2 (age) + β_3 (education) + β_4 (income) + β_5 (female) + β_6 (foreign born) + β_7 (ideology). Results of the estimations are documented in appendix tables D.5 through D.8. Sample sizes for each model vary depending on response rates, but sizes are no smaller than 779 whites, 655 blacks, 426 Asian Americans, and 656 Latinos.

40. Political theorists including Gutmann (2004) and Kymlicka (1995) argue not only that individuals are capable of holding and embracing multiple identities but that this diversity is an important characteristic supporting deliberation in democracy. The idea that multiple identities inform unique experiences is also embraced in theories of intersectionality (e.g., Crenshaw, 1991; C. Cohen, 1999; Hancock, 2004; and Strolovitch 2007).

41. This analysis included only US citizens only in order to eliminate the potential confounds of competing national loyalties among non-citizens. Differences between whites and racial minorities are significant at $p < 0.01$, and continue to be significant even after accounting for variation in age, gender, socioeconomic status, and political ideology.

Chapter 5

1. The Gallup poll has asked the question "Should immigration be increased, decreased or kept at its present level?" since 1965. Support for decreased immigration has been as high as 65% in 1993 and as low as 38% in 2000. The data are available at http://brain.gallup.com/home.aspx.

2. These characteristics also interact with one another creating unique experiences for those individuals found at the intersection (Hancock 2007; C. Cohen 1999; Crenshaw 1991).

3. Gender and class may structure agency in ways similar to race, but analysis of their effects is beyond the scope of this project.

4. High cognitive sophistication influences how respondents answer survey questions. Carmines and Stimson (1980) argue there is a relationship between attention and sophistication on the one hand and the type of survey question on the other. "Easy" questions regarding attitudes toward groups or valence issues encourage affective or immediate "top of the head" responses that do not require careful attention or high levels of sophistication. "Hard" questions ask for opinions on specific policies or events and require higher levels of knowledge. Questions on general immigration restriction and perceptions about groups, citizenship, and belonging are closer to the "easy" end of the continuum.

5. The role of immigrant contact is not only used to understand the formation of immigration policy attitudes but also to analyze intergroup conflict. See, for example, McClain et al. (2006).

6. While Citrin and colleagues show that the connection between economic outlook and immigration attitudes is weak, Hainmueller and Hiscox (2010) provide further evidence that economic threat does not directly influence immigration attitudes.

7. Factors such as economic outlook and even authoritarianism are what social psychologists consider "explicit" attitudes. In other words, these are the attitudes respondents verbally communicate to the researcher. However, evidence suggests that there are also implicit attitudes—automatic thoughts that are not consciously communicated—that influence immigration attitudes (Perez 2010).

8. Practices of so-called redlining have prevented African Americans from purchasing property in all neighborhoods (Conley 1999). This segregation has allowed discriminatory practices in how state and local resources are divided. Black neighborhoods represent those with the worst school systems, poorest maintenance, and unhealthiest living conditions (Massey and Denton 1998).

9. However, new changes in black political opportunity may be changing the contours of black public opinion. Tate (2010) finds that increased black political incorporation has caused black public opinion to move from the left toward the center-left.

10. Data for the 2008 election results are from CNN exit polls, http://www
.cnn.com/ELECTION/2008/results/president/.

11. This is not the say that blacks are a politically homogenous group. Dawson
(2001) argues that African Americans rely on a set of political ideologies developed from the black experience. Black ideologies challenge the idea that individuals are politically free and autonomous, as well as the assumption of equality.
Accounting for distinctive ideologies among minority populations is difficult,
particularly because, as Dawson suggests, scholars do not fully agree on the content of black political ideology.

12. The effects of social desirability must always be considered when asking
about potentially sensitive topics in surveys. The Faces of Immigration Survey
was administered to a random probability sample of the US population via the
Internet and conducted by the survey research firm Knowledge Networks. This
method of administration alleviates some of the potential biases introduced by
race-of-interviewer effects identified in data collected in interviews over the telephone or in person (D. Davis 1997b; Hatchett and Schuman 1975). In addition,
questions on immigration may be less affected by concerns with social desirability effects compared to questions on redistribution and racial inequality, where
scholars have found social desirability effects for white respondents (Berinsky
1999). Americans of all races are openly willing to provide negative assessments
about immigrants and immigration restriction, and the effect of social desirability on responses is less of a concern.

13. Authoritarianism is often measured by a battery of questions on childrearing practices; however Hetherington and Perez (2010) found that this measure accounts for authoritarian personality among whites but not among African
American respondents. See also Hetherington and Weiler (2009). The measure
we use asks about another key dimension of authoritarianism, preference for social order.

14. Party identification was measured on an ordinal scale with 0 representing those who are strongly Democratic and the maximum value, 1, representing
those who are strongly Republican. Solid independents (i.e., those who do not
lean Democrat or Republican) are coded at the median of the scale.

15. Cara Wong (2007) finds that both white and racial-minority respondents
overreport the size of minority populations. Even though racial groups tend to
live in highly segregated neighborhoods with others of the same race, respondents
of all races perceive a more racially diverse population than is actually the case.

16. According to the US Census, high-immigration states are the five states
that have historically experienced the most immigration (from highest to lowest): California, New York, Texas, Florida, and Illinois.

17. In addition to taking into account subjective and objective measures of intergroup contact, there are other important reasons to include these two variables. The high-immigration-state variable accounts for the type of political

culture in an area. States with long histories of immigration have developed an institutional capacity to deal with immigrant populations. In contrast, states with less experience with immigrants either in the past or recently have less capacity to handle immigrants. Hopkins (2010) found that residents in areas that had witnessed immigration growth for the first time can be more easily mobilized to support anti-immigrant initiatives than residents of traditional immigrant destinations. In contrast, the variable representing neighborhood diversity is a self-reported measure about the amount of racial diversity experienced and is not limited to contact with immigrants. This self-reported measure is the best way to test existing theories on realistic group threat (Blumer 1958; Bobo and Hutchings 1996). Those who feel more threatened by newcomers have stronger perceptions of their own group being overtaken in numbers. Cara Wong (2007) finds that how a respondent perceives diversity is a better indicator of the respondent's attitudes than the actual diversity of his or her surroundings.

18. We included a control variable for exposure to experimental primes included in the study. Substantive results from this experiment are discussed in chapter 6.

19. We used the SPost program created by Long and Freese (2006). To calculate the predicted probabilities, we set the respondent to be native born, middle-aged, middle class, having some college education, male, residing in a racially homogenous neighborhood in a state that is not among the top five in immigration. All other factors were held at their median value, and perceived linked fate is set to its highest value.

20. The same method as described above was used for those with strong group identities. For this analysis, because responses to the American-boundary measure are skewed toward the highest end of the index, respondents classified as "weak" identifiers rank at the bottom 10% or give scores of 0 to 7 on a fifteen-point scale.

21. Results for this set of model estimates are provided in appendix table A.8.

22. See appendix A for question wording and appendix table A.9 for the distribution of these items by race.

23. Although the Illegal Immigration Reform and Immigrant Responsibility Act of 1996 was signed into law by Democratic president Bill Clinton, the bill was largely considered a policy success of the Republican leaders who controlled Congress at the time (Tichenor 2002).

Chapter 6

1. The Wilson ad can be viewed at http://www.youtube.com/watch?v=lLIzzs2 HHgY. The Tancredo ad can be viewed on YouTube at http://www.youtube.com/ watch?v=j3ERcvnnsiU.

2. Although framing and priming can strongly influence public opinion, the voting public will not necessarily obey every message presented by political elites. Certain individuals are more strongly swayed by political messages than others. Cognitive sophistication, motivation, and even party identification have been found to moderate the effects of framing and priming (Chong and Druckman 2007).

3. See also García Bedolla and Michelson (2009); Hutchings et al. (2006); Perez (2011); Philpot and White (2010); Ramirez 2005; J. Wong (2005).

4. The American choice to employ the term "illegal" is also clearly seen as a purposeful political strategy when we compare the United States with other European countries. In Europe, these immigrants are framed as the "irregular population" or "without papers" (see Cornelius et al. 2004; Koopmans et al. 2005).

5. The distinction between legal and illegal immigration arguably started with the 1882 Chinese Exclusion Act. However, since this act only targeted one particular immigrant group, a clear distinction between legal and illegal immigration that would be applied to immigrants more generally did not arise until 1924 (see Ngai 2005).

6. Data on support for decreasing immigration were gleaned from multiple surveys documented in the Gallup iPOLL database, accessed August 13, 2012, http://www.ropercenter.uconn.edu/cgi-bin/hsrun.exe/roperweb/pom/pom .htx;start=ipollsearch?TopID=15. The questions were on different surveys and conducted by different survey firms, though all questions were asked of a nationally representative sample of respondents.

7. The survey was collected using computer-assisted telephone interviews conducted between February 8 and March 7, 2006. Respondents had the option of conducting the survey in either English or Spanish. This survey included a nationwide sample of 2,000 adults as well as city samples for Chicago, IL; Las Vegas, NV; Phoenix, AZ; and Raleigh-Durham, NC. We limited the analysis to the nationwide sample only. The sample sizes by racial group were whites ($n =$ 1,499), blacks ($n = 176$), and Latinos ($n = 185$). The remainder of the same was controlled for as "other race" in our analyses. The sampling error for the entire sample is ± 3.5 percentage points. For additional information about this survey see http://www.pewhispanic.org/2006/03/30/americas-immigration-quandary/.

8. One way to study framing effects is to compare public opinion on immigration before and after a major political event involving illegal immigrants or immigration policy. Media attention to events such as the Proposition 187 campaign or the passage of SB 1070 in Arizona in 2010 (which authorized racial profiling and automatic searches of those suspected to be illegal immigrants) will mean that voters are provided persistent frames in favor of or opposed to illegal immigration. These events provide scholars a natural experiment to test how American public opinion changes in response to persistent media and political attention to illegal immigration. A report by the Field Poll that tracked Californian

opinion on Proposition 187 over the last two months leading up to the election found that support for the initiative the changed most among likely white voters, while Latino support remained unchanged (Field and DiCamillo 1994). This finding supports our hypothesis that illegal immigration frames will most likely influence white attitudes. However, we recognize that more extensive analysis of these data is needed to fully verify this pattern.

9. Results for all analyses of the 2006 Pew data reported here were weighted to reflect the national sample. Sample sizes by racial group were 1,499 whites, 176 blacks, and 185 Latinos.

10. We considered responses to the "bigger problem" question to be nominal in nature. Therefore, we used multinomial logit analysis and used those who felt "illegal immigration" was the biggest problem as our comparison group. In these models, we included race, age, education, income, gender, being foreign born, and political ideology as control variables. To observe differences between whites and racial minorities as well as possible differences across racial minority groups, we ran two different multinomial models: one with whites as the excluded category and one with blacks as the excluded category. Appendix tables E.2 and E.3 detail the results.

11. The hypothesis we test here is whether or not difference in responses to illegal immigration vary systematically by race. We thus seek to show, using the control-variable approach, whether or not race is a key factor explaining attitude differences, even if assuming all else is held equal. Questions seeking to determine why these differences occur should employ comparative relational analysis. However, since we believe the existing assumption is that racial groups respond similarly to illegal immigration, we seek to discount that claim attempting to verify that group differences can be attributed systematically to race.

12. However, we excluded responses to the question "Which of the following actions do you think would be MOST effective in reducing the number of illegal immigrants who come to the U.S. across the Mexican border" because it is unclear which of the three response options (increasing border patrol, building more fences, or employer sanction) is the most restrictive option.

13. Because we needed to determine differences between whites and racial minorities as well as possible differences across racial minority groups, we ran two different regression models: one with whites as the excluded category and one with blacks as the excluded category. Appendix table E.6 details the results.

14. The sample sizes for the Asian-immigrant treatment group, the Latino-immigrant treatment group, and the control group were 140, 167, and 126 for whites; 139, 142, and 157 for blacks; 148, 113, and 124 for Asians; and 142, 128, and 140 for Latinos. Appendix A documents the experimental treatments.

15. By doing so, we sought to escape the problem that respondents might be influenced by social desirability concerns. Mendelberg (2001) argues that explicit questions about race cause white respondents to change their answers in order to

conform with existing social norms about racial equality. Therefore, it is difficult to measure white racial attitudes using direct and explicit racial messages. Rather, she advocates use of implicit or indirect messages such as images, which more subtly prime race to white respondents.

16. The treatments were taken from the US Census Bureau website (http://www.census.gov/multimedia/www/photos/facts_for_features/), which provides public-domain images of Americans.

17. We recognize that this design is distinctively different from most other designs used to test the racial-appeals hypothesis. Scholars usually choose stimuli that encourage specific negative stereotypes of racial minorities. However, in our design, we were more concerned with external validity, so we explicitly attempted to provide images of immigrants that respondents would likely encounter in their daily lives. We recognize that our stimuli may not capture extreme negative responses to immigrants, but any difference in attitudes can be directly attributed to the racial prime.

18. Because our samples of Asian American and Latino respondents include relatively larger shares of immigrants compared to the white and black samples, we also examined the effect of the treatment across only native-born Asians and Latinos. Although native-born Asians and Latinos held more negative attitudes toward immigrants compared to the full samples, we did not find significant effects from the experimental treatment for any of the three measures. Therefore, we present the results for the full Asian and Latino samples in this discussion.

19. Differences of means significant at $p < 0.01$.

20. Statistically significant results reported in this discussion are significant by at least $p < 0.10$.

Conclusion

1. In a speech to the National Federation of Republican Women, Newt Gingrich, who was then running for the 2012 Republican presidential nomination, stated: "We should replace bilingual education with immersion in English so people learn the common language of the country and they learn the language of prosperity, not the language of living in a ghetto" Associated Press (2007). See also Rutenberg and Zeleny (2012).

2. The Obama administration deported more than 1 million people in 2.5 years. Bennett (2011); O'Toole (2011).

3. Hoekstra lost the election for a seat in the US House of Representatives.

References

Abrajano, Marisa. 2010. *Campaigning to the New American Electorate: Advertising to Latino Voters*. Palo Alto, CA: Stanford University Press.

Abrajano, Marisa, and Simran Singh. 2009. "Examining the Link between Issue Attitudes and News Source: The Case of Latinos and Immigration Reform." *Political Behavior* 31 (1): 1–30.

Abrams, Dominic, Michael A. Hogg, and José Marques, eds. 2005. *Social Psychology of Inclusion and Exclusion*. New York: Psychology Press.

Adorno, Theodor, Else Frenkel-Brunswick, Daniel Levinson, and R. Nevitt Sanford. 1950. *The Authoritarian Personality*. New York: Harper.

Alba, Richard, and Victor Nee. 2005. *Remaking the American Mainstream: Assimilation and Contemporary Immigration*. Cambridge, MA: Harvard University Press.

Aleinikoff, T. Alexander. 2002. *Semblances of Sovereignty: The Constitution, the State, and American Citizenship*. Cambridge, MA: Harvard University Press.

Allport, Gordon W. 1954. *The Nature of Prejudice*. Cambridge, MA: Addison-Wesley.

Andersen, Kristi. 1979. *The Creation of a Democratic Majority, 1928–1936*. Chicago: University of Chicago Press.

Anderson, Barbara, Brian Silver, and Paul Abramson. 1988. "The Effects of the Race of the Interviewer on Race-Related Attitudes of Black Respondents in the SRC/CPS National Election Studies." *Public Opinion Quarterly* 52:289–324.

Anderson, Benedict. 1991. *Imagined Communities: Reflections on the Origin and Spread of Nationalism*. New York: Verso.

Anderson, Cameron, and Jennifer Berdahl. 2002. "The Experience of Power: Examining the Effects of Power on Approach and Inhibition Tendencies." *Journal of Personality and Social Psychology* 83:1362–1377.

Arkes, Hal, and Philip Tetlock. 2004. "Attributions of Implicit Prejudice or

'Would Jesse Jackson "Fail" the Implicit Attitudes Test?'" *Psychological Inquiry* 15 (4): 257–278.

Armor, David, and Curtis Gilroy. 2010. "Changing Minority Representation in the U.S. Military." *Armed Forces & Society* 36 (2): 223–246.

Ashburn-Nardo L., M. Knowles, and M. Monteith. 2003. "Black Americans' Implicit Racial Associations and Their Implications for Intergroup Judgment." *Social Cognition* 21:61–87.

Associated Press. 2007. "Gingrich Links Bilingual Education and 'Ghetto.'" MSNBC, March 31, 2007. Accessed August 12, 2012. http://www.msnbc.msn.com/id/17889756#.TyIxRYGwVLc.

Ayala, César, and Rafael Bernabé. 2007. *Puerto Rico in the American Century: A History since 1898.* Chapel Hill: University of North Carolina Press.

Baldus, David, George Woodworth, David Zuckerman, Neil Weiner, and Barbara Broffitt. 2001. "The Use of Peremptory Challenges in Capital Murder Trials: A Legal and Empirical Analysis." *University of Pennsylvania Journal of Constitutional Law* 3:3–169.

Barreto, Matt. 2007. "Si Se Puede! Latino Candidates and the Mobilization of Latino Voters." *American Political Science Review* 101:425–441.

———. 2010. *Ethnic Cues: The Role of Shared Ethnicity in Latino Political Participation.* Ann Arbor: University of Michigan Press.

Baumgartner, Frank R., and Bryan D. Jones. 1993. *Agendas and Instability in American Politics.* Chicago: University of Chicago Press.

Beltrán, Cristina. 2010. *The Trouble with Unity: Latino Politics and the Creation of Identity.* New York: Oxford University Press.

Bender, Steven W. 2005. *Greasers and Gringos: Latinos, Law, and the American Imagination.* New York: New York University Press.

———. 2010. *Tierra y Libertad: Land, Liberty, and Latino Housing.* New York: New York University Press.

Bennett, Brian. 2011. "Obama Administration Reports Record Number of Deportations." *Los Angeles Times*, October 18. Accessed July 9, 2012. http://articles.latimes.com/2011/oct/18/news/la-pn-deportation-ice-20111018.

Berinsky, Adam. 1999."The Two Faces of Public Opinion." *American Journal of Political Science* 43 (4): 1209–1230.

Berlin, Ira. 1992. *Slaves without Masters: The Free Negro in the Antebellum South.* New York: New Press.

Blalock, Hubert M., Jr. 1967. *Toward a Theory of Minority-Group Relations.* New York: Wiley.

Blumer, Herbert. 1958. "Race Prejudice as a Sense of Group Position." *Pacific Sociological Review* 1 (1): 3–7.

Bobo, Lawrence D., and Franklin D. Gilliam, Jr. 1990. "Race, Sociopolitical Participation, and Black Empowerment." *American Political Science Review* 84:377–393.

Bobo, Lawrence D., and Vincent Hutchings. 1996. "Perceptions of Racial Group Competition: Extending Blumer's Theory of Group Position to a Multiracial Context." *American Sociological Review* 61 (6): 951–972.

Bobo, Lawrence D., James Kluegel, and Ryan Smith. 1997. "Laissez-Faire Racism: The Crystallization of a Kinder, Gentler, Antiblack Ideology." In *Racial Attitudes in the 1990s: Continuity and Change*, edited by Steven Tuch and Jack Martin, 15–44. Westport, CT: Praeger.

Bobo, Lawrence D., and Frederick Licari. 1989. "Education and Political Tolerance: Testing the Effects of Cognitive Sophistication and Target Group Affect." *Public Opinion Quarterly* 53:285–308.

Bobo, Lawrence D., and Michael Massagli. 2001. "Stereotyping and Urban Inequality." In *Urban Inequality: Evidence from Four Cities*, edited by Alice O'Connor, Chris Tilly, and Lawrence D. Bobo, 89–162. New York: Russell Sage Foundation.

Bobo, Lawrence D., and Mia Tuan. 2006. *Prejudice in Politics: Group Position, Public Opinion, and the Wisconsin Treaty Rights Dispute*. Cambridge, MA: Harvard University Press.

Bonilla-Silva, Eduardo. 2010. *Racism without Racists: Color-Blind Racism and the Persistence of Racial Inequality in America*. 3rd ed. New York: Rowman and Littlefield.

Borjas, George. 1991. *Friends or Strangers: The Impact of Immigrants on the U.S. Economy*. New York: Basic Books.

Bosniak, Linda. 2006. *The Citizen and the Alien: Dilemmas of Contemporary Membership*. Princeton, NJ: Princeton University Press.

Bowers, William, Benjamin Steiner, and Marla Sandys. 2001. "Death Sentencing in Black and White: An Empirical Analysis of the Role of Jurors' Race and Jury Racial Composition." *University of Pennsylvania Journal of Constitutional Law* 3:171–274.

Bowler, Shaun, and Gary M. Segura. 2012. *The Future Is Ours: Minority Politics, Political Behavior, and the Multiracial Era of American Politics*. Washington, DC: CQ Press.

Brader, Ted, Nicholas Valentino, and Elizabeth Suhay. 2008. "What Triggers Public Opposition to Immigration? Anxiety, Group Cues, and Immigration Threat." *American Journal of Political Science* 52 (4): 959–978.

Branton, Regina, and Johanna Dunaway. 2009. "Slanted Newspaper Coverage of Immigration: The Importance of Economics and Geography." *Policy Studies Journal* 37:257–273.

Brewer, Marilynn. 1991. "The Social Self: On Being the Same and Different at the Same Time." *Personality and Social Psychology Bulletin* 17:475–482.

Browning, Rufus, Dale Rogers Marshall, and David Tabb. 1986. *Protest Is Not Enough: The Struggle of Blacks and Hispanics for Equality in Urban Politics*. Berkeley: University of California Press.

Brubaker, Rogers. 1998. *Citizenship and Nationhood in France and Germany.* Cambridge, MA: Harvard University Press.

Burns, Nancy. 2005. "Finding Gender." *Politics & Gender* 1 (1): 137–141.

Burns, Nancy, and Donald Kinder. 2012. "Categorical Politics: Gender, Race, and Public Opinion." In *New Directions in Public Opinion*, edited by Adam Berinsky, 139–167. New York: Routledge.

Burns, Peter, and James Gimpel. 2000. "Economic Insecurity, Prejudicial Stereotypes, and Public Opinion on Immigration Policy." *Political Science Quarterly* 115 (2): 201–225.

Calavita, Kitty. 1992. *Inside the State: The Bracero Program, Immigration, and the INS.* New York: Routledge.

Camarillo, Albert. 1984. *Chicanos in California: A History of Mexican Americans.* Sparks, NV: Materials for Today's Learning.

Campbell, Angus, Philip Converse, Warren Miller, and Donald Stokes. 1960. *The American Voter.* Chicago: University of Chicago Press.

Card, David. 1990. "The Impact of the Mariel Boatlift on the Miami Labor Market." *Industrial and Labor Relations Review* 43 (2): 245–257.

Carmines, Edward, and James Stimson. 1980. "The Two Faces of Issue Voting." *American Political Science Review* 74:78–91.

Carter, Niambi. 2007. "The Black/White Paradigm Revisited: African Americans, Immigration, Race and Nation in Durham, NC." PhD diss., Duke University.

Castano, Emanuele, Maria-Paola Paladino, Alastair Coull, and Vincent Yzerbyt. 2002. "Protecting the Ingroup Stereotype: Ingroup Identification and the Management of Deviant Ingroup Members." *British Journal of Social Psychology* 41:365–385.

Chan, Sucheng. 1991. *Asian Americans: An Interpretive History.* New York: Twayne.

Chavez, Leo. 2008. *The Latino Threat: Constructing Immigrants, Citizens, and the Nation.* Palo Alto, CA: Stanford University Press.

Chin, Gabriel. 1998. "Segregation's Last Stronghold: Racial Discrimination and the Constitutional Law of Immigration." *UCLA Law Review* 46:1–74.

Chong, Dennis, and James Druckman. 2007. "Framing Theory." *Annual Review of Political Science* 10:103–126.

Chong, Dennis, and Dukhong Kim. 2006. "The Experiences and Effects of Economic Status among Racial and Ethnic Minorities." *American Political Science Review* 100:335–351.

Citrin, Jack, Donald Green, Christopher Muse, and Cara Wong. 1997. "Public Opinion toward Immigration Reform: The Role of Economic Motivations." *Journal of Politics* 59 (3): 858–881.

Citrin, Jack, Amy Lerman, Michael Murakami, and Kathryn Pearson. 2007.

"Testing Huntington: Is Hispanic Immigration a Threat to American Identity?" *Perspectives on Politics* 5 (1): 31–48.

Citrin, Jack, Beth Reingold, and Donald Green. 1990. "American Identity and the Politics of Ethnic Change." *Journal of Politics* 52 (4): 1124–1154.

Clawson, Rosalee, Harry Neil Strine IV, and Eric Waltenburg. 2003. "Framing Supreme Court Decisions: The Mainstream versus the Black Press." *Journal of Black Studies* 33 (6): 784–800.

Cohen, Cathy. 1999. *The Boundaries of Blackness: AIDS and the Breakdown of Black Politics.* Chicago: University of Chicago Press.

Cohen, Deborah. 2011. *Braceros: Migrant Citizens and Transnational Subjects in the Postwar United States and Mexico.* Chapel Hill: University of North Carolina Press.

Conley, Dalton.1999. *Being Black, Living in the Red: Race, Wealth, and Social Policy in America.* Berkeley: University of California Press.

Conover, Pamela J. 1984. "The Influence of Group Identification on Political Perception and Evaluation." *Journal of Politics* 46 (3): 760–785.

———. 1988. "The Role of Social Groups in Political Thinking." *British Journal of Political Science* 18 (1): 51–76.

Converse, Philip. 1964. "The Nature of Belief Systems in Mass Publics." In *Ideology and Discontent,* edited by David Apter New York: Free Press.

Cornelius, Wayne, and Marc Rosenblum. 2005. "Immigration and Politics." *Annual Review of Political Science* 8:99–119.

Cornelius, Wayne, Takeyuki Tsuda, Philip Martin, and James Hollifield. 2004. *Controlling Immigration: A Global Perspective.* 2nd ed. Palo Alto, CA: Stanford University Press.

Crenshaw, Kimberle. 1991. "Mapping the Margins: Intersectionality, Identity Politics, and Violence against Women of Color." *Stanford Law Review.* 43:1241–1299.

Cuddy, Amy, Susan Fiske, and Peter Glick. 2007. "The BIAS Map: Behaviors from Intergroup Affect and Stereotypes." *Journal of Personality and Social Psychology* 92:631–648.

Dahl, Robert. 1961. *Who Governs? Democracy and Power in an American City.* New Haven, CT: Yale University Press.

Daniels, Roger. 2004a. *Guarding the Golden Door: American Immigration Policy and Immigrants since 1882.* New York: Hill and Wang.

———. 2004b. *Prisoners without Trail: Japanese Americans in World War II.* New York: Hill and Wang.

———. Davis, Winfield J. 1893. *History of Political Conventions in California, 1849–1892.* Sacramento: California State Library.

Dawson, Michael C. 1994. *Behind the Mule: Race and Class in African-American Politics.* Princeton, NJ: Princeton University Press.

———. 2001. *Black Visions: The Roots of Contemporary African-American Political Ideologies*. Chicago: University of Chicago Press.

———. 2011. *Not in Our Lifetimes: The Future of Black Politics*. Chicago: University of Chicago Press.

De Angelis, Karin, and David Segal. 2012. "Minorities in the Military." In *The Oxford Handbook of Military Psychology*, edited by Janice Laurence and Michael Matthews, 325–343. New York: Oxford University Press.

De la Garza, Rodolfo O., Louis DeSipio, F. Chris Garcia, John Garcia, and Angelo Falcon. 1992. *Latino Voices: Mexican, Puerto Rican, and Cuban Perspectives on American Politics*. Boulder, CO: Westview.

De la Garza, Rodolfo O., Angelo Falcon, and F. Chris Garcia. 1996. "Will the Real Americans Please Stand Up: Anglo and Mexican-American Support of Core American Political Values." *American Journal of Political Science* 40 (2): 335–351.

Delli Carpini, Michael X., and Scott Keeter. 1996. *What Americans Know about Politics and Why It Matters*. New Haven, CT: Yale University Press.

Department of Homeland Security. 2011. *Yearbook of Immigration Statistics: 2010*. Washington, DC: US Department of Homeland Security, Office of Immigration Statistics.

DeSipio, Louis. 1996. *Counting on the Latino Vote: Latinos as the New Electorate*. Charlottesville: University Press of Virginia.

Devine, Patricia. 1989. "Stereotypes and Prejudice: Their Automatic and Controlled Components." *Journal of Personality and Social Psychology* 56:5–18.

Devine, Patricia, and Andrew Elliot. 1995. "Are Racial Stereotypes Really Fading? The Princeton Trilogy Revisited." *Personality and Social Psychology Bulletin* 21:1139–1150.

Devos, Thierry, and Mahzarin Banaji. 2005. "American = White?" *Journal of Personality and Social Psychology* 88:447–466.

Dovidio, John F., and Samuel L. Gaertner, eds. 1986. *Prejudice, Discrimination, and Racism*. Orlando: Academic.

Dovidio, John F., Nancy Evans, and Richard Tyler. 1986. "Racial Stereotypes: The Contents of Their Cognitive Representations." *Journal of Experimental Social Psychology*. 22 (1): 22–37.

Druckman, James. 2010. "What's It All About? Framing in Political Science." In *Perspectives on Framing*, edited by Gideon Keren, 279–302. New York: Psychology Press.

Druckman, James, Cari Hennessy, Kristi St. Charles, and Jonathan Webber. 2010. "Competing Rhetoric over Time: Frames versus Cues." *Journal of Politics* 72 (1): 136–148.

Druckman, James, and Kjersten Nelson. 2003. "Framing and Deliberation: How Citizens' Conversations Limit Elite Influence." *American Journal of Political Science* 47 (4): 729–745.

Dunaway, Johanna, Regina Branton, and Marisa Abrajano. 2010. "Agenda Setting, Public Opinion, and the Issue of Immigration Reform." *Social Science Quarterly* 91 (2): 359–378.

Ellemers, Naomi, Russell Spears, and Bertjan Doosje. 1999. *Social Identity: Context, Commitment, Content.* Oxford: Blackwell.

Emirbayer, Mustafa. 1997. "Manifesto for a Relational Sociology." *American Journal of Sociology.* 103 (2): 281–317.

Entman, Robert, and Andrew Rojecki. 2000. *The Black Image in the White Mind: Media and Race in America.* Chicago: University of Chicago Press.

Espenshade, Thomas, and Katherine Hempstead. 1996. "Contemporary American Attitudes toward U.S. Immigration." *International Migration Review* 30 (2): 535–570.

Feldman, Stanley. 2003. "Enforcing Social Conformity: A Theory of Authoritarianism." *Political Psychology* 24 (1): 41–74.

Feldman, Stanley, and Karen Stenner. 1997. "Perceived Threat and Authoritarianism." *Political Psychology* 18 (4): 741–770.

Field, Mervin D., and Mark DiCamillo. 1994. "Big Drop in Support for Prop. 187, The Anti–Illegal Immigrant Measure." Field Poll Release no. 1734, Field Institute, San Francisco.

Filindra, Alexandra, and Jane Junn. 2012. "Aliens and of Color: The Multidimensional Relationship of Immigration Policy and Racial Classification in the U.S." In *Oxford Handbook of International Migration*, edited by Daniel Tichenor and Marc Rosenblum, 429–455. Oxford: Oxford University Press.

Fiske, Susan. 1993. "Controlling Other People: The Impact of Power on Stereotyping." *American Psychologist* 48 (6): 621–628.

———. 2011. *Envy Up, Scorn Down: How Status Divides Us.* New York: Russell Sage Foundation.

Foner, Eric. 1999. *The Story of American Freedom.* New York: W. W. Norton.

Fraga, Luis, John Garcia, Gary Segura, Michael Jones-Correa, Rodney Hero, and Valerie Martinez-Ebers. 2010. *Latino Lives in America: Making It Home.* Philadelphia: Temple University Press.

Fraga, Luis, and Gary Segura. 2006. "Culture Clash? Contesting Notions of American Identity and the Effects of Latin American Immigration." *Perspectives on Politics* 4 (2): 279–287.

Franklin, John Hope, and Alfred A. Moss, Jr. 1988. *From Slavery to Freedom: A History of Negro Americans.* 6th ed. New York: McGraw-Hill.

Frymer, Paul. 1999. *Uneasy Alliances: Race and Party Competition in America.* Princeton, NJ: Princeton University Press.

Gaertner, Samuel L., and John F. Dovidio. 2000. *Reducing Intergroup Bias: The Common Ingroup Identity Model.* Philadelphia: Psychology Press.

Gamson, William A. 1992. *Talking Politics.* New York: Cambridge University Press.

Gamson, William A., and Andre Modigliani. 1987. "The Changing Culture of Affirmative Action." In *Research in Political Sociology*, vol. 3, edited by Richard D. Braungart, 137–177. Greenwich, CT: JAI.

García Bedolla, Lisa. 2005. *Fluid Borders: Latino Power, Identity, and Politics in Los Angeles.* Berkeley: University of California Press.

García Bedolla, Lisa, and Melissa Michelson. 2009. "What Do Voters Need to Know? Testing the Role of Cognitive Information in Asian American Voter Mobilization." *American Politics Research* 37:254–274.

Gardner, Martha. 2005. *The Qualities of a Citizen: Women, Immigration, and Citizenship, 1870–1965.* Princeton, NJ: Princeton University Press.

Gilens, Martin. 1999. *Why Americans Hate Welfare: Race, Media, and the Politics of Antipoverty Policy.* Chicago: University of Chicago Press.

Gillion, Steven. 2000. *That's Not What We Meant to Do: Reform and Its Unintended Consequences in Twentieth-Century America.* New York: W. W. Norton.

Gladwell, Malcolm. 2008. *Outliers: The Story of Success.* New York: Little, Brown.

Glenn, Evelyn Nakano. 2002. *Unequal Freedom: How Race and Gender Shaped American Citizenship and Labor.* Cambridge, MA: Harvard University Press.

Goldstein, A., and J. Chance. 1978. "Judging Face Similarity in Own and Other Races." *Journal of Psychology* 98:185–193.

Gomez, Laura. 2008. *Manifest Destinies: The Making of the Mexican American Race.* New York: New York University Press.

Gordon, Milton. 1964. *Assimilation in American Life: The Role of Race, Religion, and National Origins.* New York: Oxford University Press.

Green, Donald, Robert Abelson, and Margaret Garnett. 1999. "The Distinctive Political Views of Hate-Crime Perpetrators and White Supremacists." In *Cultural Divides: Understanding and Overcoming Group Conflict*, edited by Deborah Prentice and Dale Miller, 429–64. New York: Russell Sage Foundation.

Green, Donald, Bradley Palmquist, and Eric Schickler. 2004. *Partisan Hearts and Minds: Political Parties and the Social Identities of Voters.* New Haven, CT: Yale University Press.

Greer, Christina. 2013. *Black Ethnics: Race, Immigration, and the Pursuit of the American Dream.* New York: Oxford University Press.

Gross, Ariela. 2008. *What Blood Won't Tell: A History of Race on Trial in America.* Cambridge, MA: Harvard University Press.

Gutmann, Amy. 2004. *Identity in Democracy.* Princeton, NJ: Princeton University Press.

Gyory, Andrew. 1998. *Closing the Gate: Race, Politics, and the Chinese Exclusion Act.* Chapel Hill: University of North Carolina Press.

Ha, Shang. 2008. "The Consequences of Multiracial Contexts on Public Attitudes toward Immigration." *Political Research Quarterly* 63 (1): 29–42.

Hainmueller, Jens, and Michael Hiscox. 2010. "Attitudes toward Highly Skilled and Low-Skilled Immigration: Evidence from a Survey Experiment." *American Political Science Review* 104:61–84.

Hajnal, Zoltan, and Taeku Lee. 2011. *Why Americans Don't Join the Party: Race, Immigration, and the Failure of Political Parties to Engage the Electorate.* Princeton, NJ: Princeton University Press.

Hancock, Ange-Marie. 2004. *The Politics of Disgust: The Public Identity of the Welfare Queen.* New York: New York University Press.

———. 2007. "When Multiplication Doesn't Equal Quick Addition: Examining Intersectionality as a Research Paradigm." *Perspectives on Politics* 5 (1): 63–79.

Haney López, Ian. 2006. *White by Law: The Legal Construction of Race.* Rev. and updated 10th Anniversary ed. New York: New York University Press.

Harris, Lasana, and Susan Fiske. 2006. "Dehumanizing the Lowest of the Low: Neuroimaging Responses to Extreme Out-groups." *Psychological Science* 17 (10): 847–853.

Harris-Lacewell, Melissa. 2003. "The Heart of the Politics of Race: Centering Black People in the Study of White Racial Attitudes." *Journal of Black Studies* 34 (2): 222–249.

Harris-Perry, Melissa. 2011. *Sister Citizen: Shame, Stereotypes, and Black Women in America.* New Haven, CT: Yale University Press.

Hartz, Louis. 1991. *The Liberal Tradition in America: An Interpretation of American Political Thought since the Revolution.* 2nd Harvest/HBJ ed. San Diego: Harcourt Brace Jovanovich.

Haslam, Nick. 2006. "Dehumanization: An Integrative Review." *Personality and Social Psychology Review* 10 (3): 252–264.

Hatchett, Shirley, and Howard Schuman. 1975. "White Respondents and Race-of-Interviewer Effects." *Public Opinion Quarterly* 39:523–528.

Hattam, Victoria. 2007. *In the Shadow of Race: Jews, Latinos, and Immigrant Politics in the United States.* Chicago: University of Chicago Press.

Henry, P. J., and David Sears. 2000. "The Symbolic Racism 2000 Scale." *Political Psychology* 23 (2): 253–283.

Hero, Rodney. 1992. *Latinos and the U.S. Political System: Two-Tiered Pluralism.* Philadelphia: Temple University Press.

Hetherington, Marc J., and Efren Perez. 2010. "How Race Can Color the Questions We Ask and the Inferences We Draw." Paper presented at the Midwest Political Science Association Annual Meeting, Chicago, April.

Hetherington, Marc J., and Jonathan D. Weiler. 2009. *Authoritarianism and Polarization in American Politics.* New York: Cambridge University Press.

Higham, John. (1955) 2002. *Strangers in the Land: Patterns of American Nativism, 1860–1925.* New Brunswick, NJ: Rutgers University Press.

Hilton, James, and William von Hippel. 1996. "Stereotypes." *Annual Review of Psychology* 47:237–271.

Hing, Bill Ong. 1994. *Making and Remaking Asian America through Immigration Policy, 1850–1990.* Palo Alto, CA: Stanford University Press.

———. 2003. *Defining America through Immigration Policy.* Philadelphia: Temple University Press.

Hochschild, Jennifer L., Vesla M. Weaver, and Traci R. Burch. 2012. *Creating a New Racial Order: How Immigration, Multiracialism, Genomics, and the Young Can Remake Race in America.* Princeton, NJ: Princeton University Press.

Hoefer, Michael, Nancy Rytina, and Bryan Baker. 2012. "Estimates of the Unauthorized Immigrant Population Residing in the United States: January 2011." Washington, DC: Department of Homeland Security, Office of Immigration Statistics.

Hofstadter, Richard. (1948) 1989. *The American Political Tradition: And the Men Who Made It.* New York: Vintage.

Hogg, Michael A., and Dominic Abrams. 1988. *Social Identifications: A Social Psychology of Intergroup Relations and Group Processes.* London: Routledge.

Hogg, Michael A., Kelly Fielding, and John Darley. 2005. "Fringe Dwellers: Processes of Deviance and Marginalization in Groups." In *The Social Psychology of Inclusion and Exclusion,* edited by Dominic Abrams, Michael A. Hogg, and José Marques, 191–210. New York: Psychology Press.

Hopkins, Daniel. 2010. "Politicized Places: Explaining Where and When Immigrants Provoke Local Opposition." *American Political Science Review* 104:40–60.

Horowitz, Donald L. 2000. *Ethnic Groups in Conflict.* Berkeley: University of California Press.

HoSang, Daniel Martinez. 2010. *Racial Propositions: Ballot Initiatives and the Making of Postwar California.* Berkeley: University of California Press.

Huddy, Leonie. 2003. "Group Identity and Political Cohesion." In *Oxford Handbook of Political Psychology,* edited by David Sears, Leonie Huddy, and Robert Jervis, 511–558. New York: Oxford University Press.

Huddy, Leonie, and Nadia Khatib. 2007. "American Patriotism, National Identity, and Political Involvement." *American Journal of Political Science* 51 (1): 63–77.

Hughes, Michael, and David Demo. 1989. "Self-Perceptions of Black Americans: Self-Esteem and Personal Efficacy." *American Journal of Sociology* 95 (1): 132–159.

Huntington, Samuel. 2004. *Who Are We? The Challenge to America's National Identity.* New York: Simon and Schuster.

Hurwitz, Jon, and Mark Peffley. 1997. "Public Perceptions of Race and Crime: The Role of Racial Stereotypes." *American Journal of Political Science* 41 (2): 375–401.

———. 2005. "Playing the Race Card in the Post–Willie Horton Era: The Impact of Racialized Code Words on Support for Punitive Crime Policy." *Public Opinion Quarterly* 69:99–112.

Hutchings, Vincent, Nicholas Valentino, Tasha Philpot, and Ismail White. 2006. "Racial Cues in Campaign News: The Effects of Candidate Strategies on Group Activation and Political Attentiveness among African Americans." In *Feeling Politics: Emotion in Political Information Processing*, edited by David P. Redlawsk, 165–186. New York: Palgrave Macmillan.

Ignatiev, Noel. 1995. *How the Irish Became White*. New York: Routledge.

Iyengar, Shanto, and Donald Kinder. 1987. *News That Matters: Television and American Opinion*. Chicago: University of Chicago Press.

Jacobson, Matthew Frye. 1998. *Whiteness of a Different Color: European Immigrants and the Alchemy of Race*. Cambridge, MA: Harvard University Press.

———. 2006. *Roots Too: White Ethnic Revival in Post–Civil Rights America*. Cambridge, MA: Harvard University Press.

Jacobson, Robin Dale. 2008. *The New Nativism: Proposition 187 and the Debate over Immigration*. Minneapolis: University of Minnesota Press.

Jennings, M. Kent, and Richard Niemi. 1975. "Continuity and Change in Political Orientations: A Longitudinal Study of Two Generations." *American Political Science Review* 69:1316–1335.

Jiménez, Tomás. 2010. *Replenished Ethnicity: Mexican Americans, Immigration, and Identity*. Berkeley: University of California Press.

Johnson, Lyndon B. "Remarks at the Signing of the Immigration Bill, Liberty Island, New York." 1965. Speech, October 3. LBJ Presidential Library. http://www.lbjlib.utexas.edu/johnson/archives.hom/speeches.hom/651003.asp.

Jones-Correa, Michael, and David Leal. 1996. "Becoming 'Hispanic': Secondary Panethnic Identification among Latin-American-Origin Populations in the United States." *Hispanic Journal of Behavioral Sciences* 18 (2): 214–254.

Jost, John, and Mahzarin Banaji. 1994. "The Role of Stereotyping in System-Justification and the Production of False Consciousness." *British Journal of Social Psychology* 33:1–27.

Jost, John, Mahzarin Banaji, and Brian Nosek. 2004. "A Decade of System Justification Theory: Accumulated Evidence of Conscious and Unconscious Bolstering of the Status Quo." *Political Psychology* 25 (6): 881–919.

Judd, C., and B. Park. 1988. "Out-group Homogeneity: Judgments of Variability at the Individual and Group Levels." *Personality and Social Psychology Bulletin*. 54:778–788.

Junn, Jane. 2007. "From Coolie to Model Minority: U.S. Immigration Policy and the Construction of Racial Identity." *Du Bois Review* 4 (2): 355–373.

Junn, Jane, and Nadia E. Brown. 2008. "What Revolution? Incorporating Intersectionality in Women and Politics." In *Political Women and American Democracy*, edited by Christina Wolbrecht, Karen Beckwith, and Lisa Baldez, 64–78. New York: Cambridge University Press.

Junn, Jane, and Natalie Masuoka. 2008a. "Asian American Identity: Shared Racial Status and Political Context." *Perspectives on Politics* 6 (4): 729–740.

——. 2008b. "Identities in Context: Racial Group Consciousness and Political Participation among Asian American and Latino Young Adults." *Applied Developmental Science* 12 (2): 93–101.

Karst, Kenneth. 1989. *Belonging to America: Equal Citizenship and the Constitution*. New Haven, CT: Yale University Press.

Katznelson, Ira. 2005. *When Affirmative Action Was White: An Untold History of Racial Inequality in Twentieth-Century America*. New York: W. W. Norton.

Kerber, Linda. 1998. *No Constitutional Right to Be Ladies: Women and the Obligations of Citizenship*. New York: Hill and Wang.

Key, V. O. 1984. *Southern Politics in State and Nation*. New ed. Knoxville: University of Tennessee Press.

Kim, Claire Jean. 1999. "The Racial Triangulation of Asian Americans." *Politics and Society*. 27 (1): 105–138.

——. 2000. *Bitter Fruit: The Politics of Black-Korean Conflict in New York City*. New Haven, CT: Yale University Press.

Kim, Hyung-Chan. 1994. *A Legal History of Asian Americans, 1790–1990*. Westport, CT: Greenwood.

Kinder, Donald, and Allison Dale-Riddle. 2012. *The End of Race? Obama, 2008, and Racial Politics in America*. New Haven, CT: Yale University Press.

Kinder, Donald, and Cindy Kam. 2009. *Us against Them: Ethnocentric Foundations of American Opinion*. Chicago: University of Chicago Press.

Kinder, Donald, and Lynn Sanders. 1996. *Divided by Color: Racial Politics and Democratic Ideals*. Chicago: University of Chicago Press.

King, Desmond S. 2002. *Making Americans: Immigration, Race, and the Origins of the Diverse Democracy*. Cambridge, MA: Harvard University Press.

King, Desmond S., and Rogers M. Smith. 2011. *Still a House Divided: Race and Politics in Obama's America*. Princeton, NJ: Princeton University Press.

Kohut, Andrew, Roberto Suro, Scott Keeter, Carroll Doherty, and Gabriel Escobar. 2006. *America's Immigration Quandary: No Consensus on Immigration Problem or Proposed Fixes*. Washington, DC: Pew Research Center for the People and the Press and Pew Hispanic Center. Accessed January 22, 2007. http://pewhispanic.org/files/reports/63.pdf.

Koopmans, Ruud, Paul Statham, Marco Guigni, and Florence Passy. 2005. *Contested Citizenship: Immigration and Cultural Diversity in Europe*. Minneapolis: University of Minnesota Press.

Kosterman, Rick, and Seymour Feshbach. 1989. "Toward a Measure of Patriotic and Nationalistic Attitudes." *Political Psychology* 10 (2): 257–274.

Kymlicka, Will. 1995. *Multicultural Citizenship*. New York: Oxford University Press.

Lapinski, John, Pia Peltola, Greg Shaw, and Alan Yang. 1997. "The Polls—Trends: Immigrants and Immigration." *Public Opinion Quarterly* 61:356–383.

Lau, Richard, and David P. Redlawsk. 2006. *How Voters Decide: Information Processing in Election Campaigns*. New York: Cambridge University Press.

Lee, Jennifer, and Frank D. Bean. 2010. *The Diversity Paradox: Immigration and the Color Line in Twenty-First Century America*. New York: Russell Sage Foundation.

Lee, Sharon, and Barry Edmonston. 2005. "New Marriages, New Families: U.S. Racial and Hispanic Intermarriage." *Population Bulletin* 60 (2): 3–36.

Lee, Taeku. 2008. "Race, Immigration, and the Identity-to-Politics Link." *Annual Review of Political Science* 11:457–478.

Leighley, Jan. 2001. *Strength in Numbers: The Political Mobilization of Racial and Ethnic Minorities*. Princeton, NJ: Princeton University Press.

Leighley, Jan, and Arnold Vedlitz. 1999. "Race, Ethnicity, and Political Participation: Competing Models and Contrasting Explanations." *Journal of Politics* 61 (4): 1092–1114.

Li, Qiong, and Marilynn Brewer. 2004. "What Does It Mean to Be an American? Patriotism, Nationalism, and American Identity after 9/11." *Political Psychology* 25 (5): 727–739.

Lieberman, Robert. 1998. *Shifting the Color Line: Race and the American Welfare State*. Cambridge, MA: Harvard University Press.

———. 2008. "Legacies of Slavery? Race and Historical Causation in American Political Development." In *Race and American Political Development*, edited by Joseph E. Lowndes, Julie Novkov, and Dorian Tod Warren, 206–233. New York: Taylor Francis.

Lien, Pei-te. 2001. *The Making of Asian America through Political Participation*. Philadelphia: Temple University Press.

Lien, Pei-te, M. Margaret Conway, and Janelle S. Wong. 2004. *The Politics of Asian Americans: Diversity and Community*. New York: Routledge.

Lippmann, Walter. 1922. *Public Opinion*. New York: Harcourt, Brace.

Lipset, Seymour Martin. 1997. *American Exceptionalism: A Double-Edged Sword*. New York: W. W. Norton.

Lipsitz, George. 1998. *Possessive Investment in Whiteness: How White People Profit from Identity Politics*. Philadelphia: Temple University Press.

Long, J. Scott, and Jeremy Freese. 2006. *Regression Models for Categorical Dependent Variables Using Stata*. 2nd ed. College Station, TX: Stata.

Lublin, David. 1999. *The Paradox of Representation: Racial Gerrymander-

ing and Minority Interests in Congress. Princeton, NJ: Princeton University Press.

Major, Brenda, and Laurie O'Brien. 2005. "The Social Psychology of Stigma." *Annual Review of Psychology* 56:393–421.

Marques, José, Dominic Abrams, Dario Páez, and Michael A. Hogg. 2001. "Social Categorization, Social Identification, and Rejection of Deviant Group Members." In *Blackwell Handbook of Social Psychology: Group Processes,* edited by Michael A. Hogg, and Scott Tindale, 400–424. Malden, MA: Blackwell.

Marques, José, Dominic Abrams, Dario Páez, and Cristina Martinez-Taboada. 1998. "The Role of Categorization and In-group Norms in Judgments of Groups and Their Members." *Journal of Personality and Social Psychology* 75:976–988.

Marx, Anthony W. 1998. *Making Race and Nation: A Comparison of South Africa, the United States, and Brazil.* New York: Cambridge University Press.

Massey, Douglas. 2007. *Categorically Unequal: The American Stratification System.* New York: Russell Sage Foundation.

Massey, Douglas, and Nancy Denton. 1998. *American Apartheid: Segregation and the Making of the Underclass.* Cambridge, MA: Harvard University Press.

Masuoka, Natalie. 2006. "Together They Become One: Examining the Predictors of Panethnic Group Consciousness among Asian Americans and Latinos." *Social Science Quarterly* 87 (5): 993–1011.

———. 2008a. "Defining the Group: Latino Identity and Political Participation." *American Politics Research* 36:33–61.

———. 2008b. "Political Attitudes and Ideologies of Multiracial Americans: The Implications of Mixed Race in the U.S." *Political Research Quarterly* 61 (2): 253–267.

McAdam, Doug. 1982. *Political Process and the Development of Black Insurgency, 1930–1970.* Chicago: University of Chicago Press.

McCall, Leslie. 2001. *Complex Inequality: Gender, Class, and Race in the New Economy.* New York: Routledge.

McClain, Paula, Niambi Carter, Victoria DeFrancesco Soto, Monique Lyle, Jeffrey Grynaviski, Shayla Nunnally, Thomas Scotto, J. Alan Kendrick, Gerald Lackey, and Kendra Davenport Cotton. 2006. "Racial Distancing in a Southern City: Latino Immigrants' Views of Black Americans." *Journal of Politics* 68 (3): 571–584.

McConnaughy, Corrine, Ismail White, David Leal, and Jason Casellas. 2010. "A Latino on the Ballot: Explaining Coethnic Voting among Latinos and Response of White Americans." *Journal of Politics* 72 (4): 1119–1211.

Menchaca, Martha. 2002. *Recovering History, Constructing Race: The Indian,*

Black, and White Roots of Mexican Americans. Austin: University of Texas Press.

Mendelberg, Tali. 2001. *The Race Card: Campaign Strategy, Implicit Messages, and the Norm of Equality.* Princeton, NJ: Princeton University Press.

Miller, Arthur H., Patricia Gurin, Gerald Gurin, and Oksana Malanchuk. 1981. "Group Consciousness and Political Participation." *American Journal of Political Science* 25 (3): 494–511.

Miller, Warren. 1992. "Generational Changes and Party Identification." *Political Behavior* 14 (3): 333–352.

Minter, Shannon. 1993. "Sodomy and Public Morality Offenses under U.S. Immigration Law: Penalizing Lesbian and Gay Identity." *Cornell International Law Journal* 26:771–818.

Montejano, David. 1987. *Anglos and Mexicans in the Making of Texas, 1836–1986.* Austin: University of Texas Press.

Morris, Irwin. 2000. "African American Voting on Proposition 187: Rethinking the Prevalence of Interminority Conflict." *Political Research Quarterly* 53 (1): 77–98.

Neiman, Max, Martin Johnson, and Shaun Bowler. 2006. "Partisanship and Views about Immigration in Southern California: Just How Partisan is the Issue of Immigration?" *International Migration* 44 (2): 35–56.

Neuman, Gerald. 1996. *Strangers to the Constitution: Immigrants, Borders, and Fundamental Law.* Princeton, NJ: Princeton University Press.

Nevins, Joseph. 2010. *Operation Gatekeeper: The Rise of the "Illegal Alien" and the Remaking of the U.S.-Mexico Border,* 2nd ed. New York: Routledge.

Newton, Lina. 2008. *Illegal, Alien, or Immigrant: The Politics of Immigration Reform.* New York: New York University Press.

Ngai, Mae. 2004. *Impossible Subjects: Illegal Aliens and the Making of Modern America.* Princeton, NJ: Princeton University Press.

Nicholson, Stephen. 2005. *Voting the Agenda: Candidates, Elections, and Ballot Propositions.* Princeton, NJ: Princeton University Press.

Nie, Norman, Jane Junn, and Kenneth Stehlik-Barry. 1996. *Education and Democratic Citizenship in America.* Chicago: University of Chicago Press.

Nobles, Melissa. 2000. *Shades of Citizenship: Race and the Census in Modern Politics.* Palo Alto, CA: Stanford University Press.

Nunnally, Shayla. 2012. *Trust in Black America: Race, Discrimination, and Politics.* New York: New York University Press.

Oliver, J. Eric, and Janelle S. Wong. 2003. "Racial Context and Inter-Group Prejudice in a Multi-Ethnic Setting." *American Journal of Political Science* 47 (4): 567–582.

Oliver, Melvin, and Thomas Shapiro. 2006. *Black Wealth/White Wealth: A New Perspective on Racial Inequality.* New York: Routledge.

Omi, Michael, and Howard Winant. 1994. *Racial Formation in the United States: From the 1960s to the 1990.* 2nd ed. New York: Routledge.

Ono, Kent, and John Sloop. 2002. *Shifting Borders: Rhetoric, Immigration, and California's Proposition 187.* Philadelphia: Temple University Press.

O'Toole, Molly. 2011. "Analysis: Obama Deportations Raise Immigration Policy Questions." Reuters, September 20, 2011. Accessed July 9, 2012. http://www.reuters.com/article/2011/09/20/us-obama-immigration-idUSTRE78J05720110920.

Padilla, Felix. 1985. *Latino Ethnic Consciousness: The Case of Mexican Americans and Puerto Ricans in Chicago.* Notre Dame, IN: University of Notre Dame Press.

Pantoja, Adrian, Ricardo Ramirez, and Gary Segura. 2001. "Citizens by Choice, Voters by Necessity: Patterns in Political Mobilization by Naturalized Latinos." *Political Research Quarterly* 54 (4): 729–750.

Parker, Christopher. 2009. *Fighting for Democracy: Black Veterans and the Struggle against White Supremacy in the Postwar South.* Princeton, NJ: Princeton University Press.

———. 2010. "Symbolic versus Blind Patriotism: Distinction without Difference?" *Political Research Quarterly* 63 (1): 97–114.

Pateman, Carole. 1988. *The Sexual Contract.* Palo Alto, CA: Stanford University Press.

Perez, Efren. 2010. "Explicit Evidence on the Import of Implicit Attitudes: The IAT and Immigration Policy Judgments." *Political Behavior* 32 (4): 517–545.

———. 2011. "Black Ice? Race and Political Psychology of Implicit Bias." Paper presented at the 2011 Annual Meeting of the Midwest Political Science Association, Chicago.

Perlmann, Joel. 2005. *Italians Then, Mexicans Now: Immigrant Origins and Second-Generation Progress, 1890–2000.* New York: Russell Sage Foundation.

Pew Research Center for the People and the Press. 2010. "Public Supports Arizona Immigration Law." Pew Research Center Publications, May 12. Accessed August 8, 2010. http://pewresearch.org/pubs/1591/public-support-arizona-immigration-law-poll.

Philpot, Tasha S. 2007. *Race, Republicans, and the Return of the Party of Lincoln.* Ann Arbor: University of Michigan Press.

Philpot, Tasha S., and Ismail White, eds. 2010. *African-American Political Psychology: Identity, Opinion, and Action in the Post–Civil Rights Era.* New York: Palgrave Macmillan.

Pickett, Cynthia, and Marilynn Brewer. 2005. "The Role of Exclusion in Maintaining Ingroup Inclusion." In *The Social Psychology of Inclusion and Exclusion,* edited by Dominic Abrams, Michael A. Hogg, and José Marques, 89–112. New York: Psychology Press.

Qian, Zhenchao. 1997. "Breaking the Racial Barriers: Variations in Interracial Marriage between 1980 and 1990." *Demography* 34 (2): 263–276.

Ramirez, Ricardo. 2005. "Giving Voice to Latino Voters: A Field Experiment on the Effectiveness of a National Nonpartisan Mobilization Effort." *Annals of the American Academy of Political and Social Science* 601:66–84.

Rim, Kathy. 2007. "Model, Victim, or Problem Minority? Examining the Socially Constructed Identities of Asian-Origin Ethnic Groups in California's Media." *Asian American Policy Review* 16.

Rodriguez, Gregory. 2008. *Mongrels, Bastards, Orphans, and Vagabonds: Mexican Immigration and the Future of Race in America.* New York: Vintage.

Roediger, David R. 2005. *Working toward Whiteness: How America's Immigrants Became White; The Strange Journey from Ellis Island to the Suburbs.* New York: Basic Books.

Rogers, Reuel R. 2006. *Afro-Caribbean Immigrants and the Politics of Incorporation: Ethnicity, Exception, or Exit.* New York: Cambridge University Press.

Rosenberg, Morris, and Roberta G. Simmons. 1971. *Black and White Self-Esteem: The Urban School Child.* Washington, DC: American Sociological Association Press.

Rutenberg, Jim, and Jeff Zeleny. 2012. "Romney Stays on the Offense with Gingrich." *New York Times*, January 26. Accessed July 9, 2012. http://www.nytimes.com/2012/01/27/us/politics/a-grueling-day-on-the-stump-then-a-debate.html?pagewanted=all.

Sanchez, Gabriel. 2006. "The Role of Group Consciousness in Latino Public Opinion." *Political Research Quarterly* 59 (3): 435–446.

Sanchez, Gabriel, and Natalie Masuoka. 2010. "Brown-Utility Heuristic? The Presence and Contributing Factors of Latino Linked Fate." *Hispanic Journal of Behavioral Sciences* 32 (4): 519–531.

Schaller, Mark, Lucian Conway, and Tracy Tanchuk. 2002. "Selective Pressures on the Once and Future Contents of Ethnic Stereotypes: Effects of the Communicability of Traits." *Journal of Personality and Social Psychology* 82:861–877.

Schildkraut, Deborah. 2005. "The Rise and Fall of Political Engagement among Latinos: The Role of Identity and Perceptions of Discrimination." *Political Behavior* 27 (3): 285–312.

———. 2011. *Americanism in the Twenty-First Century: Public Opinion in the Age of Immigration.* New York: Cambridge University Press.

Schlesinger, Arthur. 1991. *The Disuniting of America: Reflections on a Multicultural Society.* New York: W. W. Norton.

Schmidt, Ronald, Sr., Yvette M. Alex-Assensoh, Andrew L. Aoki, and Rodney E. Hero. 2010. *Newcomers, Outsiders, and Insiders: Immigrants and American Racial Politics in the Twenty-First Century.* Ann Arbor: University of Michigan Press.

Schneider, Anne Larason, and Helen Ingram. 1997. *Policy Design for Democracy.* Lawrence: University of Kansas Press.

Schneider, David J. 2004. *The Psychology of Stereotyping.* New York: Guilford.

Schrag, Peter. 2010. *Not Fit for Our Society: Immigration and Nativism in America.* Berkeley: University of California Press.

Schuck, Peter, and Rogers M. Smith. 1985. *Citizenship without Consent: Illegal Aliens in the American Polity.* New Haven, CT: Yale University Press.

Schuman, Howard, Charlotte Steeh, Lawrence D. Bobo, and Maria Krysan. 1997. *Racial Attitudes in America: Trends and Interpretation.* Cambridge, MA: Harvard University Press.

Scola, Becki, and Lisa García Bedolla. 2006. "Finding Intersection in Race, Class, and Gender in the 2003 California Recall Vote." *Politics & Gender* 2 (1): 5–27.

Sears, David, P. J. Henry, and Rick Kosterman. 2000. "Egalitarian Values and Contemporary Racial Politics." In *Racialized Politics: The Debate about Racism in America,* edited by David Sears, James Sidanius, and Lawrence D. Bobo, 75–117. Chicago: University of Chicago Press.

Sears, David, James Sidanius, and Lawrence D. Bobo, eds. 2000. *Racialized Politics: The Debate about Racism in America.* Chicago: University of Chicago Press.

Sears, David, Collete Van Laar, Mary Carrillo, and Rick Kosterman. 1997. "Is It Really Racism? The Origins of White Americans' Opposition to Race-Targeted Policies." *Public Opinion Quarterly* 61:16–53.

Segovia, Francine, and Renatta Defever. 2010. "The Polls—Trends: American Public Opinion on Immigrants and Immigration Policy." *Public Opinion Quarterly* 74:375–394.

Segura, Gary, and Shaun Bowler. 2011. *The Future Is Ours: Minority Politics, Political Behavior, and the Multiracial Era of American Politics.* Washington, DC CQ Press.

Shingles, Richard. 1981. "Black Consciousness and Political Participation: The Missing Link." *American Political Science Review* 75:76–91.

Sidanius, Jim, and Felicia Pratto. 1999. *Social Dominance: An Intergroup Theory of Social Hierarchy and Oppression.* New York: Cambridge University Press.

Sidanius, Jim, Seymour Feshbach, Shana Levin, and Felicia Pratto. 1997. "The Interface between Ethnic and National Attachment: Ethnic Pluralism or Ethnic Dominance?" *Public Opinion Quarterly* 61:102–133.

Sigelman, Lee, and Richard Niemi. 2001. "Innumeracy about Minority Populations: African Americans and Whites Compared." *Public Opinion Quarterly* 65:86–94.

Smith, Rogers M. 1997. *Civic Ideals: Conflicting Visions of Citizenship in U.S. History.* New Haven, CT: Yale University Press.

———. 2003. *Stories of Peoplehood: The Politics and Morals of Political Membership.* New York: Cambridge University Press.

Sniderman, Paul M., and Edward G. Carmines. 1999. *Reaching beyond Race.* Cambridge, MA: Harvard University Press.

Sniderman, Paul M., and Louk Hagendoorn. 2007. *When Ways of Life Collide: Multiculturalism and Its Discontents in the Netherlands.* Princeton, NJ: Princeton University Press.

Sniderman, Paul M., Pierangelo Peri, Rui de Figueiredo, and Thomas Piazza. 2000. *The Outsider: Prejudice and Politics in Italy.* Princeton, NJ: Princeton University Press.

Sniderman, Paul M., and Thomas Piazza. 1993. *The Scar of Race.* Cambridge, MA: Belknap Press of Harvard University Press.

Sniderman, Paul M., and Sean Theriault. 2004. "The Structure of Political Argument and the Logic of Issue Framing." In *Studies in Public Opinion: Attitudes, Nonattitudes, Measurement Error, and Change,* edited by Willem Saris and Paul M. Sniderman, 133–165. Princeton, NJ: Princeton University Press.

Sommers, Samuel, and Phoebe Ellsworth. 2001. "White Juror Bias: An Investigation of Prejudice against Black Defendants in the American Courtroom." *Psychology, Public Policy, and Law* 7:201–229.

Stanford, Leland. 1862. "Inaugural Address." The Governors' Library. http://governors.library.ca.gov/addresses/08-Stanford.html.

Steele, Claude. 2010. *Whistling Vivaldi and Other Clues to How Stereotypes Affect Us.* New York: W. W. Norton.

Stimson, James. 2004. *Tides of Consent: How Public Opinion Shapes American Politics.* New York: Cambridge University Press.

Stokes, Atiya Kai. 2003. "Latino Group Consciousness and Political Participation." *American Politics Research* 31:361–378.

Stouffer, Samuel. 1955. *Communism, Conformity, and Civil Liberties: A Cross-Section of the Nation Speaks Its Mind.* New York: John Wiley and Sons.

Strolovitch, Dara Z. 2007. *Affirmative Advocacy: Race, Class, and Gender in Interest Group Politics.* Chicago: University of Chicago Press.

Sullivan, John, Amy Fried, and Mary Dietz. 1992. "Patriotism, Politics, and the Presidential Election of 1988." *American Journal of Political Science* 36 (1): 200–234.

Sumner, William Graham. (1906) 2002. *Folkways: A Study of Mores, Manners, Customs, and Morals.* Mineola, NY: Dover.

Swain, Carol. 2002. *The New White Nationalism in America: Its Challenges to Integration.* New York: Cambridge University Press.

Tajfel, Henry. 1981. *Human Groups and Social Categories: Studies in Social Psychology.* Cambridge: Cambridge University Press.

Takaki, Ronald. 1998. *Strangers from a Different Shore: A History of Asian Americans.* Updated and rev. ed. New York: Little, Brown.

———. 2000. *Iron Cages: Race and Culture in 19th-Century America*. New York: Oxford University Press.

Tam Cho, Wendy. 1999. "Naturalization, Socialization, Participation: Immigrants and (Non-) Voting" *Journal of Politics* 61 (4): 1140–1155.

Tate, Katherine. 1998. *From Protest to Politics: The New Black Voters in American Elections*. Cambridge, MA: Harvard University Press.

———. 2010. *What's Going On? Political Incorporation and the Transformation of Black Public Opinion*. Washington, DC: Georgetown University Press.

Taylor, Charles. 1998. "The Dynamics of Democratic Exclusion." *Journal of Democracy* 9 (4): 143–156.

Tesler, Michael, and David Sears. 2010. *Obama's Race: The 2008 Election and the Dream of a Post-Racial America*. Chicago: University of Chicago Press.

Theiss-Morse, Elizabeth. 2009. *Who Counts as American? The Boundaries of National Identity*. New York: Cambridge University Press.

Tichenor, Daniel. 2002. *Dividing Lines: The Politics of Immigration Control in America*. Princeton, NJ: Princeton University Press.

Tilly, Charles. 1999. *Durable Inequality*. Berkeley: University of California Press.

Tocqueville, Alexis de. 1863. *Democracy in America*. Translated by Francis Bowen. Cambridge, MA: Sever and Francis.

Transue, John. 2007. "Identity Salience, Identity Acceptance, and Racial Policy Attitudes: American National Identity as a Uniting Force." *American Journal of Political Science* 51 (1): 78–91.

Tuan, Mia. 1998. *Forever Foreigners or Honorary Whites? The Asian Ethnic Experience Today*. New Brunswick, NJ: Rutgers University Press.

Vaca, Nicolas. 2004. *The Presumed Alliance: The Unspoken Conflict between Latinos and Blacks and What It Means for America*. New York: HarperCollins.

Valentino, Nicholas. 1999. "Crime News and the Priming of Racial Attitudes during Evaluations of the President." *Public Opinion Quarterly* 63:293–320.

Valentino, Nicholas, Vincent Hutchings, and Ismail White. 2002. "Cues That Matter: How Political Ads Prime Racial Attitudes during Campaigns." *American Political Science Review* 96:75–90.

Vavreck, Lynn. 2009. *The Message Matters: The Economy and Presidential Campaigns*. Princeton, NJ: Princeton University Press.

Verba, Sidney, and Norman Nie. 1972. *Participation in America: Political Democracy and Social Equality*. New York: Harper and Row.

Wallace-Sanders, Kimberly. 2008. *Mammy: A Century of Race, Gender, and Southern Memory*. Ann Arbor: University of Michigan Press.

Waters, Mary C. 1990. *Ethnic Options: Choosing Identities in America*. Berkeley: University of California Press.

———. 2000. *Black Identities: West Indian Immigrant Dreams and American Realities*. Cambridge, MA: Harvard University Press.

Weber, Max. 1930. *The Protestant Work Ethic and the Spirit of Capitalism.* Translated by Talcott Parsons. London: G. Allen and Unwin.

Weglyn, Michi. 2000. *Years of Infamy: The Untold Story of America's Concentration Camps.* Seattle: University of Washington Press.

Welch, Susan, Lee Sigelman, Timothy Bledsoe, and Michael Combs. 2001. *Race and Place: Race Relations in an American City.* New York: Cambridge University Press.

White, Ismail. 2007. "When Race Matters and When It Doesn't: Racial Group Differences in Response to Racial Cues." *American Political Science Review* 101:339–354.

Wilkins, David E., and Heidi Kiiwetinepinesiik Stark. 2011. *American Indian Politics and the American Political System.* 3rd ed. Lanham, MD: Roman and Littlefield.

Williams, Linda Faye. 2003. *The Constraint of Race: Legacies of White Skin Privilege in America.* University Park: Pennsylvania State University Press.

Wilmer, Franke, Michael E. Melody, and Margaret Maier Murdock. 1994. "Including Native American Perspectives in the Political Science Curriculum." *PS: Political Science and Politics* 27 (2):269–276.

Wilson, William Julius. 1987. *The Truly Disadvantaged: The Inner City, the Underclass, and Public Policy.* Chicago: University of Chicago Press.

———. 2009. *More Than Just Race: Being Black and Poor in the Inner City.* New York: W. W. Norton.

Wong, Cara. 2007. "'Little' and 'Big' Pictures in Our Heads: Race, Local Context, and Innumeracy about Racial Groups in the United States." *Public Opinion Quarterly* 71:392–412.

———. 2010. *Boundaries of Obligation in American Politics: Geographic, National, and Racial Communities.* New York: Cambridge University Press.

Wong, Cara, and Grace Cho. 2005. "Two-Headed Coins or Kandinskys: White Racial Identification." *Political Psychology* 26 (5): 699–720.

Wong, Janelle. 2005. "Mobilizing Asian American Voters: A Field Experiment." *Annals of the American Academy of Political and Social Science* 601:102–114.

———. 2006. *Democracy's Promise: Immigrants and American Civic Institutions.* Ann Arbor: University of Michigan Press.

Wong, Janelle, S. Karthick Ramakrishnan, Taeku Lee, and Jane Junn. 2011. *Asian American Political Participation: Emerging Constituents and Their Political Identities.* New York: Russell Sage.

Young, Richard, and Jeffrey Meiser. 2008. "Race and the Dual State in the Early American Republic." In *Race and American Political Development*, edited by Joseph Lowndes, Julie Novkov, and Dorian Warren, 31–58. New York: Taylor Francis.

Zaller, John R. 1992. *The Nature and Origins of Mass Opinion*. New York: Cambridge University Press.

Zilversmit, Arthur. 1967. *The First Emancipation: The Abolition of Slavery in the North*. Chicago: University of Chicago Press.

Zolberg, Aristide R. 2006. *A Nation by Design: Immigration Policy in the Fashioning of America*. Cambridge, MA: Harvard University Press.

Index

Abrajano, Marisa, 134
affirmative action, 116, 160
African Americans. *See* blacks
agency, political, inequality in, 25
Alabama anti-immigration law (HB 56),
    190, 194
Aleinikoff, T. Alexander, 48
Alien and Sedition Acts (1798), 201n1
Alien Land Laws (California, 1913), 55
American boundaries. *See* Americanness
American Dream narrative, 66–67
American Indians. *See* Native Americans
American Insurance Company v. Canter
    (1828), 51
American National Election Studies, 135
Americanness: abode policies and, 148–54;
    attitudes on immigration and, 187; def-
    inition of, 45–56, 92–93, 104, 208n11,
    208n17; English-only laws and, 147; im-
    migrants as out-group and, 130; linked
    fate and, 119–21; racial differences in
    perception of, 99–100, 197; restrictions
    on immigration and, 138–44, 153–54,
    189; in RPGI model, 125, 126; social
    services for immigrants and, 147–48;
    strict group boundaries, 102
American Protective League, 37
"anchor babies," 22
Anderson, Benedict, 41
anthropology, racial categories and, 54
anti-Islamism, 22
anti-Semitism, 22
Arab Americans, 22. *See also* Middle
    Easterners

Arizona immigrant-profiling law (SB
    1070), 13, 24–25, 190, 194, 216–17n8
Arizona v. United States (2012), 201n3
Asian Americans: abode policies and,
    150–52, 154–55; affirmative action and,
    116–17; Americanness and, 138–42; as
    Americans versus Asians, 92, 207n6;
    Arizona immigrant-profiling law and,
    25; Asian exclusion laws and, 18, 37,
    191–92, 194, 201n2; assimilation and
    party affiliation among, 151–52; atypi-
    cality of, 104; black-Asian conflict and,
    110; changing immigration policy and,
    20, 36, 61; changing stereotypes of,
    21–22; comparative relational approach
    and, 33; concern about racial inequal-
    ity among, 112; as "coolies," 86, 195;
    crime and, 80–81; drugs and gangs and,
    77, 78; English-language ability and,
    77, 78, 79; exclusion of, from citizen-
    ship, 54, 55, 60–61; family values and,
    81; generation of migration and, 134,
    144, 151, 218n18; geographic barriers
    to immigration and, 66; group close-
    ness among, 114–15; "illegal" immigra-
    tion and, 80–82, 169; as "inferior race,"
    199n1 (introduction); in-group bias of,
    79, 84; interracial marriage and, 210–
    11n30; landownership prohibited for,
    55; linked fate and, 108, 113–15, 138–42,
    154–55; as model minority, 61, 64, 74,
    86, 97, 99, 194–95; national identity
    and, 93, 96–104, 154; national-origin
    versus pan-ethnic identification and,

Asian Americans (*continued*)
  108; negative versus positive stereotypes and, 82–83; neighborhood diversity and, 33; as nonwhite, 54; numbers
  of, 194; party identification among,
  135–36; perceived intelligence and, 76,
  77, 79; perceptions of discrimination
  and, 115, 117–18; as peripheral members of polity, 104; as perpetual foreigners, 61, 64, 80, 81, 195, 197; political
  ideology and, 103–4, 210n28; preferences in immigration policy and, 20, 66;
  priming and, 177, 179–83; race-nation
  misalignment and, 119–20; race versus
  ethnicity and, 18; racial-group identity
  among, 108–9, 210n28; in racial hierarchy, 19–22, 65, 83; racialized tropes
  and, 80; racial profiling and, 116–17; racial resentment measures and, 116–17;
  restrictions on immigration and, 13,
  123, 138–42, 144, 154–55, 180–83; sample sizes of, in population surveys,
  200n8; school performance and, 81;
  shifting racial tropes and, 85–86; social
  desirability norms and, 78–79; social
  dominance and national attachment
  among, 207n6; on social services for
  immigrants, 14; socioeconomic status
  and, 75, 78; stereotypes of, 23, 65, 66;
  stereotyping patterns of, 83–84, 177; as
  threatening, 55–56, 80–82; welfare use
  and, 77, 78, 80–81; work ethic and, 81.
  See also specific Asian groups
Asian Indians, as racial group, 18
Asiatic Barred Zone, 37, 201n4
assimilation: abode policies and, 151, 153;
  for Asians versus Latinos, 66–67; interracial marriage and, 210–11n30; of
  new immigrants of Industrial Revolution, 48; party identification and, 135,
  151–52; stereotypes of immigrants and,
  186; territorial expansion and, 46, 50;
  theories of, 54–55; white versus Latino
  perspective on, 28
authoritarianism: abode policies and, 148,
  149, 151, 152; as antecedent to opinion,
  137; dynamics of for different racial
  groups, 136; as explicit attitude, 213n7;
  indicators of, 214n13; restrictions on

immigration and, 129, 143, 144; World
  War II and, 129
Ayala, César, 202n9

Banaji, Mahzarin: on race and core-group
  status, 95; on social acceptability concerns, 211–12n36; on social desirability norms, 203–4n5; system justification
  theory and, 71–72, 73, 76, 83
Barnabé, Rafael, 202n9
belonging: desirability and, 19–20; equality and, 56–57; in era of expansion, 50;
  group-based exclusion and, 195; "illegal" immigration and, 157; immigration
  policy and, 189–92; national identity
  and, 45; norms, rules, and practices of,
  38; patterns in perceptions of, 104; political foundations of, 39–45; racial prerequisite for, 190–91; racial shades of,
  59–62; racial taxonomy and, 38–39, 187,
  197; redefinition of, 9; stereotypes and,
  187; structure of, 20; whiteness versus
  nonwhiteness and, 6; whites and whiteness and, 188. *See also* social-group
  identity
Beltrán, Cristina, 21
Biden, Joe, 63
bilingualism. *See* language
blacks: on abode policies, 149–50, 154–55;
  affirmative action and, 116–17; Americanness and, 138–42; antebellum free
  blacks and, 43; on Arizona immigrant-
  profiling law, 13, 25; belonging and, 89;
  on bilingualism, 110; civil rights movement and, 36, 56; comparative relational approach and, 33; concern about
  racial inequality among, 111–12; conflicts with other racial groups and, 110;
  crime and, 79, 81; drugs and gangs and,
  78, 79; durability of stereotypes of, 84;
  economic disparities and, 105–6, 108,
  133; English-language ability and, 77,
  78, 79; ethnic diversity among, 108;
  ethnicity in American politics and,
  210n29; family values and, 81; group
  closeness among, 114–15; "illegal" immigration and, 11, 81–82, 169, 171–75;
  in-group bias of, 79; interracial marriage and, 210–11n30; and Latinos in

Faces of Immigration findings, 205n17; linked fate and, 105–6, 113–15, 138–42, 154–55; mammy image and, 84; national identity and, 93, 96, 98–104, 208n15; national security and, 81; party affiliation of, 135, 143–44; patriotism and, 92, 103–4; perceived intelligence and, 76, 79; perceptions of discrimination and, 115, 117–18, 211n35; as peripheral members of polity, 99, 104, 150; on perpetual foreigners, 81; political attitudes of, 133; political ideology among, 103–4, 210n28, 213n9, 214n11; political opportunity and, 213n9; priming and, 177, 180–83; race-nation misalignment and, 119–20; race-of-interviewer effects and, 211–12n36; racial-group identity among, 108–9, 210n28; in racial hierarchy, 17, 19–22, 65–66, 74; racial profiling and, 116–17; racial resentment measures and, 116–17; redlining and, 213n8; restrictions on immigration and, 13, 123, 138–44, 154–55, 180–83; school performance and, 81; second-class citizenship and, 4, 60; self-stereotyping and, 86; social desirability norms and, 203–4n5; social dominance and national attachment among, 207n6; on social services for immigrants, 14; socioeconomic status and, 75, 79; stereotypes about, 23, 63, 65–66, 82–83; stereotyping patterns of, 177; three-fifths clause and, 17; welfare queen image and, 84; welfare use and, 77, 78, 79, 81; work ethic and, 81
Bluestone, Barry, 204n6
Blumer, Herbert, 3
Bobo, Lawrence, 8, 69–70, 204n6
border fence, 194
Border Protection, Anti-Terrorism, and Illegal Immigration Control Act (2005–2006), 190, 194
Borjas, George, 132
Bowler, Shaun, 8
Bracero Program, 193
Brader, Ted, 176
Brewer, Marilynn, 93–96, 98, 100–101
Brooks, David, 203n4
Brown, Nadia, 200n10

Brown, Robert, 206n4
Browne, Irene, 204n6
Browning, Rufus, 110
Burns, Nancy, 200n9
Burns, Peter, 130–31
Bush, George H. W., 196
Bush, George W., 186

California Proposition 187: blacks' attitudes toward, 131; exclusion and, 190; framing and, 216–17n8; negative perceptions of candidates and, 197–98; political messages and, 156, 162; public imagination and, 194; public opinion on, 13; Republican support for, 148, 156
California Vagrancy Act. See Greaser Act (California, 1855)
Camarillo, Albert, 202n7
Canadians and Canadian Americans, 193
Carmines, Edward, 135, 213n4
Catholics, early nativist movements and, 47
Celler, Emanuel, 36–37
Census, US: designations for Latinos in, 18; Mexicans as white in, 51
Charles, Camille Zubrinsky, 204n6
Chinese and Chinese Americans: academic performance of, 63, 64; anti-Chinese mobs and, 37; court testimony by prohibited, 55; exclusion of, 37, 48, 49, 54, 201n2; parenting practices of, 203n4; as racial group, 18
Chinese Exclusion Act (1882), 37, 49, 157, 216n5
Chong, Dennis, 108–9, 133
Chua, Amy, 63, 64, 203n4
citizenship: Asian Americans excluded from, 54, 55; birthright, 55; for children of undocumented immigrants, 172–73; class and, 50; construction of, in early United States, 42–45; desirability and, 19–20; eligibility for public service and, 42–43; versus equality, 43–44, 60; exclusivity and, 42; for free blacks, 43–44; gender and sexism and, 44, 50, 206n2; jus soli and, 55; legal status as insufficient condition for, 6; for Native Americans, 49, 51; political rights under, 52; race and eligibility for, 17; research methods and, 212n32, 212n41; residency

citizenship (*continued*)
    requirements and, 201n1; right of soil
    versus blood and, 39, 42; second-class,
    4, 44, 52, 60, 61; similarities versus dif-
    ferences and, 28; territorial acquisition
    and, 50–53; traits of Americans and,
    26–27, 29; "US National" category and,
    53; whiteness and, 1–2, 6–7, 17, 44–45,
    51, 53–54, 191
Citrin, Jack, 213n6
Civil Rights Act (1964), 56
civil rights movement: Democrats versus
    Republicans on, 135; equality as a norm
    and, 56–57; immigration and citizen-
    ship law and, 166–67; shifting racial
    tropes and, 85; social science and, 105
class: citizenship and, 50; Industrial Revo-
    lution and, 47
Clinton, Bill, 215n23
cognitive sophistication: abode policies
    and, 151, 152; as antecedent to opinion,
    137; framing and priming and, 216n2;
    restrictions on immigration and, 143;
    types of survey questions and, 213n4
coming-to-America stories, 1
comparative relational analysis: belong-
    ing and, 197; explanatory variables and,
    32–33; importance of, 155; individual-
    versus group-level explanations and,
    124; linked fate and, 212n38; public
    opinion research and, 32–33; research
    challenges and, 74; significance of race
    and, 209n20. *See also* Racial Prism of
    Group Identity model
Constitution, US, 17, 41–42
Conway, Lucian, 85
Conway, M. Margaret, 92
Crandall v. State of Connecticut, 43
crime, 80–81, 186
Cuba, 46, 52

Dahl, Robert, 54–55
Danziger, Sheldon, 204n6
Dark Side of the Moon (Pink Floyd al-
    bum), 200n6
Dawson, Michael: on black political ide-
    ology, 214n11; on linked fate, 106, 108,
    133; on racial order in US politics, 8
Delli Carpini, Michael X., 128, 200n9
Democratic Party: abode versus admission

policies and, 148; Asian Americans in,
    152; immigration policy and, 130; Lati-
    nos and, 162; on race, 135
demographics: abode policies and, 148,
    149, 151, 152; as antecedent to opin-
    ion, 127, 134, 137, 213nn2–3; changing,
    197–98; end of black-white binary and,
    29; Immigration and Nationality Act
    (1965) and, 2–3, 36–37; National Ori-
    gins Act (1924), 191; restrictions on im-
    migration and, 142–43; simulated re-
    spondents and, 214n19
deportation, 48, 166, 186, 218n2
Devine, Patricia, 69
Devos, Thierry, 95
Dillingham Commission, 37, 49, 191
discrimination, racial: "American" identity
    labels and, 207n6; group closeness and,
    211n35; linked fate and, 115–16, 117–18,
    211n35; redlining and, 213n8; stereotyp-
    ing and, 68, 72; by whites, 211n31
diversity, racial: abode policies and, 148,
    151; opinions on immigration and,
    32–33, 143, 150; overestimation of,
    214n15, 214–15n17; policy implications
    of, 196, 197–98
Dobbs, Lou, 27–29
DREAM Act, 14
Dred Scott v. Sanford, 44
drug involvement, perceived, 76–79

economic disparities. *See* equality and
    inequality
economic outlook: abode policies and, 149,
    151, 152; attitudes on immigration and,
    213n6; as explicit attitude, 213n7
education: abode policies and, 148, 149,
    151, 152; bilingual, 146; cognitive so-
    phistication and, 127–28; definition of
    Ameicanness and, 208n17; English as
    official language and, 147; restrictions
    on immigration and, 143, 144, 167
elections, 29, 156, 183–84, 195–98
Elks v. Wilkins (1884), 53, 201n5
Emirbayer, Mustafa, 200n10
equality and inequality: abode policies
    and, 148; as antecedent to opinion,
    133–34, 137–38; citizenship and, 43–44,
    60; ethnicity versus race and, 19; in-
    group and out-group designations and,

24; issue evolution and, 135; justification of inequality and, 24; linked fate and attitudes about, 116; membership and, 56–57; norm of equality and, 57; in political agency, 25, 32; racial-group identity and, 111–12, 133; restrictions on immigration and, 143; social services for immigrants and, 146–47; in treatment by governing institutions, 183–84

ethnicity: categories of, 57; English as official language and, 147; ethnic versus national identity and, 28–29; eugenics and, 19; in official data collection, 199n4; pluralism and, 19; versus race, 17–19; among whites, 59–60, 203n14

ethnocentrism: group-contact theory and, 131; in-groups and out-groups and, 110, 130; of whites versus minorities, 110, 125

eugenics: ethnicity and, 19; immigration policy and, 37; racial categories and, 48–49, 54

expansion. See territorial expansion

Faces of Immigration Survey: conduct of, 204–5n11; design of, 199n1 (chap. 1), 200n12, 214n12; effects of priming and, 178; explanation for racial-group differences and, 208n12; independent variables in, 205n20; Latinos in racial hierarchy on, 86; versus MCSUI, 80; opinions on immigration and, 11; partisanship versus race and, 15; population samples in, 79–80, 204–5n11, 205nn13–14, 205n19; questions on, 80–81, 83, 123, 146, 205n18; regression models in, 205n20; RPGI model and, 136; self-stereotyping and, 86; stereotypes and, 10; testing of RPGI model with, 125

family values, perceived, 81–82

Farley, Reynolds, 204n6

Fiske, Susan, 72, 73

Foner, Eric, 39

Fourteenth Amendment, birthright citizenship and, 55

Fraga, Luis, 8

framing: current events in study of, 216–17n8; "illegal" immigration and,

164–65, 169, 175; immigration as dire problem and, 185, 186–87; minorities versus whites and, 189; moderation of effects of, 216n2; opinion formation and, 159, 160–62

Franklin, Benjamin, 42

Gamson, William A., 160

gang involvement, perceived, 76–79

gays and lesbians, exclusion of, 22

gender: citizenship and, 44, 50, 206n2; as control variable, 200n11; interracial marriage and, 210–11n30; pubic opinion and, 200n9. See also women

Gimpel, James, 130–31

Gingrich, Newt, 186, 218n1

Gordon, Milton, 54, 210–11n30

Greaser Act (California, 1855), 202n7

Green, Gary, 204n6

group-contact theory. See intergroup contact

Guam, 46, 52–53

Gutmann, Amy, 212n40

Hainmueller, Jens, 213n6

Hajnal, Zoltan, 135, 151–52

Hamilton, Alexander, 42

Harris-Lacewell, Melissa, 200n10

Hart-Celler Act (1965), 56

Hattam, Victoria, 18–19

Hetherington, Marc J., 129, 214n13

Higham, John, 47, 55, 122

Hiscox, Michael, 213n6

Hispanics. See Latinos

Hoekstra, Pete, 197, 218n2

Holzer, Harry, 204n6

Hopkins, Daniel, 131, 214–15nn16–17

Horton, Willie, 196

HoSang, Daniel Martinez, 8

Huddy, Leonie, 92, 101, 209–10n22

Hutchings, Vincent, 206n4

identity. See national identity; racial-group identity; social-group identity

"illegal" immigration: arrest and deportation of, 166; construction of "illegal alien" and, 165–75, 185, 216nn4–5; as crime, 58–59, 166, 168; on Faces of Immigration Survey, 80–82; framing and, 164–65, 169, 175; history of, 157;

"illegal" immigration (*continued*)
immigration quotas and, 165–66;
Latinos stereotyped as, 21, 63, 64, 155,
167, 169; legal-illegal distinction and,
165, 167–68, 170–71, 175, 216n5; legislation against, 193–95; magnitude of,
185; national belonging and, 157; origi-
nating countries and, 192–93; policies
addressing, 172–73, 190, 217n12; in political campaigns, 156; racial-group differences in opinions on, 11, 167–69,
217nn10–11; Republicans and Democrats on, 14; restrictions on immigration and, 165–67, 168; socioeconomic
status and, 66–67; terms for in Europe,
216n4
Illegal Immigration Reform and Immigrant Responsibility Act (1996), 14,
148, 186, 190, 215n23
immigration: economies of sending and
receiving countries and, 131–32; geographic barriers to, 66; high-immigration states and, 214–15nn16–17; prototypical immigrant and, 192; racial
formation and, 189, 192–95. *See also*
"illegal" immigration; immigration policy; political messages on immigration;
public opinion on immigration; restrictions on immigration
Immigration Act (1917). *See* Asiatic
Barred Zone
Immigration Act (1990), 22
Immigration and Customs Enforcement,
186
Immigration and Nationality Act (1965):
demographics and, 2–3, 192; impe-
tus for, 36–37; limits of, 58; nativism
in spite of, 122; preference system and,
20, 166–67, 187, 190, 191, 194–95; provisions of, 36; shifting racial tropes and,
85; signing of, 36, 37; unintended consequences of, 190
immigration policy: abode policies and,
125, 145–55, 190, 191–92; Asian exclusion laws and, 18, 191; belonging and,
189–92; bipartisanship and, 14–15; as
cause of shift in racial tropes, 85–86;
as cyclical, 187; English-only laws and,
145–47, 150–51, 155; eugenics and, 37;

immigration reform of 1965 and, 56–57;
increasing inclusion in, 36–37; Latinos
in racial hierarchy and, 21; mass dem-
onstrations of 2006 and, 27–29; new immigrants of Industrial Revolution and,
48, 49; nonracial justifications for exclusion and, 58; origins of restrictions
and, 58; personal effects of, 24–25;
plenary power of federal government
and, 201n3; political coalitions around,
129–30; political motives for, 48; preference system and, 20, 56–58, 66, 166–67,
187, 190; quotas and, 49, 191; restrictions on versus increases in, 123–24;
social services for immigrants and,
145–47, 153; state-by-state variations in,
48; state versus federal law and, 201n2;
territorial expansion and, 46–47; valorization of Asians and, 21. *See also*
"illegal" immigration; restrictions on
immigration
Immigration Reform and Control Act
(1986), 14, 156, 190
indentured servitude, 43
Indian Citizenship Act (1924), 49
Industrial Revolution, 47
inequality. *See* equality and inequality
in-group bias: confounding of, 212n37;
core versus peripheral group members
and, 94; ethnocentrism and, 130–31;
hierarchies within in-groups and,
207n8; Latinos and "illegal" immigration and, 169; protection of group
boundaries and, 120–21; racial-group
identity and, 111; racial hierarchy
and, 4–5, 24; social identity theory
and, 91; stereotyping and, 176; variations among racial groups and, 79, 110;
among whites, 73
In re Ah Yup, 54
In re Rodriguez (1897), 51
Insular Cases (1901–1922), 53
intelligence, perceived, 76–77, 79
intergroup contact: as antecedent to opinion, 137, 150, 213n5; group-contact theory and, 131; measurement of, 214–
15n17; stereotyping and, 70
Irish Americans, 28, 50, 53
issue evolution, theory of, 135

Italian Americans, 50, 53
Iyengar, Shanto, 160

Jackson, James, 206n4
Japanese and Japanese Americans, 18, 37, 55–56, 80, 202–3n12
Jefferson, Thomas, 45
Jews and Jewish identity, 18–19, 22, 50, 53, 193
Johnson, James, 204n6
Johnson, Lyndon, 36, 37
Johnson-Reed Act (1924), 49
Jost, John, 71–73, 76, 83, 203–4n5, 211–12n36
Junn, Jane, 200n10

Kam, Cindy, 8, 110, 125, 130, 200n9
Keeter, Scott, 128, 200n9
Khatib, Nadia, 92, 101, 209–10n22
Kim, Claire, 8, 20, 65
Kim, Dukhong, 108–9, 133
Kinder, Donald: on ethnocentrism in public opinion, 200n9; on in-group favoritism, 110; on priming, 160; on racial order in US politics, 8; on restrictionist attitudes, 125; on wariness of outgroups, 130
King, Desmond, 8
Kirschenman, Joleen, 204n6
Knowledge Networks (Palo Alto, California), 204–5n11, 214n12
Know-Nothings, 37, 53
Koreans and Korean Americans, 18
Krysan, Maria, 204n6
Kymlicka, Will, 212n40

language: associative chains of, 19; bilingualism and, 110, 146, 218n1; English as official, 145–47, 150–51, 155; exclusion of Mexicans and, 51–52; in Faces of Immigration Survey, 204–5n11; in MCSUI, 76–79, 204n6; national identity and, 98
La Raza. See National Council of La Raza
Latinos: abode policies and, 152–53, 154–55; affirmative action and, 117; Americanness and, 138–42; as Americans versus Latinos, 207n6; Arizona immigrant-profiling law, 24–25; versus Asian Americans and blacks, 86; as-similation and, 28–29, 152; atypicality of, 104; black-Latino conflict and, 110; and blacks in Faces of Immigration findings, 205n17; census designations for, 18, 19; comparative relational approach and, 33; concern about racial inequality among, 112; crime and, 79–81; as default immigrants, 182; demographic strength of, 162; drugs and gangs and, 78–79; economic disparities and, 133; economic inclusion versus belonging for, 61–62; employment sectors and, 67; English-language ability and, 77–79; as ethnicity versus race, 17–19; family values and, 81; generation of migration and, 218n18; group closeness among, 114–15; "illegal" immigration and, 11, 21, 63–64, 80–82, 155, 167, 169, 171–75; "illegal" stereotype and, 155, 193–94, 197; in-group bias of, 79; interracial marriage and, 210–11n30; lack of positive stereotypes for, 205n16; linked fate and, 108, 113–15, 138–42, 154–55; national identity and, 93, 96–97, 98–104, 154; national-origin versus pan-ethnic identification and, 108; national security and, 80–82; as new addition to racial taxonomy, 17; party identification among, 135–36; patriotism and, 92, 103–4; perceived intelligence and, 76, 79; perceptions of discrimination and, 115, 117–18; as peripheral, 80–81, 99–100, 104; political communications about, 196–97; political ideology and, 162, 210n28; priming and, 177, 179–83, 194; race-nation misalignment and, 119–20; racial-group identity and, 108–9, 210n28; in racial hierarchy, 17–22, 83, 86; racialized tropes and, 80; racial profiling and, 117; racial resentment measures and, 117; restrictions on immigration and, 123, 138–44, 154–55, 180–83; on rising number of immigrants, 13; school performance and, 81; self-stereotyping and, 86; social dominance and national attachment among, 207n6; social mobility among, 134; on social services for immigrants, 14; socioeconomic status and, 75–76, 79;

Latinos (*continued*)
  stereotypes of, 21–22, 63–66, 82–83; as
    undesirable migrants, 190; as undiffer-
    entiated political category, 21; welfare
    use and, 77–81; work ethic and, 81
Lazarus, Emma, 185–86
Lee, Taeku, 135, 151–52
liberty, 39–40
Lien, Pei-te, 92
linked fate: abode policies and, 148–53;
    affirmative action and, 116–17; as an-
    tecedent to opinion, 29; attitudes on
    immigration and, 121, 138–42, 187;
    boundaries of Americannness and,
    119–21; comparative relational analy-
    sis and, 212n38; different effects of, for
    different racial groups, 154–55, 197;
    English as official language and, 147;
    group closeness and, 114–15; group sta-
    tus versus individual opportunity and,
    106–7; indicators of perception of, 112–
    13; for minorities versus whites, 188,
    189; perceptions of discrimination and,
    114–16, 117–18; political cohesion and,
    106–7; racial-group attachment and,
    112–18; racial-group identity and, 26–
    27, 90, 105; racial hierarchy and, 126,
    140–42, 154; racial profiling and, 116–
    17; racial resentment and, 116–17; as
    research category, 211n33, 211n35; re-
    strictions on immigration and, 125–26,
    136–37, 143–45, 154–55; social mobil-
    ity and, 133; strength of perceptions of,
    34–35; variations in, by race, 113; varia-
    tions of, among racial groups, 108
Lippman, Walter, 69, 193
Lipsitz, George, 200n13
López, Ian Haney, 54
Louisiana Purchase, 45

Madison, James, 42
Manifest Destiny, 45–46
Marshall, Dale Rogers, 110
Massagli, Michael, 69–70, 204n6
McCain, Cindy, 89, 93, 206n1
McCain, John, 89
McCarran-Walter Act (1952), 191, 193, 194
McCormack, John, 36–37
MCSUI (Multi-City Study of Urban In-
    equality), 10, 23–24, 74–80, 84, 86,
    204n9, 204nn6–7

media: abode policies and, 148–49, 151–52;
    cognitive sophistication and, 128,
    134–35; influence of, 128; mainstream
    versus ethnic, 134–35, 205–6n21; re-
    strictions on immigration and, 143
melting pot narrative, 97
Mendelberg, Tali, 57, 217–18n15
methodology, 7–8, 30–32, 187–88
Mexicans and Mexican Americans: depor-
    tation of, 186; entry between 1924 and
    1965 by, 193; as greasers, 202n7; "il-
    legal" immigration and, 167, 192–93;
    language-based discrimination against,
    51–52; Operation Wetback and, 38;
    politics and migration of, 129–30; as
    second-class citizens, 52; stereotypes
    of, 202n7; as transient laborers, 62; var-
    ied racial ancestry of, 202n8; as white,
    51, 61, 201–2n6, 202n8, 202n11
Mexico, US acquisition of territory of,
    45–46, 50–51, 61–62
Middle Easterners, 201n4, 202n10. *See also*
    Arab Americans
Modigliani, Andre, 160
Morris, Irwin, 131
Moss, Philip, 204n6
Multi-City Study of Urban Inequality
    (MCSUI). *See* MCSUI (Multi-City
    Study of Urban Inequality)
Murguia, Janet, 27–29
Murrah, Hugh, 55
Muslims, anti-Islamism and, 22

National Council of La Raza, 27–28
national identity: abode policies and, 154;
    in American colonial period, 39–40; at-
    tachment and, 92–93, 96, 101–3, 104,
    209–10n22; belonging and, 45; Chi-
    nese exclusion and, 48; collective con-
    sciousness and, 41; conservative po-
    litical ideology and, 103–4; for core
    versus peripheral members of polity,
    104, 120–21; data limitations and, 92;
    in early United States, 40–42; versus
    ethnocentrism, 46; group boundaries
    and, 98, 100–101; ideals versus practice
    and, 41; identity labels and, 92; "illegal"
    immigration and, 157; indicators of,
    90–91, 101, 208n12; key political ideals
    and, 208n11; minorities as peripheral
    and, 96–97; minorities as un-American

and, 92–93; versus nationalism, 92; nation of immigrants and, 97, 122; new immigrants of Industrial Revolution and, 47–48; patriotism and, 89, 103–4, 210n27; political ideology and, 210n27; race unity versus class unity and, 41–42; versus racial and ethnic identity, 28–29, 34; racial discrimination and, 207n6; racial-group identity and, 119–21, 154; racial hierarchy and, 34, 62, 95–97; restrictions on immigration and, 138–42, 144, 153–54; scholarship on, 91; as social-group identity, 91–97; social identity theory and, 91; territorial expansion and, 45–53; traits important to, 90, 97–98, 99; Twenty-First Century Americanism survey and, 10; typicality and, 101–2, 209–10nn22–23; whiteness and, 88; white superiority and, 44–45. *See also* Americanness

nationalism, versus patriotism, 207n5

National Origins Act (1924): construction of "illegal alien" and, 165, 186; definition of America and, 49–50; demographics and, 191, 192; North American immigration and, 193; quotas in, 36, 201n4; rejection of, 56

National Politics Study: linked fate and, 118; population samples in, 112, 211n32, 212nn38–39; principal investigators for, 206n4; questions in, 90, 112, 116, 120; racial-group identity and, 10

national security, threats to, 80–82

Native Americans: citizenship and, 49, 51, 201n5; Latino lineage and, 61; omission of, from study, 199–200nn4–5; in racial taxonomy, 22

nativism, 46–48, 53, 122

Naturalization Act of 1790, 44, 51, 53, 191, 201n1

Ngai, Mae, 58, 166, 202n9

Nosek, Brian, 73, 203–4n5

Obama, Barack: birth certificate and related controversies about, 206n3; black vote for, 135; deportations under, 186, 218n2; immigration as policy issue for, 156; Joe Biden on, 63; postracial society and, 57; "proud of my country" and, 89

Obama, Michelle, 89, 93, 206n1

Office of Management and Budget, 199n4

Oliver, Melvin, 204n6

Operation Gatekeeper (1994), 165

Operation Wetback, 38, 186, 193

opportunities, theory of, 108–9, 133–34

Ozawa v. United States (1922), 202n10

Page Act (1875), 22, 194

party identification: abode policies and, 148, 149, 151, 152; assimilationist views and, 153; attitudes on immigration and, 129–30; English as official language and, 147; framing and priming and, 216n2; political attitudes and, 8; racial differences in meaning of, 14–15, 31; restrictions on immigration and, 143–44; social services for immigrants and, 147–48

patriotism, 28, 89, 92, 103–4, 207n5, 210n27

People v. George Hall (1950), 55

People v. Pablo de la Guerra (1870), 52

Perez, Efren, 214n13

Pew Immigration Survey, 11, 169–75, 189, 216n7, 217n9

Philippines, 46, 52–53, 202n9

Pickett, Cynthia, 93–96, 98, 100–101

Pink Floyd, 200n6

pluralism, 19

political messages on immigration: audience and, 162–63, 164; California's Proposition 187 and, 156, 162; communication strategies and, 158–60; in election of 2008, 156–57; "illegal" immigration and, 170, 197; immigration and terrorism and, 157; influence of, 157; negative stereotypes and, 196, 197–98; racial appeals and, 160, 162–63, 169, 175–76; racial groups' responses to, 11, 35, 158, 164, 189; racial hierarchy and, 160–64; racial prism and, 183–84. *See also* framing; priming

Pratto, Felicia, 72, 83

prejudice, racial, 3, 68

priming: choice of images for, 217–18n15, 218n17; effects of, across racial groups, 160–62, 176–77, 180–83, 189; moderation of effects of, 216n2; process of, 159–60; race of immigrants and, 164, 175–83, 194; testing effects of, 177–80

Proposition 187. *See* California Proposition 187

Protestantism, early American culture and, 39

public opinion: attitude formation and, 158–60; cognitive sophistication and, 127–28, 134; communication strategies and, 158–60; competing interests and, 159; constraint of race on, 153–55; control variables for studies of, 127; demographics and, 127, 134, 137, 213nn2–3; established model for explaining, 126–30; formation of, 69; personality and, 128–29; political context and, 129, 135–36; "public" in, 123; racial-group versus individual factors and, 132–33; racialized narratives' effect on, 85; racial undertones in policy debates and, 132; research on minorities,' 136; structural constraints on, 132–36; variables affecting, 200n9. *See also* public opinion on immigration

public opinion on immigration: Americanness and, 187; "anchor babies" and, 22; antecedents of, 11, 126–32, 136, 142–45; on Arizona immigrant-profiling law, 13; attachment to racialized status and, 7; authoritarianism and, 129, 136; authors' approach to, 3–8; closure of American frontier and, 47–48; comparative relational analysis and, 155; comparative relational approach and, 33; for core versus peripheral members of polity, 121; demographics and, 134, 189; economic outlook and, 131–32, 137–38, 149, 151–52, 213n6; education and, 127–28; elite positions on, 129; ethnocentrism and, 130; in Europe, 131; explicit versus implicit attitudes and, 213n7; generation of migration and, 134, 144; group-contact theory and, 131; group threat and, 215n17; historical and institutional context and, 187, 188; immigrants as racial minorities and, 130–31; individual-level factors in, 124; in-group and out-group designations and, 24; intergroup contact and, 137, 213n5, 214–15n17; linked fate and, 27, 29, 34–35, 105, 121, 138–42, 187; media and, 128, 134–35; national group boundaries and, 122–23; Naturalization Act of 1790 and, 201n1; partisanship versus race and, 14–15, 31; party identification and, 137; perceptions of be-

longing and, 88; personal effects of policy and, 24–25; race as control variable and, 31; race ignored in studies of, 16; racial diversity and, 32–33, 137; racial-group identity and, 2, 5–7, 26, 107, 187; racial hierarchy and, 2, 4–5, 6, 16, 34–35; rising number of immigrants and, 13; RPGI model and, 9, 136–45; social services for immigrants and, 13–14; types of survey questions and, 213n4; of whites versus minorities, 145. *See also* political messages on immigration; public opinion

Puerto Rico, 46, 52–53, 202n9

race: barriers of, misunderstood by whites, 203n14; belonging and, 195; as condition of entry and citizenship, 1–2, 17, 201n3; construction of, in early United States, 42–45; controlling for, 7–8, 30–32, 200n10; default in-group category and, 4–5; versus ethnicity, 17–19; hierarchy structure and, 2, 4–5; as highlighted characteristic of immigrants, 157; immigration quotas and, 165–66, 168; in official data collection, 199n4; "other" races in population surveys and, 200n8; party identification and political attitudes and, 8; political messages on immigration and, 160; post-racial society and, 57–58; prerequisites to belonging and, 4; race card and, 162; Republicans versus Democrats on, 135; research on public opinion and, 32–33; as social construction, 23, 195; socioeconomic status and, 75–76; as unchanging, 19; as unexceptable reason for exclusion, 58; US movement beyond, 8. *See also* racial-group identity; racial hierarchy; racial taxonomy

racial-appeals hypothesis, 175–76, 218n17

racial categories. *See* racial taxonomy

racial-group identity: Americannness and, 27, 29; attitudes on immigration and, 145–46, 187; content of, 109–12; exclusion from nation and, 104–12; expectations of racial prism and, 33–35; group closeness and, 112–14, 118; identity labels and, 92; individual's recognition of, 26; in-group bias and, 111; for Latinos,

17–19, 21, 153; marginalization and, 105–7, 111, 133; minority political coalitions and, 110; multiracial people and, 203n13; national identity and, 28–29, 34, 119–21, 154; orientation of preferences and, 90; perceptions of belonging and, 88–90; perceptions of discrimination and, 114–15; political ideology and, 210n28; politicized racial consciousness and, 105; positive in-group identity and, 203–4n5; protection of interests and, 109–10; public opinion on immigration and, 2, 5–7, 15–16, 26, 34–35, 107; racial hierarchy and, 26, 34, 86–87, 107–8, 111–12; racial prejudice and, 3; research on public opinion and, 29–30; restrictions on immigration and, 125, 138–43, 154; RPGI model and, 29, 126; shared experience and, 110–11; versus social-group identity, 107–8, 109–11; theory of opportunities and, 108–9; US legal definitions and, 17; variation in strength of, 107–9; worldview and, 107. See also linked fate; Racial Prism of Group Identity model

racial hierarchy: acceptance of, 70, 72; antebellum, 43–44; Asians and, 21–22; attitude formation and, 158; attitudes on immigration and, 146; blacks at bottom of, 17; class and, 70–71; desirability of values and behaviors and, 163; diamond shape of, 5, 9, 19–23; Dillingham Commission report and, 37; history of, 9–10; "illegal" immigration and, 168, 175; individual-level agency and, 187; in-group favoritism and, 73, 176; Latinos in, 17–22, 86; legal maintenance of, 165; linked fate and, 105, 140–42, 154; national identity and, 34, 62, 95–97, 119; patterns of stereotyping and, 146; persistence of, 120; personal behavior and, 67; political agency and, 25–26; political appeals and, 160–64; power relationships and, 73; priming and, 176–77; public opinion on immigration and, 2, 4–5, 6, 16; racial-group identity and, 26, 34, 86–87, 107–8, 111–12; response to political messages and, 183–84; restrictions on immigration and, 181; RPGI model and, 29; shades

of belonging and, 59–62; social dominance theory and, 71–72, 73; stability of, 195; stereotypes and, 4, 10, 68–71, 73–74, 83, 188; support for versus opposition to, 67; system justification theory on, 71–72, 73; unequal constraints and, 32; valence of stereotypical traits and, 64–66; whites at top of, 17

Racial Prism of Group Identity model: antecedents of public opinion in, 137; constraints on attitudes about immigration and, 29; creation of, 9, 26; empirical expectations and, 33–35, 123; linked fate and, 118; race's significance for different races and, 153–55; racial-group attachments and, 10; racial hierarchy and, 90, 145–46; restrictions on immigration and, 136, 142–45; simulated respondents in, 139, 215nn19–20; strong support for, 189; testing of, 125–26; visual representation of, 200n6; working of, 27–28. See also comparative relational analysis

racial profiling, 25, 116

racial taxonomy: as antecedent to opinion, 133; anthropology and, 54; belonging and, 187, 197; creation of racial categories and, 38–39; definition of America and, 49–50; eugenics and, 48–49, 54; immigration in formation of, 189, 192–95; immigration reform of 1965 and, 57; Latinos in, 17; among Mexicans, 202n8; Middle Easterners and, 202n11; multiracial Americans and, 203n13; Native Americans in, 22; postracial society and, 57; territorial expansion and, 50, 53–56

racism: antecedents of racial attitudes and, 10–11; conservative ideology and, 148–49; institutionalized, 2, 5; racial-group identity and, 116; social desirability norms and, 211–12n36

rational-actor theories, 131–32, 134

redlining, 213n8

Republican Party: abode versus admission policies and, 148; Asian Americans in, 151–52; blacks and, 143–44; English as official language and, 151; immigration reform and, 129–30; Latinos and, 162; on race, 135 restrictions on immigration: antecedents of attitudes about, 142–45; assimilationist views and, 153; eastern and southern Europeans and, 166; Gallup polling on, 213n1; "illegal" immigration and, 165–67, 168; linked fate and, 136–37, 154–55; national identity and, 153–54; priming and, 180–83; quotas and, 165–66; race and positions on, 123–24; racial-group identity and, 123–25, 138–42, 189; racial hierarchy and, 181; RPGI model and, 136; stereotypes and, 196; titles of federal legislation and, 190

restrictive covenants, 202n7
Rodriguez, Ricardo, 51
Romney, Mitt, 19
RPGI. *See* Racial Prism of Group Identity model

Santorum, Rick, 63, 64
Save Our State initiative. *See* California Proposition 187
SB 1070. *See* Arizona immigrant-profiling law (SB 1070)
Schaller, Mark, 85
Schildkraut, Deborah, 93, 206n4, 207n6, 208n11
Schmidt, Ronald, 8
school performance, perceived, 81–82
Sears, David, 8
segregation, racial, 213n8
Segura, Gary, 8
Sensenbrenner bill. *See* Border Protection, Anti-Terrorism, and Illegal Immigration Control Act (2005–2006)
sexism. *See* women
Sidanius, Jim, 72, 83, 93, 207n6
Simpson-Mazzoli Act. *See* Immigration Reform and Control Act (1986)
Singh, Simran, 134
slavery, 17, 41–42, 43
Smith, Rogers, 8, 40–41
Sniderman, Paul M., 131, 159
social desirability norms, 73, 78–79, 217–18n15
social dominance theory, 71, 207n6, 207n8
social-group identity: chosen versus unchosen identities and, 91–92; core versus peripheral, 93–96, 100–101, 102, 207n8; excluded versus peripheral members

and, 207n7; group boundaries and, 94–95, 100–101, 102–4; group closeness and, 113–14, 211n35; group commonality measures and, 211n33; in-groups and out-groups and, 91–97; multiple identities and, 212n40; national identity as, 91–97; priming and, 182–83; versus racial-group identity, 107–8, 109–11; social dominance theory and, 207n8; social identity theory and, 91. *See also* belonging; racial-group identity
socioeconomic status, perceived, 75–79
SPost program, 215n19
Stanford, Leland, 199n1 (introduction)
Statue of Liberty, 185–86
Steele, Claude, 87, 207n7
stereotypes: acceptance of, for own group, 67, 71–72, 73, 76–77, 86; automatic activation of, 69; belonging and, 187; categorical thinking and, 24; changes in, over time, 21–22; choices about application of, 72; cognitive theories on, 70; as commonplace, 23; decision making and, 68–69; dehumanization of out-groups and, 68, 72; durability and change in, 84–86; electoral politics and, 196, 197–98; framing of, 69–70; "illegal alien" and, 193–94; individual versus cultural origins of, 68–72; institutionalized norms and, 85; institutionalized racism and, 2; justification of inequality and, 24; in media, 205–6n21; mobilization against immigration and, 35; negative versus positive, 64–66, 67–77, 79, 80–84, 205n18; politicians' statements and, 63; power relationships and, 72–73; prejudice and, 68; priming and, 176–77; psychological function of, 68–69; racial appeals and, 176; racial hierarchy and, 4, 10, 68–71, 73–74, 83, 146, 176, 188; through racial prism, 71–84; in social conversations, 85; social desirability norms and, 73, 78–79; social dominance theory on, 71–72, 73; social-group identity and, 94; stereotype threat and, 207n7; strength of, 23–24; system justification theory on, 71–72, 73; white versus nonwhite practices and, 72–74
Stimson, James, 135, 213n4

Suhay, Elizabeth, 176
system justification theory, 71–72, 73

Tabb, David, 110
Tanchuk, Tracy, 85
Tancredo, Tom, 156–57, 196
Tate, Katherine, 213n9
territorial expansion: assimilation and, 46,
    50; citizenship and, 50–53, 201n5; im-
    migration policy and, 46–47, 186; incor-
    poration versus nonincorporation of
    territory and, 202n9; Latinos' belong-
    ing and, 61–62; national identity
    and, 45–53; racial taxonomy and, 50,
    53–56
Tesler, Michael, 8
Theiss-Morse, Elizabeth, 92, 93, 101,
    209–10nn21–22
Theriault, Sean, 159
Tichenor, Daniel, 50, 129
Tilly, Chris, 204n6
Tocqueville, Alexis de, 40–41
Treaty of Guadalupe Hidalgo (1848),
    45–46, 50, 51
Treaty of Paris (1898), 52
Tuan, Mia, 8
Twenty-First Century Americanism sur-
    vey: American-boundary measure in,
    98, 100, 102, 103–4; conduct of, 207n9;
    national identity and, 10; perceptions of
    belonging and, 104; population samples
    in, 97, 207–8n10, 208nn13–14, 209n21;
    principal investigator for, 206n4; ques-
    tions on, 90, 97–98, 209–10n22; scoring
    of responses on, 207–8n10

undocumented immigrants. See "illegal"
    immigration
United States Immigration Commission.
    See Dillingham Commission
United States v. Thind (1923), 202n10

Vaca, Nicolas, 110
Valentino, Nicholas, 176
Viles, Peter, 28
voting rights: European immigrants and,
    54; free blacks and, 43; language and,
    52; legal protection of, 56; property-
    holding and, 45; for Puerto Ricans, 53
Voting Rights Act (1965), 56

Warren, Earl, 55–56
Waters, Mary, 203n14
Weiler, Jonathan D., 129
welfare use, perceived, on Faces of Immi-
    gration Survey, 76–81
White, Ismail, 162–63, 169, 176
white as default category: belonging and,
    38, 88, 195; hidden power of white-
    ness and, 200n13; national identity and,
    59–60, 95–96, 188; race-nation align-
    ment and, 6–7, 26–27, 119; racial hier-
    archy and, 22–23; in research, 15, 30,
    31–32, 162, 200n12. See also whites and
    whiteness
whites and whiteness: on abode policies,
    147–49; affirmative action and, 116–
    17; Americanness and, 34, 125, 138–42;
    Anglo-Saxons versus other European
    immigrants and, 53–54; Arizona immi-
    grant-profiling law and, 13, 24–25; as-
    similation promoted by, 28; citizenship
    and, 1–2, 6–7, 17, 44–45, 51, 53–54, 191;
    as core members of polity, 104; crime
    and, 81; discrimination by, 211n31;
    drugs and gangs and, 77, 78; durability
    of desirability attached to, 84; English-
    language ability and, 77, 78; equality-
    enhancing measures and, 211–12n36;
    ethnic identification of, 203n14; family
    values and, 81; group closeness among,
    114–15; groups included in, 17; hidden
    power of whiteness and, 200n13; "ille-
    gal" immigration and, 81–82, 168, 170–
    75; immigration quotas and, 49; inden-
    tured servitude and, 43; in-group bias
    of, 79; in-group favoritism of, 73; le-
    gal definition of, 54, 202n10; "less than
    white" Europeans and, 49; linked fate
    and, 113–14, 125, 136–42, 154; Mexi-
    cans in acquired territories and, 51, 61,
    201–2n6, 202n8, 202n11; national iden-
    tity and, 44–45, 88, 92–93, 98–104, 154;
    national security and, 81; neighborhood
    diversity and, 33; off-whiteness and,
    201–2n6; patriotism and political ideol-
    ogy and, 103–4; perceived intelligence
    and, 76, 79; perceptions of discrimina-
    tion and, 115–16, 117–18; on perpetual
    foreigners, 81; priming and, 176, 180–
    83; public opinion on immigration and,

whites and whiteness (*continued*)
34; race-nation alignment among, 119, 120; racial-group identity and, 108–9, 111; in racial hierarchy, 17, 19–23; racial profiling and, 116–17; racial resentment and, 110, 116–17, 160, 162, 175–76; ratings of Latinos by, 205n17; as reference category in experiments, 15–16; responses to "illegal" immigration by, 11; restrictions on immigration and, 123, 125, 136–43, 180–83; on rising number of immigrants, 13; school performance and, 81; social desirability norms and, 78–79, 203–4n5, 211–12n36, 214n12, 217–18n15; social dominance and national attachment among, 207n6; on social services for immigrants, 14; socioeconomic status and, 75–76, 77; stereotypes and, 65–66, 82–84, 176–

77; susceptibility to framing and priming and, 164; welfare use and, 77, 78, 81; work ethic and, 81. *See also* white as default category

Williams, Linda Faye, 8

Wilson, Pete, 156, 162, 196, 197

women: "anchor babies" and, 22; black, stereotypes of, 84; perceived sexual threat to, 202n7; political exclusion of, 22, 44; public safety and, 25. *See also* gender

Wong, Cara, 206n4, 214n15, 214n17

Wong, Janelle S., 92

Wong Kim Ark, 55

Wong Wing v. United States (1898), 201n3

work ethic, perceived, 81–82

Zaller, John, 158

Series titles, continued from front matter:

OBAMA'S RACE: THE 2008 ELECTION AND THE DREAM OF A POST-RACIAL AMERICA *by Michael Tesler and David O. Sears*

FILIBUSTERING: A POLITICAL HISTORY OF OBSTRUCTION IN THE HOUSE AND SENATE *by Gregory Koger*

IN TIME OF WAR: UNDERSTANDING AMERICAN PUBLIC OPINION FROM WORLD WAR II TO IRAQ *by Adam J. Berinsky*

US AGAINST THEM: ETHNOCENTRIC FOUNDATIONS OF AMERICAN OPINION *by Donald R. Kinder and Cindy D. Kam*

THE PARTISAN SORT: HOW LIBERALS BECAME DEMOCRATS AND CONSERVATIVES BECAME REPUBLICANS *by Matthew Levendusky*

DEMOCRACY AT RISK: HOW TERRORIST THREATS AFFECT THE PUBLIC *by Jennifer L. Merolla and Elizabeth J. Zechmeister*

AGENDAS AND INSTABILITY IN AMERICAN POLITICS, SECOND EDITION *by Frank R. Baumgartner and Bryan D. Jones*

THE PRIVATE ABUSE OF THE PUBLIC INTEREST *by Lawrence D. Brown and Lawrence R. Jacobs*

THE PARTY DECIDES: PRESIDENTIAL NOMINATIONS BEFORE AND AFTER REFORM *by Marty Cohen, David Karol, Hans Noel, and John Zaller*

SAME SEX, DIFFERENT POLITICS: SUCCESS AND FAILURE IN THE STRUGGLES OVER GAY RIGHTS *by Gary Mucciaroni*